NEOTROPICAL TREEBOAS

NATURAL HISTORY OF
THE *CORALLUS HORTULANUS* COMPLEX

NEOTROPICAL TREEBOAS
NATURAL HISTORY OF
THE *CORALLUS HORTULANUS* COMPLEX

Robert W. Henderson

Milwaukee Public Museum
Milwaukee, Wisconsin

Krieger Publishing Company
Malabar, Florida
2002

Original Edition 2002

Printed and Published by
KRIEGER PUBLISHING COMPANY
KRIEGER DRIVE
MALABAR, FLORIDA 32950

Copyright © 2002 by Krieger Publishing Company

Library of Congress Cataloging-in-Publication Data

Henderson, Robert W., 1945–
    Neotropical treeboas: natural history of the corallus hortulanus complex/Robert W. Henderson.
      p. cm.
    Includes bibliographical references and index.
    ISBN 1-57524-038-6 (alk. paper)
     1. Corallus hortulanus. I. Title.

QL666.O63 H46 2002
597.96′7—dc21

                                      2001020672

10   9   8   7   6   5   4   3   2

To the people who shared
the joy and excitement
of learning something new about
Corallus grenadensis
every day we were in the field
(listed in order of the amount of time spent in the field):

AL WINSTEL
ROSE HENDERSON
RICH SAJDAK
KY HENDERSON
JOEL FRIESCH
GARY HAAS

Contents

Preface

   If you're ever in Grenada, do yourself a favor and follow these simple instructions. Rent a car. Spend an hour or so on the beach at Grand Anse. If you haven't had lunch, you might go to The Nutmeg on the Carenage in St. George's. Take a window seat and you'll have a terrific view of the harbor and get a swell breeze. Try the chicken (or shrimp or conch) roti; it's tasty (especially if you like curry powder), nutritious, and inexpensive. Wash it down with a lime squash. In the late afternoon, throw a loaf of bread and a jar of peanut butter ("Creamy" for me) into the car. Some cookies would be good, too (I prefer chocolate chip, but some of the local coconut cookies are great.), and something to drink. (It's hard to beat an ice-cold Grape Fanta or Solo.) Make sure you have a good flashlight or, preferably, a headlamp. On some nights at some sites insect repellent is a good idea. ("Off®" is effective.) Assuming your starting point is somewhere in the neighborhood of St. George's, drive southeast towards Westerhall, up the leeward coast to Beausejour, or, if you're in a real adventuresome mood, head up and over the mountains at Grand Etang and begin your descent towards Grenville and the windward coast. Make sure you drive with the windows open so that you can smell the wonderful fragrances of food being prepared over wood fires as you pass through small towns and villages. It should still be light, so look for an area of mixed agriculture with lots of trees (especially mango) at an elevation between sea level and 100 m, and keep your eye out for unpaved roads leading off the paved road on which you're traveling. Pull into the dirt road, away from people's homes, and find a place to park. Get out of the car and look for someone to talk to. Shake hands, introduce yourself, and let them know that you'd like to look for "serpents" that night, and that you'll not molest the fruit trees. Tell him or her that you'll be walking around at night with a light and you don't want anyone to think that you're "up to no good," that you just want to look for serpents, and that you're not going to take them away (although they might not mind if you did). If you can tell more than one person what you're up to, that's even better. Now go back to your car, have a couple of peanut butter sandwiches, some cookies, and something to drink. By the time you've finished your dinner, it will be close to nightfall and you should hear *Eleutherodactylus johnstonei* (and perhaps *E. euphronides*) calling. Put on your headlamp and use the insect repellent. When it's dark, the real fun starts. Shine your light over the vegetation, concentrating on the tips of branches. Look for the reflected orange-red glow of the eyeshine of *Corallus grenadensis*. You might have a few false alarms provided by moths, geckos, birds, rats, and, maybe, opossums. When you find a treeboa, and you will, watch it for a few minutes. Catch it if you must; handle and admire it for a few minutes and try to avoid being bitten (but if you do, it's no big deal), and then release it into the same tree from which you took it. Take some time to appreciate where you are, what you're doing, and especially *Corallus grenadensis*. You won't be sorry and, who knows, they might not be there forever.

Acknowledgments

I am appreciative of the cooperation I have received from forestry and wildlife officials in the West Indies and Trinidad and Tobago: Alan Joseph, Rolax Frederick, Robert Dunn, and George Vincent (Grenada); Brian Johnson, Calvin Nicholls, and Cornelius Richards (St. Vincent and The Grenadines); and Nadra Nathai-Gyan and Howard Nelson (Trinidad and Tobago).

For loans (sometimes multiple) of *Corallus* specimens, or information regarding specimens, I am indebted to personnel at the following institutions: Academy of Natural Sciences of Philadelphia (ANSP); American Museum of Natural History (AMNH) (including specimens from Guyana collected under the Smithsonian Institution's Biological Diversity of the Guianas Program, University of Guyana coordinator, I. Ramdass; Smithsonian coordinator, V. Funk); British Museum of Natural History (BMNH); California Academy of Sciences (CAS); Carnegie Museum of Natural History (CMNH); Field Museum of Natural History (FMNH); Florida Museum of Natural History (University of Florida; UF); Instituto Butantan (IB); Louisiana State University Museum of Zoology (LSUMZ); Museo de Ciencias (Venezuela); Museo de Ciencias Naturales La Salle (Venezuela); Museum of Comparative Zoology (Harvard University; MCZ); Muséum National d'Histoire Naturelle (Paris; MNHN); Museu de Ciências da Pontifica Universidade Catolica de Rio Grande do Sul (Brazil; MCP); Museu de Historia Natural "Capão de Imbuia" (Curitiba, Paraná, Brazil); Museu de Zoologia (Universidade de São Paulo; MZUSP); National Museum of Natural History (The Netherlands); National Museum of Natural History (USA; USNM); Natural History Museum of Los Angeles County (LACM); Texas Cooperative Wildlife Collection (Texas A&M University; TCWC); University of California at Berkeley Museum of Vertebrate Zoology (UC-MVZ); University of Illinois Museum of Natural History (UIMNH); University of Kansas (KU, including the Albert Schwartz Field Series [ASFS]); University of Miami (CRE); University of Michigan (UMMZ); and University of Texas at Arlington (UTACV).

Field work with *Corallus hortulanus* and *C. ruschenbergerii* has been generously funded by the Milwaukee Public Museum (often via Allen M.

Young), the late Albert Schwartz, the late Jack A. Puelicher, Robert W. Bourgeois, the Central Florida Herpetological Society, and indirectly by the Chicago Zoological Society and the Institute of Museum Services. In the field I have benefitted from the companionship of Hans Boos, Ken Caesar, Joel Friesch, Gary Haas, Rose Henderson, Ky Henderson, Bill Holmstrom, Jim Kranz, Kirsten Kranz, Tim McCarthy, María Muñoz, Jesus Rivas, Rich Sajdak, John Thorbjarnarson, and Al Winstel. I have been the recipient of many *Corallus*-related favors, and these have come from Tommy Allison, Hans Boos, Bob Bourgeois, John Cadle, Ken Caesar, Olga Victoria Castaño, C. J. Cole, Jacques Daudin, Craig R. Dethloff, William E. Duellman, Paul Freed, S. Blair Hedges, Mats Höggren, William F. Holmstrom, Marinus Hoogmoed, Paul Huang, William W. Lamar, James D. Lazell, Alan Markezich, Rita Mehta, Danny Mendez, Flavio de Barros Molina, John S. Parmerlee, Jr. (for the maps included herein), Ray Pawley, Joanne Peterson, Giuseppe Puorto, A. Stanley Rand, Janis Roze, Peter J. Stafford, Andrew Stimson, Peter J. Tolson, Laurie J. Vitt, Allen M. Young, and personnel of the Maffiken Apartments.

Bill Lamar critically reviewed the manuscript and offered valuable observations based on his many years of field work in the American tropics. Likewise, Laurie Vitt provided quantifiable data for *Corallus hortulanus* in Amazonia.

Rich Sajdak volunteered to read every draft of this book, and always had constructive comments. Similarly, aware of my ineptitude with computer graphics, Bob Powell graciously offered to do the final graphs for me. Rich and Bob are friends in the truest sense of the word.

For the use of photographs I am grateful to Jan Caldwell, Phil DeVries, Ky Henderson, Bill Lamar, Mark O'Shea, Giuseppe Puorto, Rich Sajdak, Ivan Sazima, Alejandro Solórzano, Laurie Vitt, and Al Winstel.

Finally, I thank Henry S. Fitch. Although it is virtually impossible to emulate his contributions to snake natural history, he has nevertheless set the standard to which we should strive.

Chapter 1

Introduction, Methods, Species, and Study Sites

When the snake is in motion ..., if he can be induced to move in sunlight he presents a remarkably beautiful appearance ... as he wends his sinuous way along the branches.

Mole and Urich (1894) describing *Corallus ruschenbergerii*

In the early 1960s, some months after an early childhood interest in snakes had been rekindled by an encounter with a *Thamnophis sirtalis*, I was home from school, sick with some long-forgotten illness. More or less confined to bed for a few days, my mom took it upon herself to go to the local library and check out what few snake books were then available. Those books, especially Ditmars' *Snakes of the World*, Kauffeld's *Snakes and Snake Hunting*, and Schmidt and Inger's *Living Reptiles of the World*, opened a wonderful world for me. I was, of course, quite taken with some of the obvious eye-catchers like gaboon and rhinoceros vipers, bushmasters, and emerald treeboas. But I was also intrigued by less spectacular species, those that were eye-catching for different reasons: the amazingly slim body and chunky head of *Imantodes cenchoa*, the attenuated heads of neotropical vine snakes (*Oxybelis*), and the peculiar supra-orbital scales of *Bothriechis* (then *Bothrops*) *schlegelii*. Among my favorite photos were the those of yellow treeboas in Ditmars (1942: Plate 11) and Schmidt and Inger (1957: Plate 69). I often daydreamed about visiting the Neotropics in order to search for the wonderful snakes I saw in the photos.

A quarter of a century later, knowing that I was headed for the Windward Islands in the Lesser Antilles, the late Albert Schwartz offhandedly remarked that he believed the populations of *Corallus* on St. Vincent were taxonomically distinct from populations on Grenada. Al did not want to tackle the problem himself as it would require examining many specimens from outside of the West Indies, something that was unappealing to him. His comments brought back memories of my youthful enthusiasm for treeboas. Before long I began requesting loans of preserved specimens of what was then called *Corallus enydris*. Shortly thereafter, I initiated field work with *Corallus* in the West Indies.

My first treeboa collecting effort in the West Indies was auspicious. It was 1987 and, aside from collecting one *C. hortulanus* in Peru, I was ignorant of preferred habitat for treeboas when I arrived in St. Vincent, accompanied by my wife Rose and Rich Sajdak, for the express purpose of finding and collecting *Corallus*. After renting a car and finding a hotel in Kingstown, it was too late to do any reconnoitering for potential collecting sites. We set out at dusk, found a road that headed out of Kingstown, and drove into the night, unaware of where to look for treeboas, or even of where we were. We eventually left the main highway, made turns here and there, ascended a bit, and finally found a place that was relatively unpopulated by humans. Rich was the first one out of the car, followed by Rose. While I was still fumbling for my headlamp, Rich announced that he had spotted an eyeshine, and that a snake was attached to it. Climbing a tree and displaying acrobatics of which I am pretty sure I am now incapable, we collected the snake, which was, indeed, a treeboa. While I was still taking notes, Rich announced that he had already found another snake, and a second later Rose proclaimed that she, too, had found a treeboa. Now, keep in mind that we had set-out blind: we didn't know what habitat treeboas preferred, and we didn't know what habitat we were in. In fact, we didn't really know where we were! But we kept finding treeboas that night, and the next night, and the next. (As was his wont, Barbour [1937] suggested that *Corallus* no longer existed on St. Vincent.) I have not been back to that site in 7 or 8 years, but I will bet I could return there and still find *Corallus*.

Between 1987 and 2000, many more trips to the West Indian range of *Corallus* followed. Grenada received the lion's share of my attention, but return trips to St. Vincent also took place. I also visited several of the Grenadine islands, as well as Trinidad and Venezuela. Gary Haas, a Peace Corps Volunteer working in St. Vincent, visited a number of the Grenadine islands on my behalf. Initial efforts concentrated on determining where *Corallus* occurred in the West Indies, and where it did not occur, from both macro- and microgeographic perspectives. Hundreds of encounters with treeboas provided insights into various aspects of their ecology: habitat preference, diet, foraging behavior, daily activity, etc. With the probable exceptions of *Epicrates monensis* (e.g., Tolson 1988) and *Eunectes murinus*—based on the Venezuelan anaconda project (Rivas 1999)— I believe that we know more about the natural history of *C. grenadensis* than of any other snake species in the American tropics. I do not believe, however, that any aspect of *Corallus* natural history is adequately covered, or that I have a definitive grasp on any facet of *Corallus* natural history. And that paradox illustrates how little is known about the natural history of neotropical snakes.

I had two rather broad goals regarding my research with treeboas (and especially *C. grenadensis*): 1) to learn about treeboa natural history; and 2) to assess the impact of human history on the ecology of *Corallus*, especially in the West Indies. What is presented here is, in essence, a progress report: what we know and, just as importantly, what we do not know. I have little to offer regarding some topics (e.g., long-term movements, reproduction, and growth); nevertheless, I present what I do know so that others can see where we are and, hopefully, build upon it. Field work with *Corallus* in the West Indies and elsewhere continues.

MATERIALS AND METHODS

The vast majority of the data presented herein is concerned with *Corallus grenadensis*, a species with its distribution confined to the Grenada Bank. Most of the data were collected on Grenada, with significantly lesser amounts gleaned from snakes on several of the Grenadine islands. Because of the emphasis on *C. grenadensis*, I present more background information for that species. Throughout the book, I sometimes use the first person singular, and at other times the first person plural. When using the latter, I am merely indicating that I was accompanied by one or more of the following persons while on the Grenada Bank, and that they shared the pleasure and excitement of learning something new about *Corallus*: Joel Friesch, Gary Haas, Ky Henderson, Rose Henderson, Rich Sajdak, and Al Winstel; all have made multiple excursions in pursuit of treeboas.

On Grenada observations were made at night, usually between 1800 and 2400 h, although additional observations were made between 2400 and 0600 h. Searches were made with the aid of headlamps, and, rather than develop a search image for a treeboa, one develops a search image for a treeboa's telltale red-orange eyeshine. The eyeshine may be produced by the *tapetum lucidum*— meaning "bright carpet"—a mirroring device located somewhere behind the rod-and-cone layer (Walls 1942). The reflections from the tapetum increase the absolute and relative differential between an object and its surroundings, and thereby increase their discriminability (Walls 1942). With experience, one can learn to discriminate between the eyeshine of a treeboa and that of a variety of other animals. If two eyes are visible at once, it is most likely an opossum (*Didelphis marsupialis*) or a roof rat (*Rattus rattus*). Spiders also produce eyeshines, but often they have a greenish hue. Moths and some birds (i.e., caprimulgids) produce the eyeshines most often confused with *C. grenadensis*. If the eyeshine moos, it most likely belongs to a cow.

Snakes were invariably caught by hand, either from the ground or after ascending into a tree. We were often aided by bamboo poles or tree branches of varying length (up to about 8 m long) which increased our ability to capture treeboas that were beyond our grasp from either the ground or the branch we were standing on or hanging from. Only rarely during the initial collecting phase of the research did I resort to using a small saw to cut the branch or small tree harboring a treeboa.

One must just resign oneself to the fact that when working with *Corallus* you are going to get bitten. The bites are sometimes painful but never dangerous; they bleed a bit but never inhibit further collecting efforts. We never attempted the capture technique so vividly described by Mole and Urich (1894) for *C. ruschenbergerii*, but it probably has some merit. "The teeth are numerous, long, and sharp, and when disturbed the snakes are always ready to bite, throwing their heads forward with a ferocious lunge ...; but they are not at all sure of their aim, and their widely distended jaws can be easily avoided. They rarely if ever retreat when threatened. This makes their capture very easy, and the boys who catch them do so by advancing upon them boldly, presenting to them the palm of the open hand, fingers and thumb erect and close together. The snake thrusts forward its muzzle to examine the strange object, and the boy simply closes his hand and secures its head. The reptile can then be disentangled from the branches and placed in a bag."

A few *Corallus grenadensis* were marked with radio transmitters (see Henderson and Winstel 1992 for details), but as they were monitored for only 2–3 weeks, we view those data with some caution. Coupe (1997) determined that there was an approximately 20-day temporal effect from use of telemetry, and that the first 20 days of data should be eliminated from the data set. Telemetry data are used to describe how treeboas utilize parts of their habitat.

Some *Corallus grenadensis* were paint-marked (see Henderson and Winstel 1995 for details), or marked with Sanford "Sharpie" permanent marking pens. Observations were made with the aid of headlamps, sometimes affixed with a red filter in order to minimize disturbance to the snakes. Binoculars were used routinely to identify individual snakes and to observe foraging behavior, aided by illumination from one or more headlamps. Night vision binoculars and a night vision scope were used on a short-term basis, and both were found to be inadequate for observing foraging snakes, as it was difficult to separate the snake from the vegetation in which it was foraging.

Field work with a species as irascible as *Corallus grenadensis* poses some problems when working alone. When prolonged handling is necessary (for marking, examining for scars, recording notes on color and pattern), I have adopted a modified version of a technique used for much larger snakes (Rivas et al. 1995). To compensate for the much smaller size of *C. hortulanus*, instead of a sock, I cut the fingers off a glove (child's or adult's, depending on the size of the snake). When placed over the head of a treeboa, the snake would calm immediately and it could be handled without having to avoid repeated strikes. The "finger" did not have to be kept in place over the snake's head with tape or any other material.

All statistical procedures were performed using SAS (1990), and an alpha level of 0.05 was used for statistical significance. Means are presented ± 1 SE. Although I include common names for each of the four species in the next section, I use their scientific names throughout the remaining text.

THE *CORALLUS HORTULANUS* COMPLEX

Until recently (Henderson 1997a), the four species which are the focus of this publication (Table 1.1) were under the umbrella of a single name, *Corallus hortulanus*. Prior to the widespread use of the name *C. hortulanus*, this snake was generally referred to as *C. enydris*, and there was considerable disagreement over how many taxa were involved, and at what level. Many felt that two subspecies should be recognized (*C. e. enydris* and *C. e. cookii*), others considered the species monotypic (e.g., Chippaux 1986), and Hoge et al. (1978) considered *cookii* (their "*coocky*") a distinct species. McDiarmid et al. (1996) carefully documented the misuse of the name *C. enydris*, and presented a thorough synonymy for the species. Those interested in the nomenclatural history of the complex should review the papers by Henderson (1993a, 1997a) and McDiarmid et al. (1996, 1999).

Definition and Diagnosis. Members of the complex usually have nasals in contact (usually not in contact in *C. annulatus*, *C. blombergi*, *C. caninus*, and *C. cropanii*); subcaudals 94–137 (79–88 in *C. annulatus*, 65–74 in *C. caninus*, and less than 60 in *C. cropanii*). Other scale counts include maximum number of dorsal scale rows 37–63, ventrals 251–297, infraloreals 0–9, and scales between supraorbitals 3–14. In less than 1.0% of samples a supralabial scale is not separated from the orbit by a circumorbital scale (a diagnostic characteristic of the widely sympatric *Epicrates cenchria*).

Distribution. Southern Central America (south of 10° N) and some associated islets, northern South America (including the continental islands Isla Margarita, Trinidad, and Tobago), throughout the Guianas, Orinoquía, and Amazonia, to southeastern Brazil (Atlantic forests) to at least 26°08′ S; also St. Vincent and the Grenada Bank in the West Indies (Fig. 1.1).

KEY TO THE SPECIES OF THE *CORALLUS HORTULANUS* COMPLEX

1. Maximum number of dorsal scales usually greater than 50; main element in the dorsal pattern usually an irregular ellipsoid; dorsal ground color variable; occurs in southern Colombia, southern Venezuela, the Guianas, Ecuador, Peru, Brazil, and Bolivia .... *C. hortulanus*

Table 1.1. Distribution, size, habitat, and diet for members of the *Corallus hortulanus* complex.

Species	Range	Maximum known snout-vent length	Habitat	Diet
Corallus cookii	St. Vincent, West Indies	1374 mm	Rainforest; secondary forest; fruit orchards; dry scrub woodlands	Primarily lizards and rodents
Corallus grenadensis	Grenada Bank, West Indies	1625 mm	Rainforest; secondary forest; dry scrub woodlands; fruit orchards; mangroves	Primarily lizards and rodents
Corallus hortulanus	Amazonia, Guianas, southeastern Brazil	1787 mm	Primarily rainforest and secondary forest	Primarily birds, bats, and rodents
Corallus ruschenbergerii	Costa Rica, Panama, northern Colombia, northern Venezuela, Trinidad and Tobago	1870 mm	Rainforest; secondary forest; dry scrub woodland; mangrove forest; fruit orchards	Primarily lizards, birds, and rodents

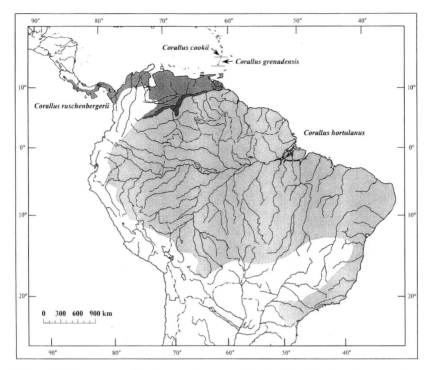

Figure 1.1. The ranges of the four species comprising the *Corallus hortulanus* complex of treeboas. See also Figure 1.3.

    Maximum number of dorsal scale rows always less than 50; main element of dorsal pattern spade shaped, rhomboidal (diamond-shaped), or an irregular hourglass, or free edge of dorsal scales edged with dark brown or black, or dorsal ground color yellowish with pale flecking 2

2.   Dorsal ground color taupe, brown, or gray, never yellowish, orange, or red; main element of dorsal pattern a ragged (and often squat) hourglass shape; occurs only on St. Vincent, West Indies . . . . *C. cookii*

    Dorsal ground color variable, including shades of yellow (khaki, tan, beige, etc.), orange, and red; main element of dorsal pattern usually spade-shaped or diamond-shaped, or free edge of dorsal scales edged in black or dark brown (occasionally devoid of a distinct dorsal pattern; rarely a ragged hourglass shape) 3

3.   Main element of dorsal pattern usually a spade shape, but if dorsal ground color yellowish, pattern may be faint or absent, or may be reduced to light flecking; dorsal ground color variable (taupe, brown, gray, dark brown,

shades of orange, shades of red, yellowish); occurs only on islands of the Grenada Bank, West Indies .... *C. grenadensis*

Main element of dorsal pattern often a rhomboid (diamond shape), or free edge of dorsal scales individually edged with black or dark brown; dorsal ground color khaki brown to rich mahogany brown, sooty gray or nearly black (depending on age), rarely taupe; occurs in Costa Rica, Panama, northern Colombia, northern Venezuela (including Isla Margarita), Trinidad, and Tobago .... *C. ruschenbergerii*

Corallus cookii Gray
St. Vincent Treeboa

Plates 1–3

Holotype. BMNH 1946.1.1.50, collected by Edward Cooke (date of collection unknown), male, 861 mm snout-vent length (SVL). Type-locality "America"; amended to "West Indies" by Gray (1849); restricted to St. Vincent by Henderson (1997a).

Definition. A species with maximum number of dorsal scale rows 39–48; ventrals 257–278; subcaudals 100–122; scales between supraoculars 7–13; infraloreals 0–4. Dorsal ground color always taupe, gray, or brown. The main element of the dorsal pattern is a ragged hourglass shape (Fig. 1.2:E) in some shade of gray or brown. A color photograph appears in Stafford and Henderson (1996: Plate 10, as *C. hortulanus*)

Diagnosis. Corallus cookii is most easily distinguished from other members of the *C. hortulanus* complex by its color pattern. It lacks the color variation (pale yellow, orange, red, many shades of brown) found in *C. hortulanus* and *C. grenadensis*. Likewise, the main element of the dorsal pattern is relatively constant, and it rarely occurs in populations outside of St. Vincent. The diamond-shaped pattern characteristic of *C. ruschenbergerii* does not occur in this species. *Corallus cookii* is distinguishable from mainland *C. hortulanus* by maximum number of dorsal scale rows: invariably less than 50 in *C. cookii* (39–48; $\bar{x}$ = 43.9 ± 0.34) and almost always more than 50 in *C. hortulanus* (47–63; $\bar{x}$ = 55.0 ± 0.17; specimens with less than 50 occur occasionally in Guyana, Suriname, Bolivia, and Peru).

Description of Holotype. A male, 861 mm SVL, tail 226 mm; maximum rows of dorsal scales 48; ventrals 269; subcaudals 119; infraloreals 5; circumorbital scales 14; scales between supraoculars 14; head width 15.4 mm, head length 26.2 mm. The dorsal ground color is taupe, and the body has 39 distorted, medium brown, hourglass-shaped markings; top of head with a somewhat

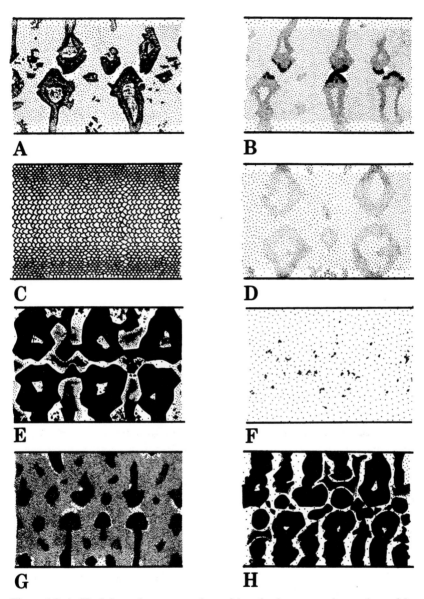

Figure 1.2. A–H. Schematic representations of dorsal color patterns in members of the *Corallus hortulanus* complex. From Henderson (1997a), and reproduced with permission of *Caribbean Journal of Science*. **A.** *C. hortulanus*—Bolivia (CMNH 2756); **B.** *C. hortulanus*—Guyana (USNM 145463); **C.** *C. ruschenbergerii*—Trinidad (AMNH 73097); **D.** *C. ruschenbergerii*—Costa Rica (UMMZ 131314); **E.** *C. cookii*—St. Vincent (MPM 23302); **F.** *C. hortulanus*—Guyana (USNM 145470); **G.** *C. grenadensis*—Grenada (USNM 167398); **H.** *C. grenadensis*—Grenada (USNM 67233).

vermiculate pattern; postorbital stripes are interrupted; underside of head off-white with several small taupe smudges; ventrals off-white to pale yellow with scattered medium brown flecks and smudges over the entire length of body; the dorsal pattern encroaches onto the lateral edges of the ventrals.

Distribution. St. Vincent (Fig. 1.3). Altitudinal distribution is uncertain; there is a record from Kingstown (MCZ 140154), but that could be anywhere from sea level to about 100 m. The highest elevation at which I have encountered *C. cookii* is 425 m (St. Patrick, Hermitage: Milwaukee Public Museum (MPM) specimens 26148-49). The distribution does not overlap with other *Corallus* species.

Remarks. Problems regarding the type-locality and holotype were discussed by Henderson (1997a). The distinctiveness of the St. Vincent populations of *Corallus* was previously noted by Underwood (1964), and Albert Schwartz (pers. comm., 1986) also alluded to it.

Corallus grenadensis (Barbour)
Grenada Bank Treeboa

Plates 4–10

Holotype. MCZ 7791, collected 20 August 1910 by G.M. Allen, male, 1170 mm SVL. Type-locality "St. George's, Grenada."

Definition. A species with maximum number of dorsal scale rows 37–46; ventrals 251–278; subcaudals 100–119; scales between supraoculars 3–9; infraloreals 0–4. Dorsal ground color variable (yellowish, orange, gray, taupe, brown), but yellowish (30.4% in a sample of 194) and taupe (64.9%) predominate; collecting sites dictate which color predominates. The main element in the dorsal pattern is usually spade-shaped (80.0%), either with sharp or rounded edges (Fig. 1.2:G, H), but other pattern elements are more prevalent in *C. grenadensis* than in other members of the complex. The anteriormost pattern elements are diamond-shaped. In The Grenadines, yellow snakes have been collected only on Bequia, but they have been observed on Union Island (J. Daudin, pers. comm.), and Garman (1887) reported a "uniform dingy yellow" treeboa "from the Grenadines." Snakes with an orange dorsal ground color have been collected on Mayreau. Color photographs appear in Stafford and Henderson (1996: Plates 6–8, 11, and 13–14, as *C. hortulanus*).

Diagnosis. *Corallus grenadensis* is distinguished from *C. hortulanus* by maximum rows of dorsal scales (37–46, $\bar{x} = 41.0 \pm 0.12$ in *grenadensis* vs. 47–63,

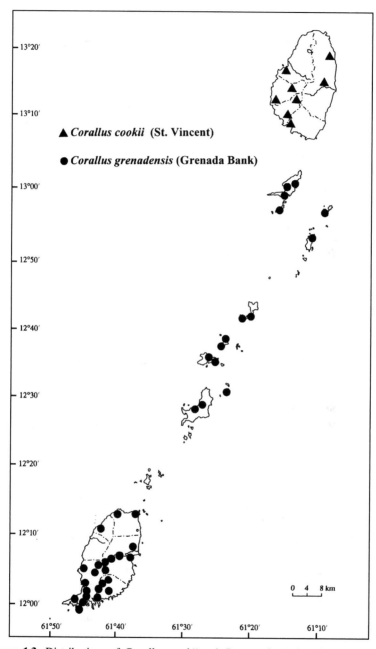

Figure 1.3. Distributions of *Corallus cookii* and *C. grenadensis* based on specimens examined.

$\bar{x} = 55.0 \pm 0.17$ in *hortulanus*). The primary spadelike element of the dorsal pattern occasionally occurs on the mainland (primarily the Guianas and northeastern Brazil), but not on St. Vincent (*C. cookii*). The rhomb pattern typical of *C. ruschenbergerii* does not occur in *C. grenadensis*.

Description of the Holotype. An adult male, 1170 mm SVL, tail 316 mm; maximum rows of dorsal scales 42; ventrals 270; subcaudals 112; infraloreals 2; circumorbital scales 10; scales between supraoculars 6; head width 20.3 mm; head length 35.0 mm. The dorsum is pale yellow with taupe flecking and no discernible pattern; top of head with some taupe flecks and small blotches; underside of head immaculate; postorbital stripes reduced to small blotches near angle of jaw; venter dull yellow, anteriorly immaculate and posteriorly with some taupe flecks.

Distribution. Islands of the Grenada Bank (see Fig. 1.3). It has been collected on Bequia, Île à Quatre, Baliceaux, Mustique, Canouan, Mayreau, Union, Petite Martinique, Carriacou and Grenada. I suspect it occurs on other islands on the bank, including some that have been unsuccessfully searched for the species, e.g., Prune Island (= Palm Island on some newer maps). The range of *C. grenadensis* does not overlap with other *Corallus* species. On Grenada, altitudinal distribution is from sea level (including mangrove branches overhanging the Caribbean) to at least 520 m. It is unlikely that *C. grenadensis* is altitudinally precluded anywhere on The Grenadines. The Grenadines which are known to harbor *C. grenadensis* range in size from 0.7 km^2 (Petite Martinique) to 32.0 km^2 (Carriacou); the highest peak is only 305 m (on Union); and annual rainfall ranges from about 900 mm (Mayreau) to about 1880 mm (Bequia) (Howard 1952). The forests are all secondary, having been cleared for agriculture or in order to make room for the human population (Howard 1952).

Corallus hortulanus (Linnaeus)
Amazon Treeboa

Plates 11–25

Holotype. Naturhistoriska Riksmuseet, Stockholm (NRS) Lin. 7, collector and date of collection unknown. Type-locality, "America."

Definition. A species with maximum number of dorsal scale rows 47–63; ventrals 258–297; subcaudals 105–137; scales between supraoculars 5–14; infraloreals 0–9; circumorbital scales 8–17. Dorsal ground color variable (yellow, gray, taupe, brown, pink, or reddish), but taupe predominates (71.5% in a sample of 256), and taupe+brown+gray account for 80.9%; yellow-brown (yellow, khaki, beige, brownish yellow) is much less common (19.1% of sample). The main element of the dorsal pattern is usually a dorsoventrally oriented ellipsoid with the dorsal end broader than the ventral end (Fig. 1.2:A, B); many variations of this shape appear throughout the range (Fig. 1.2:F). The anteriormost elements of the dorsal pattern are diamond-shaped. Maximum SVL is at least 1787 mm (W.W. Lamar, in litt., April 2000). Color photographs appear in Stafford and Henderson (1996: Plates 23–25 and 27–33).

Diagnosis. *Corallus hortulanus* is distinguishable from other species in the complex by the maximum number of dorsal scale rows (almost always over 50 in *hortulanus*, always less than 50 in *cookii*, *grenadensis*, and *ruschenbergerii*). Populations of *C. hortulanus* which harbor snakes with less than 50 dorsal scale rows occur in Guyana, Suriname, Bolivia, and Peru. In general, *C. hortulanus* has higher counts for meristic characters (Table 1.2) than other members of the complex. The shape of the main element in the dorsal pattern at midbody is more or less ellipsoidal, whereas it is a ragged hourglass in *cookii* (Fig. 1.2:E) and is usually spade-shaped in *grenadensis* (Table 1.3; Fig. 1.2:G, H).

Distribution. The Guianas and Amazonia (southern Colombia, southern Venezuela, Ecuador, Peru, Bolivia, Brazil) (see Fig. 1.1). The distribution in Brazil also includes Cerrado, mesic enclaves in Caatinga (Puorto and Henderson 1994), sand dune areas in Caatinga (Rodrigues 1996), Atlantic rainforest to about 26°08′ (Puorto and Henderson 1994), and Ilha Grande (off southeastern Brazil). Its distribution is widely sympatric (and probably syntopic) with *C. caninus*, sympatric with *C. cropanii*, and marginally sympatric or parapatric with *C. ruschenbergerii* (see below). Altitudinal distribution is from sea level to about 915 m (USNM 60694 from the Río Cosireni, Cuzco, Peru). In general, collection localities above 200–300 m are rare. The record for *C. hortulanus* collected between La Aguadita and Fusagasugá, Cundinamarca, Colombia, at 1900 m (Pérez-Santos and Moreno 1988) is based on a misidentified *Chironius monticola* (O. Victoria Castaño, in litt., 17 Sept 1993).

Remarks. McDiarmid et al. (1996) determined that *Corallus hortulanus* is the correct name for snakes long referred to as *C. enydris*. Based on the scale counts and inadequate color and pattern description given in Linnaeus (1758) and Andersson (1899), the type of *Boa enydris* is most likely *C. hortulanus*.

Corallus ruschenbergerii (Cope)
Caribbean Coastal Treeboa

Plates 26–32

Holotype. ANSP 10325, collected by W.S.W. Ruschenberger, female, 1530 mm SVL. Type-locality "Panama."

Table 1.2. Mean ± SE (range; N) for selected meristic characters in species of the *Corallus hortulanus* complex. None of the species exhibited significant sexual dimorphism in any of the characters.

	C. hortulanus	C. grenadensis	C. cookii	C. ruschenbergerii
Ventrals	278.6 ± 0.43 (258–297; 252)	263.7 ± 0.30 (251–278; 187)	268.4 ± 0.65 (257–278; 42)	262.9 ± 0.47 (250–272; 119)
Subcaudals	117.9 ± 0.37 (105–137; 234)	109.0 ± 0.32 (100–119; 174)	115.2 ± 0.61 (100–122; 35)	105.8 ± 0.35 (94–115; 113)
Scales between supraoculars	10.2 ± 0.10 (5–14; 252)	6.3 ± 0.08 (3–9; 193)	9.7 ± 0.25 (7–13; 42)	6.0 ± 0.12 (3–10; 125)
Infraloreals	3.7 ± 0.09 (0–9; 257)	1.8 ± 0.07 (0–4; 189)	2.0 ± 0.17 (0–4; 43)	2.7 ± 0.08 (0–6; 126)
Circumorbital scales	14.6 ± 0.08 (8–17; 249)	11.5 ± 0.08 (8–14; 186)	12.5 ± 0.17 (10–14; 39)	13.5 ± 0.09 (11–16; 122)
Maximum number of dorsal scale rows	55.0 ± 0.17 (47–63; 255)	41.0 ± 0.12 (37–46; 192)	43.9 ± 0.34 (39–48; 42)	43.8 ± 0.19 (38–48; 123)

Table 1.3. Summary of predominant color and pattern characteristics in tree-boas of the *Corallus hortulanus* complex. All figures are percentages within each species.

	Species			
	hortulanus	*cookii*	*grenadensis*	*ruschenbergerii*
Dorsal color				
Taupe	80.9	100.0	65.0	60.2
Yellow	19.1	0.0	30.4	39.8
Orange	0.0	0.0	4.6	0.0
Pattern				
Ellipse	64.7	0.0	5.4	0.0
Rhomb	2.4	0.0	0.0	59.7
Hourglass	2.7	87.8	1.1	0.0
Spade	9.0	2.4	80.0	0.0
Dorsals edged with black	0.0	0.0	0.0	27.1
Flecks	2.0	0.0	7.0	0.0
Patternless	3.9	0.0	2.2	9.8
Other	15.3	9.8	4.3	3.4

Definition. A very large species; maximum SVL at least 1870 mm; maximum total length at least 2311 mm based on preserved material, but surely reaching at least 2500 mm (the specimen with the longest SVL, FMNH 49918, has a stub tail). Maximum number of dorsal scale rows 38–48, ventrals 250–272, subcaudals 94–115, infraloreals 1–6, circumorbital scales 11–16. The hemipenes are bilobed. The dorsal ground color ranges from yellow-brown to deep copper brown and sooty gray (to nearly black in some individuals: W.W. Lamar, in litt., April 2000); the dorsal pattern may be as follows: 1) a series of diamonds or rhombs (59.7% in a sample of 134) (Fig. 1.2:D); 2) the free edge of most or all dorsal scales dark brown or black (27.1%) (Fig. 1.2:C); 3) a combination of 1 and 2 (3.4%); or 4) lacking any discernible pattern (9.8%) (see Table 1.2). The ground color of the venter ranges from white to lemon yellow, often without conspicuous markings, but if present more prominent posteriorly. Color photographs appear in Stafford and Henderson (1996: Plates 17 and 19–22, as *C. hortulanus*).

Diagnosis. *Corallus ruschenbergerii* is easily distinguished from all other species of *Corallus* except *C. grenadensis*. The maximum number of dorsal scale rows in *C. cropanii* is fewer than 35 (38–48 in *C. ruschenbergerii*). *Corallus annulatus*, the only congener with which there is significant sympatry, has a maximum of 50–57 dorsal scale rows and only 79–88 subcaudals (94–115 in *C. ruschenbergerii*). *Corallus caninus* has a maximum of 63–77 dorsal scale rows, and 186–209 ventrals (250–272 in *C. ruschenbergerii*). With very few exceptions, *C. hortulanus* from mainland South America and Ilha Grande off southeastern Brazil have 50 or more maximum dorsal scale rows (individuals from Guyana, Suriname, Peru, and Bolivia rarely have 47 or 48) and color pattern is extremely variable.

Corallus from St. Vincent and the Grenada Bank are the shortest and most slender of the Neotropical treeboas, and this can be related to aspects of their ecology. They exhibit great overlap in lepidosis with *C. ruschenbergerii*, but *C. ruschenbergerii* is much larger (maximum SVL in West Indian *Corallus* is 1625 mm), and *C. grenadensis* exhibits tremendous color and pattern variation. Despite the pattern variation in the West Indian populations, none of it duplicates that found in *C. ruschenbergerii*, with the exception of yellow-brown individuals that have no discernible pattern.

Description of the Holotype. An adult female, 1530 mm SVL, tail 353 mm; maximum rows of dorsal scales 48; ventrals 270; subcaudals 107; infraloreals 2; circumorbital scales 14; scales between supraoculars 5; head width 28.2 mm; head length 53.8 mm. Dorsal ground color pale yellow to pale khaki, with about 37 pale taupe to brown rhomboid markings on left side of the laterally compressed body (shapes of the markings are more diamondlike near head and near tail); dorsal markings more prominent on posterior part of body and on tail; top of head with pale smudges posteriorly; underside of head immaculate pale yellow; postorbital stripes pale and ill defined; ventrals dull yellow, immaculate anteriorly (but with slight lateral encroachment of the dorsal pattern), and with brown blotches appearing near midventer and becoming more prominent posteriorly; dull yellow subcaudals moderately to heavily marked with brown.

Distribution. *Corallus ruschenbergerii* occurs from southern Costa Rica (south of 10° N), through Panama (including the offshore islands of Isla del Rey, Isla Contadora, Isla de Cébaco, and Isla Suscantupu); in Colombia east of the Andes in the llanos and adjacent foothills, and more or less north of the cordilleras Central and Oriental; and in Venezuela north of the Cordillera de Mérida and the Río Orinoco (and on Isla Margarita), and north and west of the Guiana Shield. Although Lancini and Kornacker (1989) depict *Corallus* (which, on the basis of geography, must be *C. ruschenbergerii*) as occurring on the northern tip of the Península de Paraguaná, I am not aware of specimens documenting its presence there. The eastward edge of the range appears to be the Orinoco Delta. The species also occurs on Trinidad and Tobago (see Fig. 1.1).

The ranges of *Corallus ruschenbergerii* and *C. hortulanus* may exhibit a narrow zone of sympatry just south of the Río Orinoco in Venezuela and just east of the Cordillera Oriental in Departamento Meta, Colombia. Altitudinal distribution of *C. ruschenbergerii* is largely under 200 m, but it has a limited distribution to at least 600 m above sea level (asl) (above Villavicencio, Meta, Colombia: W.W. Lamar, in litt.). The distribution of *C. ruschenbergerii* largely excludes areas of tropical rainforest on the South American mainland (based on vegetation maps in Hueck and Seibert [1972], Ewel et al. [1976], and Campbell and Lamar [1989]), and on the system of morphoclimatic domains (Ab'Saber, 1977). Instead, it has a wide distribution in lowland dry forest, thorn forest, savanna/grassland with woody species (llanos with gallery forests), and lower montane dry forest. It also occurs in coastal mangrove stands (Isla Salamanca, Colombia; Río Sierpè, Costa Rica: W.W. Lamar, in litt., April 2000). On Trinidad and Tobago and in Central America it occurs in tropical moist forest. In contrast, *C. caninus* is largely restricted to lowland rainforest (although it does occur at altitudes reaching at least 1000 m asl: Lehr 2001) and Cerrado, while *C. hortulanus* has a limited distribution outside of lowland tropical rainforest (with limited distribution in Atlantic forest, Caatinga, Cerrado, and gallery forests in savanna/grassland: Henderson et al. 1995). Rainfall over most of the range of *C. ruschenbergerii* is depressed: usually 1000–2000 mm annually, although it does occur in areas that receive less than 1000 mm annually. In Central America and the Chocó of Colombia, annual rainfall within its range may reach 4000 mm (Snow 1976). By contrast, *Corallus caninus* occurs only in rainfall regimes of 1500–4000 mm annually. The vast majority of the range of *C. hortulanus* occurs in areas that receive annual precipitation of 1500–4000 mm; it also has limited distribution in areas that receive less than 1500 mm annually (including areas in Caatinga that receive about 700 mm annually: Rodrigues 1996).

Remarks. The largest *C. ruschenbergerii* SVL is more than 230 mm greater than the largest *C. hortulanus*, and 245 mm larger than the largest *C. cookii* or *C. grenadensis.* Although the available prey in the range of *C. ruschenbergerii* is, in a broad taxonomic sense, essentially the same as for *C. hortulanus* (including high species diversity for lizards, but with population densities much lower than in the West Indies), because of its large size *C. ruschenbergerii* exploits prey species (e.g., *Marmosa, Herpestes*) probably not taken by *C. hortulanus*.

A BRIEF DESCRIPTION OF GRENADA AND SELECTED LOCALITIES

The southernmost of the main islands in the Lesser Antilles, Grenada is situated about 135 km off the north coast of Trinidad, and about 140 km off the north coast of Venezuela on the Península de Paria. It is about 34 km long and 19 km wide, and has an area of 311.0 km². It is a moderately eroded volcanic pile, apparently intermediate in age between young St. Vincent and old St. Lucia. The highest peak, Morne St. Catherine (839 m), rises in the northern half of the island as the center of a massif surrounded by lesser peaks and ridges. South of this peak is a low depression, and beyond it the land rises again into a long curving ridge (or system of ridges), running first toward the south and then to the east and northeast. This chain contains numerous peaks and high points: Fedon's Camp (840 m), Morne QuaQua (735 m), Mt. Sinai (701 m), and Southeast Mountain (219 m), and embraces several old crater basins, one of which is the lake occupied by Grand Etang. From these central mountains the land descends gradually to the sea. There is no coastal plain, but there are lowlands in the northeast at Levera and in the southwest where a long low peninsula runs out to Point Salines. Except in the higher parts of the mountains, slopes are not excessively steep and, with the small size of the island, this has led to a large proportion of the area being cleared for cultivation. Orchard crops form the bulk of the cultivations. Because of the gentle topography along most of the coastline, eroded hills covered with poor bush are not a common feature except in the extreme south (rough grazing land with acacia covers most of the Point Salines peninsula). In the interior, nearly all of the land to the mountain tops was sold to estates, and cultivations were pushed to the highest practicable limit in most cases (though some estate owners preserved belts of forest on ridges for protective purposes: Beard 1949).

Following are brief descriptions of the habitat at several localities that are referred to throughout the text (Fig. 1.4). The most intensive work was conducted at Mt. Hartman Bay and Westerhall Estate.

Beausejour Estate. Situated just off the leeward coast in St. George Parish at about 55 m asl, this site is trisected by a dirt road and by the Beausejour River. It is a mosaic of cleared areas, orchard crops, and native vegetation (much of it second growth); a few large (ca. 30 m tall) trees (*Ceiba*), remnants of forests cut long ago, are situated along the river (Fig. 1.5). The road cut and the river, which more or less parallel one another, provide long stretches of edge habitat which are critical for *Corallus grenadensis*. Rainfall is moderate (1500-2000 mm/year) and there is a short dry season (i.e., mean number of relatively dry months/year is between 3 and 4). Additional photographs of the site appear in Henderson and Winstel (1992) and Henderson (1993b).

Mt. Hartman Bay. This site borders Mt. Hartman Bay (Mosquito Bay on some older maps) along one of the peninsulas on the southwest coast of the island. It is described in some detail in Henderson et al. (1998), and photographs of it appear in Henderson (1997b, 1998), and Henderson et al. (1998). It is adjacent to the Grenada Dove (*Leptotila wellsi*) Reserve, the last stronghold of this endan-

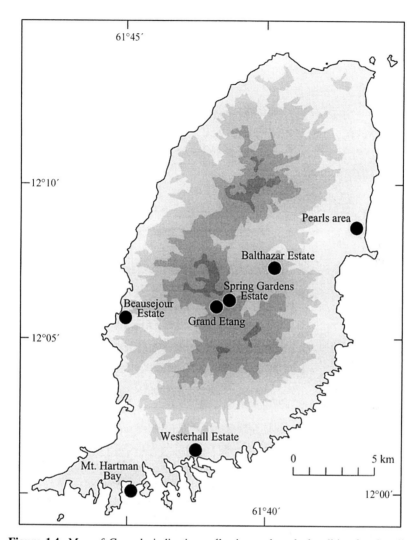

Figure 1.4. Map of Grenada indicating collecting and study localities for *Corallus grenadensis*. Contour lines are at 120 m, 365 m, and 610 m.

gered species and the national bird of Grenada. A 550-m transect marked off in 10-m segments was established along a narrow path which ran along a mangrove-acacia interface (Fig. 1.6). Low hills (60 m asl) rise above the bay on the narrow peninsula, and although *C. grenadensis* occurs virtually to the tops of the hills, we could not observe these snakes from the transect path. All of our

Figure 1.5. *Corallus grenadensis* habitat along the Beausejour River, St. George Parish, Grenada (Oct. 1991). Photo by R.W. Henderson.

Figure 1.6. Acacia-mangrove habitat along Mt. Hartman Bay, St. George Parish, Grenada (Feb. 1998). Photo by R.A. Sajdak.

observations at this site occurred at or near (<10 m asl) sea level. A dense stand of mangroves (largely *Rhizophora mangle*, but including *Avicennia*, *Laguncularia*, and *Conocarpus*) borders much of the bay side of the transect, but is edged by *Acacia nilotica* and other thorny scrub vegetation on the southern end of the transect. Manchineel (*Hippomane mancinella*) was also a common associate with the mangroves. The side of the transect away from the bay is completely devoid of mangrove; vegetation there is dominated by dense stands of *Acacia nilotica*. Other conspicuous vegetation includes logwood (*Haematoxylum campechianum*) and gumbo limbo (*Bursera simaruba*). At the southernmost section of the transect, at the mouth of the bay, only the eastern portion of the transect remains, with open water to the west. Here a steep eroded cliff harbors a high concentration of prickly pear (*Opuntia dellenii*), organ pipe cactus (*Cephalocereus royenii*), and century plant (*Agave caribaeicola*), interspersed with other thorny vegetation; *C. grenadensis* occurred occasionally in this habitat, also (Fig. 1.7). Although portions of this site are adjacent to agricultural activities (mostly sugarcane), only about 1% of the transect had any agricultural activity (corn) and, although this occurred late in the study, it did eliminate a section of the site that had until then produced the most snakes and observations. There was also some cutting of trees at the site for charcoal production.

Figure 1.7. Cactus-acacia scrub at the mouth of Mt. Hartman Bay. *Corallus grenadensis* would occasionally be encountered on the steep cliff face (Feb. 1998). Photo by R.A. Sajdak.

<u>Westerhall Estate.</u> At about 45 m asl in St. David Parish, this site is a wonderful mosaic of mixed agriculture (banana, nutmeg, breadfruit, citrus, cacao, coconut, pineapple, mango, sugarcane, corn), dry scrub woodlands (*fide* Beard 1949), and open treeless areas. A 610-m transect (19–46 m asl) was established along a north-south unpaved road that rarely received vehicular traffic. Habitat east and west of the road was considered part of the study site (Fig. 1.8). The transect was marked at 10-m segments using numbered biodegradable flags. The transect more or less paralleled, but did not include, the St. Louis River. Because the road was constructed along a hillside, portions of the transect rose above the road (west side) or dropped off toward the river (east side). Vegetation in the uncultivated sections of the transect included *Bursera simaruba, Pisonia fragrans, Tabebuia pallida, Ficus* sp., *Leucaena leucocephala, Lonchocarpus, Acacia* spp., *Amyris* sp., *Pithecellobium* sp., and *Randia* sp. The uncultivated areas occasionally included bamboo (*Bambusa* sp.) and/or harbored a solitary tree of mango, breadfruit, or *Annona* spp. Coconut palms (*Cocos nucifera*) bordered the road in many segments of the transect. Additional photographs of the site appear in Henderson and Winstel (1995), Henderson (1996), and Henderson et al. (1998). The area receives 1500–2000 mm of rain annually, and the mean number of relatively dry months is between 3 and 4/year. The site has been under cultivation for over 200 years (Hall 1982; Brizan 1984). The

Figure 1.8. *Corallus grenadensis* habitat in an area of mixed agriculture at Westerhall Estate, St. David Parish, Grenada (April 1993). Photo by R.A. Winstel.

Westerhall Rum Factory is adjacent to the site. The original building of the distillery was built in 1800 and is still in use; personnel at the factory informed me that sugarcane cultivation was much more extensive in the nineteenth century than it is currently. Similarly, a local gentleman (Clifton Noel) who was 80 years old in 1993 and had lived in the area all of his life told me that sugarcane cultivation within the study site was much more widespread during his boyhood than now. He observed that rats (*Rattus*) were common, and were especially attracted to sugarcane and corn. During field work in April 2000, Ky Henderson and I encountered new houses immediately to the south of the transect. We also encountered more *C. grenadensis* than I had recorded since 1993, including some within a few meters of one of the new houses.

Grand Etang Forest Reserve. Located in St. Andrew Parish, and the site of a volcanic crater lake, this is the highest site (525 m) at which I have collected *Corallus grenadensis*. This area is often cloaked in cloud cover. Rainfall is heavy (4000 mm/year), and there is no dry season (the mean number of relatively dry months is <1.0/year). The percentage of possible sunshine is low. According to Beard (1949), the dominant trees form a closed canopy, with *Dacryodes excelsa* and *Licania ternatensis* being especially conspicuous. Other dominant species include *Sloanea caribaea*, *Euterpe* sp., and *Cassipourea elliptica*. Epiphytes are rare, as are large rope lianas. According to Barbour and McAndrews (1995), based on radiocarbon-dated fossilized pollen taken from a 13-m core extracted from Grand Etang, rainforest has persisted at this site for at least 25,000 years. Beard (1949) commented on the paucity of tree species in rainforest on Grenada.

I have encountered few treeboas here, and it is always an event when one is finally found. The Grand Etang Forest Reserve is a national park, nicely maintained, and therefore devoid of agricultural activity in the immediate area. Treeboas collected/observed here often have a dark brown dorsal ground color.

Spring Gardens Estate. At 460 m asl in St. Andrew Parish, this site is at the highest elevation that intermittently (i.e., more often than Grand Etang) produced treeboas; we had many more unsuccessful trips to this site (i.e., devoid of treeboas) than we had successful ones. Part of the Grand Etang rainforest, and about 1.6 km from the Grand Etang Forest Reserve headquarters, this site is devoted largely to nutmeg and banana cultivation, with some mango and citrus (Fig. 1.9). The trees are lush and the leaves are often dripping moisture. Annual rainfall is 3000–4000 mm (there is no dry season, i.e., the mean number of relatively dry months/year is <1.0), and cloud cover is heavy much of the time. Treeboas at this site often had a dark brown dorsal ground color. Visits to this site from 1989 to 1998 indicated little alteration of the habitat. Field work in

Figure 1.9. *Corallus grenadensis* habitat at Spring Gardens Estate, St. Andrew Parish, Grenada (Feb. 1998). Photo by R.A. Sajdak.

April 2000 saw clearing of hillsides in close proximity to where our search efforts had been concentrated since 1989.

Balthazar Estate. Located in St. Andrew Parish along the Balthazar River at about 75 m asl, this is an area of mixed agriculture on low rolling hills. Predominant fruit trees include mango, banana, nutmeg, citrus, breadfruit, and coconut (Fig. 1.10). Treeboas were encountered in the vines of passion fruit (*Passiflora edulis*), as well as in stands of bamboo (*Bambusa* sp.) along the river at this site. The hillsides above the site support a nice stand of royal palms (*Roystonea regia*). Rainfall is moderate (1500–2000 mm/year), and the mean number of relatively dry months/year is between 3 and 4. In April 2000, this site was still very much intact and treeboas were not uncommon.

Pearls. Situated at about 30 m asl in St. Andrew Parish, this site is less than 1 km from the windward coast. It is a lush area of mixed agriculture, interspersed with tall trees (25+ m) that are forest remnants. Fruit trees include banana, citrus, breadfruit, coconut, and lots of mango (Fig. 1.11). The study areas were in an agro-climatic transition area, where annual rainfall is 1000–2000 mm, and

Figure 1.10. Area of mixed agriculture at Balthazar Estate along the Balthazar River, St. Andrew Parish, Grenada (Feb 1998). This was a productive site for *Corallus grenadensis* between 1989 and 2000. Photo by R.A. Sajdak.

Figure 1.11. Area of mixed agriculture at Pearls Estate, St. Andrew Parish, Grenada (Feb. 1998). This was a productive site for *Corallus grenadensis* between 1988 and 2000. Photo by R.A. Sajdak.

the mean number of dry months/year is between 3 and 6. In April 2000, this site was still very much intact and treeboas were very common.

THE GRENADINES

The Grenadine islands are part of the Grenada Bank (Grenada and The Grenadines) and are situated between St. Vincent to the north and Grenada to the south (see Fig. 1.3; Fig. 1.12). Approximately 120 islands comprise the group, and the entire surface of the islands is about 130.0 km². According to Howard (1952), if the current sea level was lowered 38 m, all of the islands between Bequia and Carriacou would be united. Although only nine of the Grenadine islands are currently known to harbor populations of *Corallus grenadensis*, locals have informed us that they occur on additional islands; these rumors await verification.

The Grenadines have been inhabited continuously by Europeans since 1650, and deforestation, poor farming practices, and rapidly increasing erosion have helped to deteriorate agriculture over the past 200 years (Kingsbury 1960). The islands were divided into estates, with the smaller islands representing single plantations. The human population on The Grenadines waxed and waned

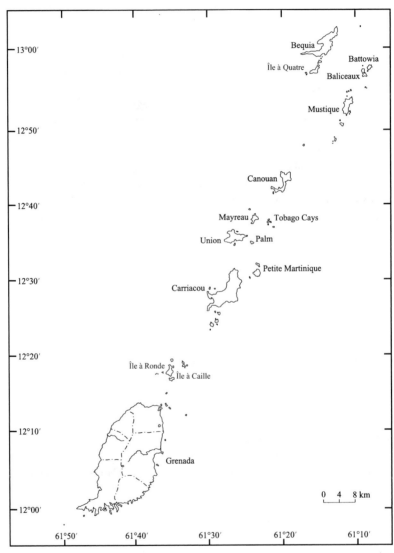

Figure 1.12. Grenada and The Grenadines.

with the sugar economy and the slave population. In 1831 the total human population was 9500, of which 6000 were slaves, and sugar production was about 25,000 tons. There was a more or less gradual population decline through the remainder of the nineteenth century, and by 1859 sugar production was down to 8000 tons. By 1910 the human population was reported to be 2500 persons. The twentieth century, however, saw a gradual increase in human population on the islands (Howard 1952), but sugar was grown only for local consumption. With the abolition of slavery and the sugar crisis, cotton became the important crop in the economy of The Grenadines in the latter half of the nineteenth century, and it continues to some degree today. Both sugar and cotton rely on having open treeless (or near-treeless) fields, and the impact of this on *Corallus grenadensis* populations is obvious. However, as on Grenada and St. Vincent, cutting of forests on The Grenadines probably increased potential treeboa habitat by creating more edge situations.

Howard (1952) presents detailed descriptions of the vegetation for each of the main Grenadine islands. Here I touch on factors that may impact on the distribution of *Corallus grenadensis* on each of the islands. To that end, this quote from Howard (1952) is significant: "The forested areas of the Grenadines are secondary formations. At one time practically every possible acre of land has been under cultivation and those not cultivated have been extensively cut back by the pressure of [human] population needs." Nearly 50 years later, his reference to the pressures of human population needs is just as critical.

The Grenadines offer almost endless possibilities for treeboa research; hopefully, field work there will be initiated before the islands are decimated.

Carriacou. The largest of The Grenadines with an area of 32.0 km^2, its highest elevation is 226 m. Annual rainfall is about 1310 mm (Howard 1952). Carriacou had a long history of sugar cultivation, followed by cotton. Lime trees were also extensively planted. In the remaining woodland areas, the dominant tree species are *Bursera simaruba*, *Pisonia fragrans*, *Ficus lentiginosa*, and *Lonchocarpus benthamianus*. Beard (1949) encountered a woodland of almost pure mahogany (*Swietenia mahogani*), about 18 m high; he considered it pioneer community on old agricultural land. According to Kingsbury (1960), Carriacou is the longest continually occupied of The Grenadines, and in 1784 it had about 50 estates varying in size from 6.5 to 223 hectares (ha). In the late 1950s, 64% of the island's area was divided into 2270 "peasant holdings," cultivable land amounted to 1700 ha, lime production was on the increase, and 162 ha were designated forest reserves (Kingsbury 1960). Today, Carriacou is being discovered by tourists and accommodations for them are proliferating. In 1989, Rose Henderson and I, based on a single night of collecting and on interviews with residents, got the impression that *Corallus* was ubiquitous on the island. Everyone we spoke with was aware of the snake and we were told they occurred everywhere. We encountered them in roadside scrub and in a large expanse of *Coccoloba uvifera* and *Cocos nucifera*.

Bequia. The northernmost of the larger islands, Bequia has an area of 18.0 km^2 and its highest elevation is 262 m. Annual precipitation is about 1880 mm (Howard 1952). Bequia has been heavily populated and cultivated for a long time, and the vegetation is much altered with secondary brush predominating. In the 1820s, nearly 1500 ha were planted in sugarcane (about 83% of the island's area). Sea island cotton was introduced to Bequia in 1930, and that was the principal crop on the island during Howard's field work, but Kingsbury (1960) reported that very little commercial cotton was grown. Nichols (1891) provided a list of "the most conspicuous plants" he encountered, and these included *Bursera simaruba, Ceiba pentandra, Cocos nucifera, Tabebuia pallida, Opuntia, Agave,* and *Hippomane.* Howard (1952) encountered undisturbed woodland only on the northern slopes or cliffs of the southwest peninsula, with trees reaching 8–10 m in height. *Corallus* was collected in stands of acacia in 1992.

Union. Union is the most rugged of The Grenadines, with an area of 8.1 km^2 and highest elevation reaching 305 m (the highest point in The Grenadines). Rainfall is about 960 mm annually (Howard 1952). Cotton has been the primary crop here, with virtually every acre (save the highest ridges and swamps) devoted to it. According to Howard (1952), "the current vegetation has been at least 50 and perhaps as much as 120 years in developing." At the time of Howard's visit (1950) to the island, raising stock (cattle, sheep, goats, and chickens) was the principal industry, with large areas devoted to pasture. According to Kingsbury (1960), cotton was still the main commercial crop, and livestock (goats, sheep, poultry, pigs, and cattle) had the run of the island. At the time of my visit (1990), Union had a serviceable airstrip and was a hub for getting to other islands in the group. Development of the island for tourism is gathering momentum. Dominant tree species include *Bursera simaruba, Ficus* sp., *Hippomane mancinella,* and *Coccoloba* sp. In 1990 there were small areas of mangrove that were very productive for *Corallus grenadensis,* and in 1992 Gary Haas found treeboas in residential areas of Clifton.

Canouan (also spelled Cannouan). Canouan has an area of 7.4 km^2 and the highest point on the island is 247 m. Annually the island receives about 1100 mm of rain (Howard 1952). Dominant tree species include *Bursera simaruba, Pisonia fragrans, Tabebuia pallida,* and *Ficus* sp. According to Howard (1952), "Cannouan has been heavily cultivated in the past but the lack of rainfall, erosion of the land and general exhaustion of the soil have reduced the acreage under cultivation in recent years," and only the slopes of Mt. Royal in the northeast corner of the island have never been under cultivation. Commercial crops include cotton, coconuts, and limes (Kingsbury 1960). In 1990, Gary Haas and I found *Corallus* associated with scrubby thorn-laden vegetation, and saw it foraging in *Opuntia dillenii*; in 1992 Haas encountered two treeboas in flamboyant trees (*Delonix regia*) and another in a tamarind tree (*Tamarindus indica*).

Mustique. The highest elevation on Mustique is 152 m, and the island has an area of 5.2 km². Between 1827 and 1829, an average of 360 ha was under sugarcane cultivation (about 70% of the total area of the island). During Howard's field work, the island was used for livestock, especially horses; cotton was the primary agricultural crop. Common tree species include *Acacia nilotica, Bursera simaruba, Leucaena glauca, Tabebuia pallida*, and *Eugenia ligustrina*. Stands of mangroves (*Avicennia, Rhizophora*) occur at Grand Bay. When I visited Mustique with Gary Haas in 1990, the island was semiprivate and catered to the well-to-do (e.g., Princess Margaret, Mick Jagger). Perhaps for this reason it is well maintained, disturbances are kept to a minimum, and treeboas should continue to do well there.

Mayreau (sometimes spelled Mayero). This island has an area of 2.6 km², and a maximum elevation of 61 m. Annual rainfall is about 900 mm. According to Howard (1952), cotton has been grown on the island since 1831. In 1950 Mayreau was still heavily planted in cotton, and Howard commented that they were the poorest crop plants he had seen anywhere in The Grenadines. As on other islands on the bank, dominant trees include *Bursera simaruba, Tabebuia pallida*, and *Pisonia fragrans*. In 1991 Gary Haas collected *Corallus grenadensis* in acacia around Salt Whistle Bay and Saline Bay, and in cactus (probably *Opuntia*) near Station Hill; all treeboas we have taken on Mayreau have been associated with thorny scrub vegetation. According to Kingsbury (1960), about one-third of the island is arable, and cotton was still the major commercial crop.

Île à Quatre. The area of this island is 2.0 km² and its highest elevation is 104 m. Kingsbury (1960) reported an abundance of mango, guava, lime, coconut, and other fruit, largely growing wild, and certainly able to provide *Corallus* habitat. In 1992, Gary Haas encountered *C. grenadensis* in acacia.

Baliceaux. Baliceaux has an area of 1.0 km² and elevation reaches ca. 183 m. Apparently used as a stock island as early as the 1820s, Howard (1952) reported remains of a sugar mill indicating that sugarcane was ground and boiled. *Acacia nilotica* is present, as are small stands of *Hippomane, Capparis* spp., *Pisonia fragrans*, and *Tabebuia pallida*. The *Hippomane* and *T. pallida* are cut for firewood. Kingsbury (1960) states that the island was once a cotton plantation, and Howard (1952) indicated that cotton was cultivated during his visit. Gary Haas found *C. grenadensis* in a "fruit" tree near the ruins in 1992.

Petit Martinique. This is the smallest of The Grenadines (0.7 km^2) known to harbor a population of *Corallus grenadensis*, and it is known from only a single specimen (MCZ 6112, collected in 1879). Neither I nor any of my associates have been to this island. The highest elevation on Petit Martinique is 226 m. Interestingly, there have been reports of a species of *Bothrops* on this island (Howard 1952), and Campbell and Lamar (1989), referring to those rumors, reported that there were no snakes extant on Petit Martinique. It is, however, not uncommon for species of *Corallus* to be mistaken for species of *Bothrops* (see Chapter 10). According to Howard (1952), most of Petit Martinique's area is devoted to crops and pasture for grazing animals, and what woodlands remain are badly decimated. The dominant and largest tree species is gumbo limbo (*Bursera simaruba*), with lesser amounts of *Hippomane mancinella*, *Tabebuia pallida*, and *Ficus laevigata*.

Chapter 2

Color and Pattern, Meristic Characters, and Size

Adult [treeboas] *are cryptically coloured a pale yellowish or greyish brown ...,*
but within a single litter ... it is not unusual to find every colour from amber to
yellow to brick red and sepia.

Parker 1963

With the possible exception of *Corallus cropanii*, members of the genus
Corallus are easily identified as treeboas based on characteristics of their external
morphology: 1) a laterally compressed body; 2) a large chunky head on a relatively slender neck; 3) conspicuous labial pits; 4) relatively long anterior teeth
on the maxilla and mandible; and 5) a prehensile tail. Lateral compression of the
body and a prehensile tail are characteristics shared by many arboreal snakes
(Lillywhite and Henderson 1993). Likewise, a relatively large head supported
by a comparatively slender neck is a trait seen in other tree-dwelling snakes
(e.g., some *Boiga* and *Dipsas, Imantodes*), and heat-sensitive labial pits occur in
a number of boids. The greatly enlarged anterior teeth on the maxilla and mandible do not commonly occur in other snake species, and they are another adaptation to an arboreal life-style. Once a prey item is captured, it cannot be released,
either during immobilization (which is accomplished by constriction) or deglutition. The enlarged anterior teeth function as meat hooks which allow for some ma-
neuvering of prey while reducing the chances of losing it to the ground below.

It is, however, other morphological variables found among members of
the *Corallus hortulanus* complex that are especially intriguing.

COLOR AND PATTERN

Two members of the complex display relatively little variation in pattern
and color: *Corallus cookii* and *C. ruschenbergerii*. Ironically, the species that

33

exhibits the most variation (*C. grenadensis*) is sandwiched geographically between *C. cookii* and *C. ruschenbergerii*.

Corallus cookii

The dorsal coloration is uniform, considering the remarkable variability in *C. hortulanus* and *C. grenadensis*. Out of 47 specimens for which I was able to score dorsal ground color, 41 (87.2%) were taupe and the others were gray or brown. The main element of the dorsal pattern is best described as an hourglass or dumbbell shape, rarely like a very stout spade; the dorsalmost portion of the shape is hollow. The main elements are usually edged in black, with or without white margins. Between the main elements there is only dorsal ground color, or a dorsoventrally elongated blotch. Unlike other species in the *hortulanus* complex, the anteriormost blotches are not rhomboidal. Near middorsum, the dorsal pattern may become a series of longitudinally elongated blotches with another longitudinally elongated series situated more laterally. Milwaukee Public Museum (MPM) specimens 23302 and 23304 exhibit fusion of the main pattern elements across their dorsalmost portions, creating a middorsal stripe. In addition to triangle shapes on the dorsum, MPM 23297 has a taupe ground color with markings similar to *C. hortulanus*. The underside of the head is immaculate but the ventrals may be lightly to heavily patterned; lateral encroachment of the dorsal pattern onto the ventrals is common. The top of the head has rounded blotches or a vermiculate pattern. Whereas other *C. hortulanus* complex treeboas usually have well-defined postorbital stripes, in *C. cookii* it is more of a postorbital blotch. Mental and gular regions are white, but marked (often heavily) with brown.

Corallus grenadensis

The spadelike element in the dorsal pattern occurs throughout the Grenada Bank, with the greatest variation being whether the spade has sharp angles (53.5%) or is rounded (26.5%). Although the rounded spades may appear in any habitat, they predominate at higher elevations on Grenada. A dorsal ground color of taupe predominates on all of the islands except Mayreau, where orange is predominant (seven of eight specimens). The primary element in the dorsal pattern in snakes from Mayreau is also consistently different from other populations on the bank (more of a balloon shape rather than a spade; a similar pattern occurs on the other islands on the bank, but not to the exclusion of the more typical spade shape). The samples from Petit Martinique, Baliceaux, and Mustique are too small to make a detailed assessment of pattern variation. Based on the examination of living *C. grenadensis*, it appears that dorsal ground color is correlated with iris color and tongue color (i.e., snakes with a yellowish dorsal ground color usually have yellowish irises and a pale-colored tongue; snakes that are taupe to dark brown have very dark irises and dark brown to black tongues). The ventral ground color is usually dull yellow, but it may be white or cream. It may also be immaculate (in snakes with a yellowish dorsal ground color), marked with flecks, spots, large blotches, or almost completely covered with dark brown. The ventral pattern usually becomes denser more posteriorly. *Corallus grenadensis* on Grenada exhibits the widest range of dorsal ground colors anywhere within the range of the *hortulanus* complex. The predominating dorsal ground color at any locality is associated with elevation, rainfall, and percent possible sunshine. Spearman Correlation indicates that the incidence of "yellow" *C. grenadensis* at four localities (Mt. Hartman Bay, Pearls, Westerhall, and the Grand Etang forest area) is correlated with altitude ($P < 0.0001$), annual precipitation ($P < 0.0001$) and percent possible sunshine ($P < 0.0001$). An initial analysis (Henderson 1990a, 1990b) was based in part on the collecting whims of myself and, quite possibly, others. That is, because the species is so common in some areas, during the collecting phase of my field work I selectively collected certain color morphs and not others, and did not always keep a record of each snake that I observed. Subsequent efforts have been more objective (noted briefly in Henderson 1996) and have confirmed the results of the initial effort (Table 2.1).

It seems likely that the differences in the incidence of predominant dorsal ground color at different altitudes and in different climatic regimes has a thermoregulatory function. Yellowish (i.e., pale) snakes occur most frequently in low areas of high ambient temperature, high percentage of possible sunshine, and depressed rainfall. Based on personal observations, these areas are usually dominated by dry scrub vegetation, often thorny (e.g., large stands of *Acacia nilotica*), and open (i.e., do not provide deep shade). In these situations a dorsal ground color that has some reflective capabilities might be advantageous. Perhaps examination of the microdermatoglyphics (e.g., Hoge and Souza Santos 1953; Price 1982) in snakes from different climatic regimes would be instructive. Conversely, treeboas that are dark brown usually occur at elevations greater than 400 m in areas that receive lots of rain, and have depressed ambient temperatures and percent of possible sunshine, e.g., the Grand Etang forest area (Figs. 2.1, 2.2, 2.3, and 2.4). In these situations it would be advantageous to be able to utilize the reduced periods of insolation in the most effective manner (for foraging efficiency and prey assimilation), and a dark dorsum is more absorptive than one that is pale-colored. Nevertheless, in a study of growth rate in an insular population of the adder (*Vipera berus*) in the Baltic Sea, Forsman (1993) determined that, although melanistic snakes had faster heating rates and higher body temperatures than nonmelanistic *V. berus*, growth rates did not differ significantly between color morphs. In fact, melanistic snakes grew slightly more slowly during several years, and Forsman con-

Table 2.1. Distribution of color phases of *Corallus grenadensis* at four sites on Grenada. NDA = no data available.

	Mt. Hartman Bay[1]	Pearls[2]	Westerhall Area[3]	Grand Etang Forest Area[4]
Sample Size	38	35	72	8
Color Phase (%)				
Yellow	71.1	37.1	15.3	0.0
Taupe	21.0	45.7	83.3	37.5
Dark Brown	2.6	0.0	0.0	50.0
Altitude (m)	0–15	30	65	450–525
Annual rainfall (cm)	111.8	154.4	167.1	351.5
Percent possible sunshine	NDA	NDA	62.8	35.5
Temperature				
mean C_{min}	24.2	NDA	23.1	19.7
mean C_{max}	30.1	NDA	28.5	25.6

[1]Rainfall and temperature data were collected at Point Salines Airport. Rainfall data are from 1988–92, and the number represents the sum of the monthly means from each of those years.
[2]Rainfall data were collected at Paradise Estate, and only in 1986.
[3]Rainfall, percent possible sunshine, and temperature data were collected at the CARDI Agro-Met Station.
[4]Rainfall, percent possible sunshine, and temperature data were collected at Grand Etang.

cluded that there was "no evidence to indicate any significant effect of melanism on snake growth rate." Although Forsman's results do not preclude a significant advantage for *C. grenadensis*, it does suggest that predominant dorsal color may confer a selective advantage other than foraging efficiency, prey assimilation, and growth.

Similar altitudinal/climatic variation in dorsal coloration has been documented for *Anolis* lizards on mountains, and single-anole islands in the Lesser Antilles (e.g., Hertz 1981; Malhotra and Thorpe 1991) and, like the anoles, *C. grenadensis* has possibly evolved behavioral and ecological flexibility (e.g., foraging and thermoregulatory efficiency: *fide* Henderson and Henderson 1995) to compensate for altitudinal changes in ambient thermal regimes. A parallel situation has been found in the Bananaquit (*Coereba flaveola*) on Grenada: the yellow morph occurred in dry deciduous scrub woodlands, whereas the black morph was found throughout the island but predominantly in wet areas. Steep

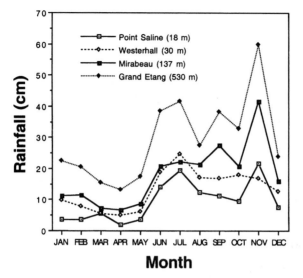

Figure 2.1. Monthly rainfall at four sites on Grenada.

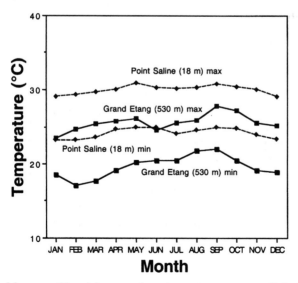

Figure 2.2. Mean monthly minimum and maximum temperatures at Point Salines and Grand Etang, St. Andrew Parish, Grenada.

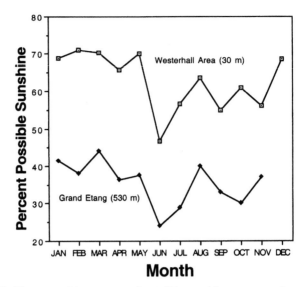

Figure 2.3. Mean monthly percent of possible sunshine at a weather station near Westerhall Estate, and at Grand Etang.

morph ratio clines, with widths of 2.5–4.8 km, were highly correlated with rainfall and altitude (Wunderle 1981a). In 1981, Wunderle (1981b) documented a shift in the morph ratio cline (3 years after his last census), including a decrease in the number of black morph Bananaquits at Mt. Hartman Estate. He found that 65% of the Bananaquits at Mt. Hartman were yellow; I found 71.1% of the treeboas at Mt. Hartman Bay (adjacent to Mt. Hartman Estate) were yellow. Documentation of a shift in the morph ratio cline goes back to the 1800s, and Wunderle (1981b) felt that field evidence suggested that the shift might be associated with habitat disturbance (e.g., changes in sugarcane cultivation); I previously suggested (Henderson 1990b) that agricultural practices on Grenada have contributed to the color and pattern variation in *C. grenadensis* that occurs on the island. Seutin et al. (1994) found no relationship between mtDNA haplotype and Bananaquit color phase.

Besides a maintenance (i.e., thermoregulatory) basis to color variation in *Corallus grenadensis*, crypsis may also be a factor. In the more open acacia forests and other scrub habitats, where sunlight penetrates and illuminates treeboa habitat, a pale-colored snake is less conspicuous than a dark one. At the Mt. Hartman Bay site I have observed that, during the dry season, about 50% of the tree crown foliage is yellow; this would, seemingly, confer further advantage to the yellow morph *C. grenadensis* that occur with such high frequency at

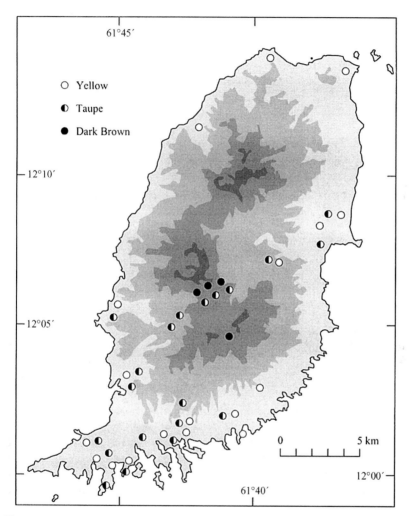

Figure 2.4. Map of Grenada indicating the distribution of three color morphs of *Corallus grenadensis*. Symbols merely indicate the presence of a color morph, but not frequency of that morph. Adjacent symbols imply that more than one color morph occurred at the same locality. Contour lines are at 120 m, 365 m, and 610 m.

Mt. Hartman. Conversely, in lush forests with dense foliage and relatively little sunlight penetration, a dark-colored snake would be less conspicuous. It is likely that dorsal color confers more than one adaptive advantage.

At a given elevation on Grenada, there is, in addition to color variation, pattern variation. This is, I believe, attributable, in part, to agricultural practices. A very large proportion of Grenada has been cleared for agriculture (Beard 1949; Anonymous 1982). *Corallus grenadensis* is most abundant in disturbed situations, especially on estates where fruit groves are mixed with native vegetation. Grenada has a long agricultural history (Bullen 1964), slopes are not exceptionally steep, and active cultivation was pushed to the highest practicable limits in most cases (Beard 1949). In 1824, at least 324 estates on Grenada effectively parceled the land into many isolated patches of trees (i.e., "islands"). Although there are many fewer active estates now (Fig. 2.5), agricultural activities from 100–200 years ago may still impact the ecology of an arboreal snake. The treeless areas between these "islands" may have acted (and continue to act) as effective barriers to gene flow. Field data indicate that *C. grenadensis* is distributed in many demes throughout much of Grenada, and many of the demes may be predominated by a unique dorsal pattern (i.e., combination of dorsal color and pattern element), thereby creating a mosaic of color pattern variation over a wide area. For example, I have encountered treeboas at Calvigny Estate with a color pattern that I have seen nowhere else on the island. Likewise, a unique pattern was observed in several snakes found near the southern tip of the Mt. Hartman peninsula.

It is interesting that the Grenada Bank—and especially Grenada—harbors treeboa populations that exhibit spectacular color pattern diversity, but that St. Vincent populations (about 100 km from Grenada, and only 8.5 km from Bequia) display little. Since St. Vincent has undergone habitat modifications due to agricultural practices and logging similar to those that occurred on Grenada, and since the species evolved from stock that originated on the South American mainland and dispersed overwater to their respective banks, it is likely that the color and pattern dichotomy between the two islands is attributable to founder effect and genetic serendipity.

Corallus hortulanus

Treeboas with a predominantly taupe dorsal ground color accounted for 70–100% of the samples in southern Venezuela, Suriname, French Guiana, Ecuador, Peru, Bolivia, Brazil north of the Rio Amazonas, Brazil's Atlantic forest, and Ilha Grande off southeastern Brazil. Snakes from Guyana and southeastern Brazil had a higher percentage of "yellow" individuals; Guyana had the highest percentage (43.5%) of yellow snakes. The Bolivia sample (n = 28) contained no yellow snakes, nor did the samples from Ilha Grande (n = 6)

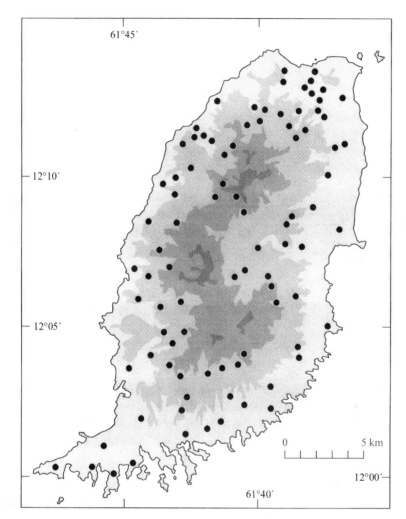

Figure 2.5. Map of Grenada indicating locations of estates during 1958–1988. Contour lines are at 120 m, 365 m, and 610 m.

or French Guiana (n = 7). Chippaux (1986) and Starace (1998), however, described beige snakes from that country, and Starace (1998) described yellow and orange individuals, also. There is a great deal of variation in the shape of the main element of the dorsal pattern at midbody, but in general an ellipselike shape was present. Snakes from southern Venezuela exhibited some possible *ruschenbergerii* influence, and snakes from the Guianas had more spade shapes than those elsewhere in the range of *C. hortulanus*. Treeboas from Ilha Grande had a uniformly distinctive dorsal pattern, reminiscent of a hot-air balloon (also noted by Machado 1945). The venter is predominantly dull yellow, but may also be white or cream; it may be immaculate—usually in snakes with a yellowish dorsal ground color—or patterned with a few flecks, scattered spots and blotches, or nearly covered with dark brown. Lateral encroachment of the dorsal pattern onto the ventrals is common. The ventral pattern becomes more densely patterned posteriorly.

Corallus ruschenbergerii

With the exception of *Corallus cookii*, *C. ruschenbergerii* exhibits less variation in dorsal pattern than other members of the complex. The middorsal rhomb (or diamond shape) is relatively uniform throughout the range of the species, and it is rarely encountered in other members of the complex (see Table 1.2). The rhomb is especially prevalent in Costa Rica (80.0%) and Panama (90.5%). Treeboas with the free edge of the dorsals edged in black occur only in *C. ruschenbergerii* (see Table 1.2). This pattern occurs most often in northern Venezuela (32.6%) and on Trinidad (20.5%); it is least common in Panama (7.1%) and northern Colombia (4.2%); according to W.W. Lamar (in litt., April 2000) it is common in treeboas from the Colombian llanos. The ventral ground color is usually dull yellow, but it may be white or cream. It may also be bright yellow, immaculate, or patterned with a few flecks, scattered spots and blotches, or nearly covered with dark brown to black. The ventral pattern becomes heavier posteriorly.

Ontogenetic Changes

Neonate treeboas of the *Corallus hortulanus* complex often exhibit conspicuous pink or salmon color, usually bordering the major elements of the dorsal pattern. By the time the snakes are a few months old, the pink and salmon-colored areas become white or off-white. Those *Corallus grenadensis* that have an orange, red or reddish dorsal ground color when young are brown when adult; this probably applies to *C. hortulanus* as well. Yellow or yellowish dorsal ground color in young *C. grenadensis*, *C. hortulanus*, and *C. ruschenbergerii* becomes darker with age, often approaching a medium brown in adults. There may be slight modification of the elements of the dorsal pattern, primarily in which the elements become somewhat less sharply defined.

Discussion

Available evidence suggests that color variation confers more than one selective advantage to *Corallus grenadensis*. The habitat-associated variation in morph frequencies (see Table 2.1) is well documented, and spatial hetero-geneity has potentially generated associations between color and ecology in *C. grenadensis*. Color and pattern in reptiles has widespread significance, and can influence social behavior, predatory and antipredatory behavior, and mainte-nance (e.g., thermoregulation). As noted by Cooper and Greenberg (1992), "Because the potentially optimal coloration may differ for each of several roles and may vary in time and space, the resultant coloration may in many cases best be viewed as an adaptive compromise between conflicting selective pressures exerted by social, predatory, antipredatory, thermoregulatory, and perhaps other demands." Shine et al. (1998) found that in a sample of 2063 specimens, four color morphs of the blood python (*Python brongersmai*) differed signifi-cantly in temporal and spatial abundances, sex ratios, age structures, mean adult body sizes, body shapes (tail length and body mass relative to SVL), energy stores, numbers of gut parasites, prey types, feeding frequencies, and clutch sizes. They felt the causal basis for these associations was based on the following three processes: 1) direct effects of dorsal color; 2) linkages between genes for color and morphological and ecological traits; and 3) correlated spatial heterogeneity in color, morphology, and ecology; and that all three explanations "are likely to be true to some extent" and that no single hypothesis would be likely to provide a complete explanation as to what processes maintain chromatic polymorphism in *P. brongersmai*. They noted the conver-gent evolution of polychromatism in heavy-bodied sit-and-wait predators of several reptile lineages, suggesting that there is "some underlying adaptive significance to the development of multiple colour morphs in these kinds of snakes." They considered frequency-dependent selection a plausible explana-tion, as well as genotype-specific habitat selection. They concluded that "Our data do not show that colour *per se* is important, but they indicate that dorsal colour is associated with a host of other traits involving size, shape and ecology," and that the color variation is not trivial.

The sympatric/syntopic color and pattern variation seen in *C. grenadensis* and *C. hortulanus* is unparalleled (or exceeded) in any other snake species; variation in, for example, *Lampropeltis triangulum*, is geographic (Williams 1988; Greene 1997). It is interesting that, among snake species that exhibit extremes in color variation, some are arboreal, e.g., *Atheris s. squamiger* (Porras 1997), *Bothriechis schlegelii* (Campbell and Lamar 1989), and others are arboreal, occur on islands, and are either always yellow (i.e., *Oxybelis wilsoni* from Isla de Roatán, Islas de la Bahía, Honduras: Villa and McCranie 1995) or are represented by a yellow morph that is confined to an island, i.e., *Candoia bibroni australis* in the Solomon Islands (Conway 1998); and *Trimere-surus albolabris* on the Indonesian island of Wetar, in the Lesser Sunda Archipelago (How et al. 1996; How and Kitchener 1997). This parallels the high incidence of yellowish *C. grenadensis* on Grenada.

Figure 2.6. Map of South America showing distribution of "yellow" morph *Corallus hortulanus*. The larger dots indicate a higher incidence of yellow treeboas.

Although the color variation on Grenada is correlated with environmental variables, I cannot with any confidence demonstrate a similar association in the distribution of yellowish phase *C. hortulanus*. Figure 2.6 presents the distribution of yellow (beige, khaki, tan, light brown) *C. hortulanus*. The color phase occurs throughout the range of the species, but, based on the specimens available, there do appear to be areas where the color is more prevalent: coastal Guyana and Suriname, and coastal areas in southeastern Brazil (Bahia, Minas Gerais, Espírito Santo, Rio de Janiero, and São Paulo). Coastal Guyana and Suriname include open savanna habitat, and it is predictable that the yellowish color phase would be more prevalent there, much like it is in open scrub woodland on Grenada. The coastal area of southeastern Brazil was, at least formerly, Atlantic forest (semideciduous or seasonal, with more limited areas of rich dense forest), and perhaps it is open enough to make the yellowish dorsal color selectively advantageous (for thermoregulation or crypsis or both). Henderson and Hedges (1995) suggested that the *Corallus* populations on Grenada may have originated in Guyana and dispersed to Grenada via the North Equatorial Current. The high incidence of yellow *Corallus* on the northeastern coast of South America might help explain the potential for a high incidence of yellow snakes on Grenada.

Yellowish colored snakes are more common in *Corallus ruschenbergerii* than in any other member of the complex. Yellowish representatives seem especially common in the Darien region of Panama (an area of rainforest and high rainfall) and northernmost Venezuela just south of the Penisula de Paria (an area of dry scrub vegetation and low rainfall). Yellowish representatives occur in Trinidad at rainforest edge, and on Isla Margarita in more xeric situations. In short, based on the material currently available to me, I can detect no pattern in the distribution of the yellowish color phase in *C. ruschenbergerii*.

Yellowish phase treeboas appear to be more common at latitudinal extremes of the *Corallus hortulanus* complex range (north: Central America, northern South America, Grenada Bank; south: southernmost area of the range in southeastern Brazil). *Corallus cookii*, of course, includes the northernmost-occurring populations of the complex, and it is the only member of the complex that does not have yellowish colored representatives.

MERISTIC CHARACTERS

Utilizing principal component analysis (PCA), I examined variation in scale characters for *Corallus grenadensis* at seven sites on Grenada: Beausejour Estate, Grand Anse-Point Salines area, Calvigny Estate, Westerhall Estate, Grand Etang-Spring Gardens Estate area, Balthazar Estate, and Pearls. These sites range in altitude from sea level to 525 m. All of the areas are disturbed to one degree or another, and agricultural activity is obvious at all sites except Grand Etang. A PCA scatter diagram (Fig. 2.7) showed great overlap for all sites, with only Pearls somewhat divergent at principal component 2, with a high loading for subcaudals. I ran another PCA for islands on the Grenada Bank for which we have specimens of *C. grenadensis*. Again, there was overlap among all of the islands for which there were adequate samples (Fig. 2.8), and the Grenada sample encompassed virtually all of the samples from The Grenadines, with a significant portion of only the Mayreau sample falling outside of the Grenada sample. As noted previously, the Mayreau sample is also distinctive due to the high incidence of snakes with an orange dorsal ground color and distinctive dorsal markings.

A third PCA was run with the same data set, only instead of a geographic variable I used predominant dorsal ground color. Again, there was tremendous

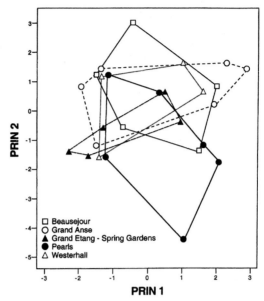

Figure 2.7. Plot of first and second principal component axes based on six meristic characters from five localities on Grenada. For clarity, only peripheral points are shown for each locality.

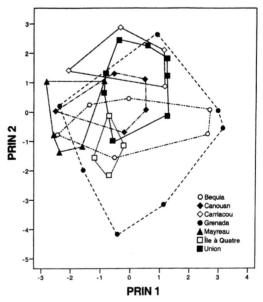

Figure 2.8. Plot of first and second principal component axes based on six meristic characters from seven islands on the Grenada Bank. For clarity, only the peripheral points are shown for each island.

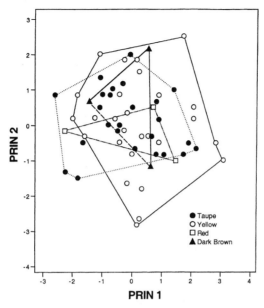

Figure 2.9. Plot of first and second principal component axes based on six meristic characters for four color morphs of *Corallus grenadensis* on Grenada.

overlap among the color variables taupe and "yellow," and dark brown snakes fell in with either taupe or "yellow" snakes (Fig. 2.9).

SIZE

There is considerable disparity in size within the *Corallus hortulanus* complex. The smallest snakes are *C. cookii* and *C. grenadensis* and the largest is *C. ruschenbergerii* (Table 2.2). Using only the 10% of each species with the longest SVLs, an analysis of variance (ANOVA) indicated significant differences at 0.0001 (F = 42.06). Tukey's Studentized Range Test (TSRT) indicated significant differences ($\alpha = 0.05$) between *C. ruschenbergerii* and the other three species, and between *C. hortulanus* and *C. cookii*. A Waller-Duncan K-ratio *t*-test indicated significant differences between *C. ruschenbergerii* and the other three species, and between *C. cookii* and the other three species; *C. grenadensis* and *C. hortulanus* were not significantly different from each other. Although *C. ruschenbergerii* includes both mainland and insular populations, the insular populations harbor the largest snakes (Trinidad and Tobago), and all of the *C. cookii* and *C. grenadensis* populations are insular (see Table 2.2).

Significant size discrepancies between mainland and insular populations of a snake species are not uncommon, and usually the members of the insular

Table 2.2. Mean SVL ± SE (range) of the largest 10% of each sample (if fewer than 15 in sample, only maximum SVL is given) for *Corallus hortulanus* complex snakes from mainland and island localities. All maximum SVLs are for females unless marked by an asterisk (*). N = the total sample size for each location. All West Indian populations are *C. grenadensis* except for St. Vincent. All continental island populations are *C. ruschenbergerii* except for Ilha Grande.

Location	Maximum SVL (mm)	N
Mainland		
Central America	1625.5 ± 16.9	42
(*C. ruschenbergerii*)	(1590–1665)	
Northern So. America	1683.3 ± 43.3	33
(*C. ruschenbergerii*)	(1640–1770)	
Guianas	1536.4 ± 11.1	51
(*C. hortulanus*)	(1510–1565)	
Amazonia	1437.7 ± 25.8	175
(*C. hortulanus*)	(1305–1640)	

Island	Island Area (km²)		N
West Indies			
Petit Martinique	0.7	985*	1
Baliceaux	1.0	705?	2
Quatre	2.0	887	4
Mayreau	2.6	911*	8
Mustique	5.2	960	3
Canouan	7.4	932*	11
Union	8.1	1237.5 ± 12.5	15
		(1225–1250)	
Bequia	18.0	1250.0 ± 30.0	15
		(1220–1280)	
Carriacou	32.0	1282.5 ± 269.5	8
		(1013–1552)	
Grenada	311.0	1418.5 ± 23.1	143
		(1300–1625)	
St. Vincent	345.0	1295.8 ± 32.5	41
(*C. cookii*)		(1215–1374)	

Table 2.2. (*Continued*)

Location	Island Area (km²)	Maximum SVL (mm)	N
Continental Islands			
Contadora			
(Panama)	5.0	1445	6
Tobago	301.0	1790	7
Margarita			
(Venezuela)	373.0	1725	3
Trinidad	4827.0	1773.0 ± 54.0	34
		(1650–1870)	
Ilha Grande			
(Brazil)	179.8	1276.5 ± 38.5	18
(*C. hortulanus*)		(1238–1315)	

populations are smaller (Case 1978) than those occurring on the mainland, but not always (Schwaner 1985; Schwaner and Sarre 1988). Prey availability has been identified as the critical variable in determining snake size in these situations (Case 1978). In the West Indies, small, diurnal, scansorial lizards (*Anolis* spp.) are ubiquitous and often occur at phenomenally high densities, and are much more common than on the mainland (Henderson and Powell 1999). On St. Vincent and the Grenada Bank, *Corallus cookii* and *C. grenadensis*, respectively, prey predominantly on *Anolis* until they attain a SVL of about 900 mm, at which time rodents become the predominant prey. In contrast, on the South American mainland lizards are absent from the diet of *C. hortulanus*, but endothermic prey (birds, bats, rodents) is much more prevalent (Henderson 1993b, c). Although the lizard fauna of, for example, Amazonia is very rich in species, population densities of the lizards pale by comparison to populations in the West Indies. A similar pattern exists between insular and mainland populations of *Crotalus* (Viperidae) in the Gulf of California (Case 1978), and a phylogenetic analysis by Rodríguez-Robles and Greene (1996) supported the hypothesis that a shift to an adult diet of lizard prey was a likely factor in the evolution of smaller body size in some West Indian species of *Epicrates* (Boidae). It is likely that the evolution of smaller body size in West Indian *Corallus* was due, at least in part, to the prevalence of lizard prey. Treeboas responded first behaviorally and then morphologically to the ubiquity and abundance of *Anolis*.

The large size attained by *Corallus ruschenbergerii* is more perplexing.

The largest *C. ruschenbergerii* SVL is more than 230 mm greater than the largest *C. hortulanus*, and 245 mm larger than the largest *C. cookii*. The available prey fauna in the range of *C. ruschenbergerii* is essentially the same as for *C. hortulanus* (including high species diversity for lizards, but with population densities much lower than in the West Indies), yet, because of its large size, *C. ruschenbergerii* exploits prey species (e.g., *Marmosa, Herpestes*) not utilized by *C. hortulanus*. I offer a hypothesis to explain the large size of *C. ruschenbergerii* based on the following information: 1) five species of *Corallus* occur in northern South America (*C. annulatus*, *C. blombergi*, *C. caninus*, *C. hortulanus*, *C. ruschenbergerii*) (Figs. 2.10 and 2.11) (*C. blombergi* is not sympatric with any other species of *Corallus*); 2) *C. caninus* and *C. hortulanus* are widely sympatric and syntopic, with *C. hortulanus* possibly being longer, but *C. caninus* more massive; 3) *C. annulatus* and *C. ruschenbergerii* are sympatric over portions of their ranges in Central America and northern South America, with *C. ruschenbergerii* longer and more massive than *C. annulatus*; 4) the ranges of massive *C. caninus* and massive *C. ruschenbergerii* are virtually nonoverlapping (see Fig. 2.11); and 5) the ranges of morphologically similar

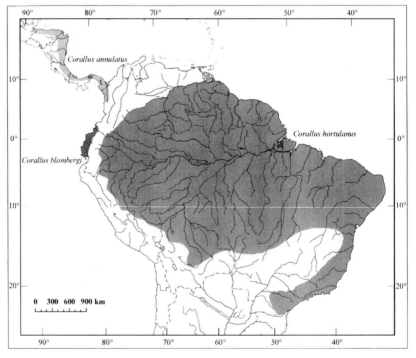

Figure 2.10. Map delineating the ranges of *Corallus annulatus*, *C. blombergi*, and *C. hortulanus*.

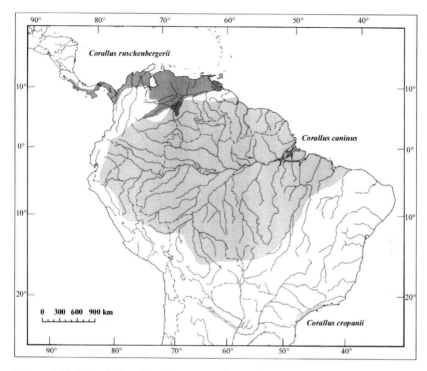

Figure 2.11. Map delineating the ranges of *Corallus caninus*, *C. cropanii*, and *C. ruschenbergerii*.

C. annulatus and *C. hortulanus* are non-overlapping (see Fig. 2.10). I suggest, then, that the sympatric/syntopic taxa exhibit size disparity that may reflect differences in diet and those portions of the arboreal habitat utilized for foraging, thereby alleviating or avoiding potential competition between congenerics.

Snout-Vent Length-Mass Relationship

Even the smallest *C. ruschenbergerii* are more massive than comparably sized *C. cookii* or *C. grenadensis*. The longest female *C. cookii* (n = 33) that I have weighed and measured was 1374 mm SVL and 510 g; the largest male was 1188 mm SVL with a mass of 272 g. The largest female *C. grenadensis* (n = 207) had a SVL of 1493 mm and a mass of 912 g, and the largest male was 1340 mm SVL and 690 g. The longest female *C. hortulanus* (n = 45) for which I have field data (supplied by L.J. Vitt, in litt., 5 Feb 1999) was 1606 mm SVL with a mass of 600 g; a smaller snake (1510 mm SVL) weighed 610 g; the largest male was 1429 mm SVL and 435 g. The largest freshly captured female *C.*

ruschenbergerii (n = 15) was 1700 mm SVL with a mass of 1458 g; a smaller snake (1640 mm SVL) had a mass of 1958 g. *Corallus ruschenbergerii* attains a greater length than the other two species, and at any given SVL is more massive. The greatest disparities occur among young (= small) snakes, with the lizard-eating West Indian species being much less massive than the primarily bird-eating (when young) *C. ruschenbergerii*.

Snout-Vent Length vs. Head Size and Body Girth

Figure 2.12 presents a plot of the first and second principal components using the variables SVL, head width, and midbody circumference for three members of the *Corallus hortulanus* complex and *C. caninus*. There is considerable overlap among the three members of the *C. hortulanus* complex, from the most slender *C. grenadensis* to the most heavy-bodied *C. ruschenbergerii*; *C. hortulanus* is intermediate between the two extremes. Only *C. ruschenbergerii* exhibits substantial overlap with *C. caninus*, the most massive species of *Corallus*.

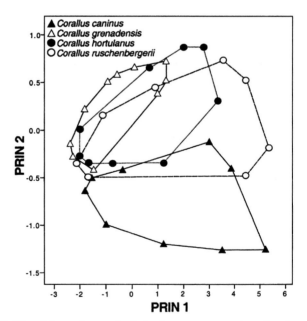

Figure 2.12. Plot of first and second principal component axes based on three characters (snout-vent length, head width, and midbody circumference) that impact the size of prey that can be killed and ingested by four species of *Corallus*. For clarity, only the peripheral points are shown for each species.

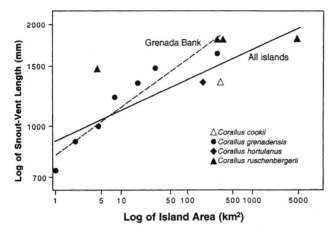

Figure 2.13. Relationship between treeboa snout-vent length and island area. The dashed line is fitted just for islands on the Grenada Bank (Y = 0.14x + 6.7; r = 0.947), and the solid line is for many insular populations within the *Corallus hortulanus* complex (Y = 0.09x + 6.8; r = 0.828).

Snout-Vent Length vs. Island Area

Based on available data, there was a positive correlation between maximum SVL and island area for *Corallus* populations on the Grenada Bank (Pearson Correlation, r = 0.94732, *P* < 0.0012; n = 7 islands) and for all insular populations of *C. hortulanus* complex treeboas (Pearson Correlation, r = 0.82792, *P* < 0.0005; n = 13 islands) (Fig. 2.13). If the largest snake from an island was not a female, that island was excluded from the analysis. It is highly unlikely that I had a snake representing maximum SVL for each island; nevertheless, the correlation coefficients are high enough to make the results of the test intriguing.

Chapter 3

Habitat, Habitat Selection, and Habitat Use

Later I asked Pasqual to get me an orchid in a large tree ..., and he almost fell off when he discovered another snake in a bunch of orchids ... This species is evidently a splendid climber.

Bartsch (in Cochran 1934) describing *Corallus grenadensis*

Not surprisingly, all *Corallus hortulanus* complex treeboas spend most of their time above ground level in trees and bushes. They occur in a wide range of habitats, but usually occur in edge situations regardless of the habitat. Edge habitat can have multiple layers, and it is not as limiting as one might envision. For example, at our Mt. Hartman Bay study site, the line of mangroves provided two edge situations (water side and land side), a narrow stand of acacia and other trees and shrubs close to sea level provided another two layers of edge, and a gentle hillside ascending above the bay provided several additional layers from close to sea level to about 60 m asl (Fig. 3.1).

Despite the relative abundance of *Corallus hortulanus* complex treeboas, we have quantifiable data only for *C. grenadensis*. It is likely that at least some of our findings regarding *C. grenadensis* are applicable to other members of the complex, but that can be verified only with field work.

CORALLUS COOKII

St. Vincent has a dense human population and an agriculturally based economy, especially bananas (*Musa*). Over the past 400 to 500 years there has been significant modification of the landscape, with most of the forest sacrificed to agriculture. My knowledge of the geographic and ecological distribution of *C. cookii* is inadequate. Although I do not believe that it is as ecologically versatile as *C. grenadensis*, I feel certain that its distribution is more widespread

Figure 3.1. Profile illustrating the various levels of edge habitat. Arrows indicate edge situations in which treeboas might be encountered. *Corallus grenadensis* at Mt. Hartman Bay was encountered in each of these situations. Drawing by James Hempel.

than currently documented, and that it occurs in more ecological situations than have been recorded to date.

I have observed *C. cookii* at elevations between 70 m (near Orange Hill in Charlotte Parish) and about 500 m asl (in the Vermont Nature Reserve, Buccament Valley, Dalaway watershed, St. Andrew Parish), but it has been collected at the Botanic Garden in Kingstown (St. George Parish), so it does occur closer to sealevel. In the mid-1980s, *C. cookii* was common in the Layou Valley (St. Patrick Parish), in an area of second growth and mixed agriculture interspersed by human residences. It was collected and/or observed foraging in mango (*Mangifera indica*), coconut (*Cocos nucifera*), nutmeg (*Myristica fragrans*), and cacao (*Theobroma cacao*) trees. In the Vermont Nature Reserve (about 500 m asl), an area of lush forest, *C. cookii* has been observed foraging in strangler fig (*Ficus* sp.) and tree ferns (*Cyathea* sp.). At Hermitage (425 m, Cumberland watershed), it has been observed loosely coiled on a dead *Cyathea* frond, and on the trunk of a Caribbean Pine (*Pinus caribbaea*). *Corallus cookii* has been observed foraging in bamboo (*Bambusa* sp.) in the Orange Hill area and the Vermont Nature Reserve. At Camden Park (150 m, St. Andrew Parish), *C. cookii* occurred above a heavily disturbed residential area, and Mrs. I. Earle Kirby informed Gary Haas that treeboas used to occur in her backyard in Kingstown. By day, I have observed this species roosting in a mango tree at

1430 h on a road cut along the Chateaubelair River (St. David Parish). I have never observed *C. cookii* alive or dead on a road, and I have seen only one moving at ground level (at the top of a road cut in viny vegetation in the Vermont Nature Reserve).

CORALLUS GRENADENSIS

Geographically widespread snake species (e.g., *Boa constrictor*, *Epicrates cenchria*, *Drymarchon corais*, *Spilotes pullatus*) exhibit tolerance of a broad spectrum of ecological conditions, both abiotic (e.g., precipitation) and biotic (e.g., plant communities). Since the *Corallus hortulanus* complex has a broad range over the Neotropics, that its members occur in a wide range of habitats is to be anticipated (e.g., Henderson et al. 1995). What is especially impressive about the ecological plasticity exhibited by *C. grenadensis* is its occurrence in so many habitats on Grenada (Table 3.1) that exhibit such a wide range of environmental variables, e.g., temperature, rainfall, insolation, vegetation (Henderson 1996; Henderson and Henderson 1995). About 72% of the land area of Grenada is devoted to agriculture, whereas the remaining native vegetation covers only about 23% (the remaining 5% is devoted to urban habitat and pastures). Since *C. grenadensis* is often common in agricultural areas where there is a contiguous canopy of fruit trees (Henderson and Winstel 1995; Henderson et al. 1996; Henderson et al. 1998), the large amount of land devoted to agriculture is not detrimental to *C. grenadensis* distribution or population densities. That is not to say that some agricultural practices (e.g., use of pesticides, clear-cutting) do not have serious ramifications for *C. grenadensis*.

On Grenada, in the Morne Rouge area of Grande Anse (St. George Parish) near sea level, *Corallus grenadensis* has been observed foraging within 15 m of an upscale hotel. In the same area I have seen it foraging within 5 m of a bright streetlight at 0040 h. At Pearls, at 2145 h, a foraging treeboa fell from a citrus tree into a shallow, temporary body of water and took refuge in a *Cocos* husk under the water. This species has been observed foraging at Woburn (St. George Parish) in a flamboyant tree (*Delonix regia*; native to Madagascar), in bananas at Mt. Pleasant (St. Andrew Parish, 275 m), in mimosa (*Mimosa pudica*), and at 4.5 m and 7.0 m in the crowns of unidentified palms at Beausejour Estate. Also at Beausejour, treeboas were seen by day coiled on branches and at night foraging on branches overhanging the Beausejour River. At Mt. Hartman Bay, *C. grenadensis* was inactive by day in mangroves (mostly *Rhizophora mangle*), coiled on branches hanging over the Caribbean Sea; by night it forages in the same branches, often over water. Additional observations at Mt. Hartman Bay include *C. grenadensis* foraging in acacia trees devoid of foliage, among spines 25–30 mm long and upon which anoles sleep; and coiled or sprawled on a nearly vertical cliffside covered with rocks, cactus (*Cephalocereus* and *Opun-*

Table 3.1. Land use on Grenada, and the status of *Corallus grenadensis* in each category: present (+), absent (−), or unknown because inadequately collected (?).

Vegatation Category	Hectares[1] of Total Area	Percentage	*Corallus* status
Foodcrops and vegetables	591	1.9	−
Foodcrops, vegetables, and fruit trees	684	2.2	+
Mixed cultivation	15,298	49.7	+
Sugarcane	534	1.7	−
Bananas	344	1.1	+
Bananas with cacao and/or nutmeg	2477	8.0	+
Cacao	328	1.1	+
Coconut	943	3.1	+
Nutmeg	996	3.2	+
Montane rainforest	1688	5.5	?
Lower montane rainforest	2279	7.4	+
Deciduous	1752	5.7	+
Scrub/cactus	1226	4.0	+
Mangrove	190	0.6	+
Inland swamp	28	0.1	?
Pastures	166	0.5	−
Open scrub	291	0.9	−
Urban/suburban	988	3.2	+

[1]Based on 1982 map, Land Use Division, Ministry of Agriculture.

tia), *Agave*, and other thorny vegetation overlooking the bay. One *C. grenadensis* spent daylight hours coiled in the abandoned nest of a Bananaquit (*Coereba flaveola*) at mangrove edge, and at dusk emerged from the nest and initiated foraging behavior. By day at Lower Woburn (St. George Parish, sea level), I have encountered a treeboa at 2.5 m in mangrove saplings completely surrounded by water in a bay of the Caribbean. I have detected the eye shine of *Corallus grenadensis* foraging in a nutmeg tree from the headlights of my jeep along a narrow paved road in a residential area near Vendome (St. George Parish, 350 m). Although I have encountered few *C. grenadensis* foraging in *Musa* (because, I believe, the structure of banana trees is not conducive to treeboa foraging), Alan Joseph (pers. comm., 17 April 1996) told me that, as a boy in Birch Grove (St. Andrew Parish), treeboas were frequently encountered in stalks of bananas after they had been cut from the trees. Perhaps, then, although *Musa* trees are not favored by foraging *C. grenadensis*, they are exploited as daytime retreats. At Grand Etang I have watched this snake foraging in a steel-roofed lean-to in a forest clearing, and many people have told me that *C. grenadensis* is not shy about entering houses. In fact, Groome (1970) observed that "It will readily enter houses and keep them free of rodents in exchange for an occasional bath—a habit which should not be discouraged."

In The Grenadines, where undisturbed habitat is virtually nonexistent (Shepard 1831; Howard 1952; RWH pers. obs., Oct. 1989, Oct. 1990) *Corallus grenadensis* has been observed foraging in *Opuntia* cactus along a road cut (Canouan), in mangroves and mangrove associates (Union), and in a large area of *Cocos nucifera* and *Coccoloba uvifera* (Carriacou), in addition to the widespread dry scrub vegetation (e.g., *Acacia nilotica*) typical of The Grenadines (Beard 1949; Howard 1952).

Treeboas are nowhere more common on Grenada than in areas of mixed agriculture between 30 m and 100 m asl. In such areas—most notably Beausejour (St. George Parish), Westerhall (St. David Parish), Balthazar and Pearls (both St. Andrew Parish)—*C. grenadensis* has been observed foraging in mango, nutmeg, coconut, breadfruit, citrus, cacao, and banana trees, and among passion fruit vines. On the Point Salines and L'anse aux Epine peninsulas, treeboas are often found associated with the thorn-laden alien *Acacia nilotica*.

Although I have spent hundreds of hours driving over much of Grenada, from sea level to more than 500 m and in a wide range of habitats, I have yet to personally find a treeboa alive or dead on the road. However, UF 73145, a 1326-mm pregnant female, was found dead on the road (DOR) on 9 May near Woburn (St. George Parish), and Al Schwartz collected a DOR boa 1.6 km NE of Grand Etang at 455 m on 9 May. Robert Dunn (in litt., 16 March 2000) encountered two DOR *C. grenadensis* on 15 March 2000 in the Balthazar Estate-Pearls area, and Alan Joseph (pers. comm., 3 April 2000), has seen "many" DOR treeboas on Grenada.

Habitat utilization by treeboas on Grenada has received special attention at two sites: Mt. Hartman Bay and Westerhall Estate. Much of the data collected at those two sites has been previously published (Henderson and Winstel 1995; Henderson et al. 1998), but because those studies are informative regarding many aspects of *Corallus* ecology, I present them again in some detail.

Study Sites and Methods

Westerhall. The Westerhall site was located in the area of Westerhall Estate, St. David's Parish. This site is described in detail in Chapter 1.

For each individual captured we recorded sex, SVL, weight (measured with Pesola spring scales while the snake was in a bag of known weight), and predominant dorsal ground color. Over 21 transect nights (19 April–3 May 1993 and 14–20 October 1993), 55 snakes were paint-marked and subsequently observed on 62 occasions (range 0–11/individual). An additional 84 observations were made of snakes we were unable to capture and mark for a total of 201 observations of marked and unmarked *Corallus grenadensis*.

Mt. Hartman Bay. This site is described in some detail in Chapter 1. Unlike at Westerhall, snakes from the Mt. Hartman site were processed at our living quarters rather than in the field, and they were released on the night following their capture. They were marked for short-term identification with ink (Sanford "Sharpie®" fine point permanent markers) in a variety of colors (depending in part on snake color), and scale clipped for long-term identification. Ink marking apparently had no ill effect on ecdysis, as we observed ink-marked snakes while they were shedding and also postshed. Snakes were collected (by hand and with long poles) and released (into the same tree or bush as collected) in the same manner as at Westerhall; a colored flag was tied to the branch from which a snake was removed, and the snake was usually placed on the same branch the next night. As at Westerhall, if a snake was later encountered on the same night it was released, we did not record habitat data for that snake. Data from individual snakes were never recorded more than once a night regardless of the number of sightings.

Over 51 nights (29 Nov–9 Dec 1995; 15–27 Apr 1996; 30 Sep–26 Oct 1996), 33 snakes were marked and subsequently observed 46 times (0–8 observations/marked snake); seven observations were made on unmarked snakes. A preliminary visit to the site on 15–25 Apr 1994 provided some data on structural habitat (54 observations), but the transect was not established until the 1995 visit; 18 different snakes were observed during the preliminary visit to the site, but not permanently marked. It was rare to see a snake at the Mt. Hartman site and not be able to capture it.

There are two species of *Anolis* on Grenada (*A. aeneus* and *A. richardi*). *Anolis aeneus* favors open sunny habitats (Schoener and Gorman 1968), and is more common in xeric areas (Roughgarden 1995). On 3 nights in October 1996 we made counts of anoles (mostly *Anolis aeneus*, fewer *A. richardi*) in the transect. One person was assigned to each side of the transect and in each of the 55 sections was given 1 minute to count anoles. The same person did not count anoles on the same side of the transect on successive nights in order to allow for differences in ability to find the sleeping lizards.

At both sites we viewed the road/path bisecting each transect as a corridor with two-dimensional walls of vegetation on either side. Each 10-m segment of the wall was characterized by the percentage that a particular type of vegetation, or a particular species of tree, occupied (as viewed from the road). Vegetation not visible from the road was excluded from our assessment of the two-dimensional corridor. For example, one segment could be 100% mangrove, whereas another could comprise 70% acacia, 15% mangroves, and 15% herbaceous groundcover. At Westerhall, some segments were open fields with graz-ing livestock, while others were 100% noncultivated woodland. At Mt. Hart-man, only two sections of the transect included land under cultivation, and this did not occur until 1996. This allowed us to quantify gross characteristics of each of the 122 sections of the transect (i.e., east and west portions of 61 segments) at Westerhall and 110 sections at Mt. Hartman (east and west portions of 55 segments). To prevent sampling bias, the vegetation characteristics of each segment were determined very early at the two study sites (i.e., before we became aware of possible patterns in the distribution of *C. grenadensis*).

Data were analyzed using Spearman Rank Correlation procedures, *t*-test, ANOVA, TSRT, chi-square, and PCA. For some tests, snakes were divided into three size classes based on an ontogenetic shift in diet described by Henderson (1993b, 1993c: Chapter 5): small = snakes <600 mm SVL (diet consists entirely of anoles); medium = 600–1100 mm SVL (diet of anoles and small endotherms, especially rodents); large = >1100 mm SVL (diet exclusively of endotherms, primarily rodents).

Results

At both sites combined, 341 observations yielded information on structural habitat and habitat utilization. Using Spearman Rank Correlation, perch height was positively correlated with snake SVL (r = 0.23350, $P = 0.0005$, n = 219) and mass (r = 0.30222, $P = 0.0001$, n = 211), as were perch diameter (SVL: r = 0.48564, $P = 0.0001$, n = 192; mass: r = 0.43259, $P = 0.0001$, n = 185) and distance from the distal end of the branch (SVL: r = 0.22496, $P = 0.0025$, n = 178; mass: r = 0.23689, $P = 0.0017$) but not with distance from the proximal end of the branch. Perch height of a snake was correlated with the distal (r = 0.15023, $P = 0.0221$, n = 232) and proximal (r = 0.25741, $P = 0.0013$, n = 154) positions on a branch, and perch diameter was correlated with the distal position (r = 0.48150, $P = 0.0001$, n = 215) (i.e., perch diameter was narrower more distally along a branch, and the higher the branch was above ground level). Small snakes were more likely to be closer to the distal end of a branch than were larger snakes. Perch characteristics for each site are summarized in Table 3.2. Using the three snake size categories and ANOVA (with TSRT for determining where significant differences occurred), we examined within and between site differences in perch characteristics. The large Westerhall snakes chose perch diameters that were significantly larger than those exploited by small and medium size snakes at both localities. Large snakes at Mt. Hartman used perches of significantly greater diameter than small snakes at either locality. A PCA was run primarily to generate a visual image of perch choice by the three size-classes at the two sites combined (Fig. 3.2). There is considerable overlap

Table 3.2. Summary of snake and perch characteristics for *Corallus grenadensis* in three size-classes and at two sites on Grenada.

	<600 mm SVL		600–1100 mm SVL		>1100 mm SVL	
	Westerhall	Mt. Hartman	Westerhall	Mt. Hartman	Westerhall	Mt. Hartman
SVL (mm)	496.5 ± 12.6 (360–560) 14	450.6 ± 12.9 (350–530) 17	821.6 ± 27.1 (620–964) 14	837.6 ± 44.6 (625–1060) 13	1280.1 ± 37.8 (1164–1485) 8	1189.6 ± 46.0 (1110–1332) 5
Weight (g)	24.7 ± 1.5 (7.5–33.5) 14	12.6 ± 1.1 (7.0–20.0) 16	104.2 ± 10.1 (25.0–213.0) 13	95.3 ± 19.3 (20.0–228.0) 13	523.8 ± 62.6 (305.0–818.0) 8	297.0 ± 42.6 (222.0–459.0) 5
Perch height (m)	4.1 ± 0.3 (0.3–16.0) 65	2.4 ± 0.1 (0.4–5.1) 49	4.0 ± 0.3 (0.3–9.0) 34	2.9 ± 0.4 (0.5–12.0) 36	6.3 ± 0.69 (0.5–12.8) 27	3.8 ± 1.0 (0.3–12) 12
Perch diameter (mm)	4.5 ± 0.6 (1–20) 59	5.4 ± 0.6 (2–18) 44	8.4 ± 1.2 (1.5–30) 32	6.7 ± 0.8 (2–18) 32	15.9 ± 2.10 (3–42) 20	13.2 ± 1.5 (5–19) 9
Distance from distal end of branch (m)	0.2 ± 0.04 (0–2.0) 57	0.2 ± 0.03 (0.2–4.0) 40	0.4 ± 0.1 (0–2.0) 31	0.3 ± 0.1 (0–2.0) 27	0.4 ± 0.1 (0–2.0) 18	0.4 ± 0.2 (0–1.8) 9
Distance from proximal end of branch (m)	1.4 ± 0.1 (0.2–3.8) 34	1.3 ± 0.2 (0.2–4.0) 34	1.7 ± 0.2 (0.3–3.4) 19	1.3 ± 0.3 (0–4.5) 22	1.1 ± 0.2 (0.2–2.0) 11	1.6 ± 0.3 (0.3–3.0) 9

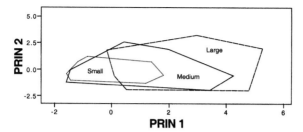

Figure 3.2. Plot of first and second principal component axes based on three variables used in describing the structural habitat of *Corallus grenadensis*. PRIN1 has high values for perch diameter and for distance from the distal end of the perch. PRIN2 has a high loading for perch height. PRIN1 (55%) and PRIN2 (29%) account for 84% of the variation. The line of short dashes encloses all of the records for snakes in the small size category (<600 mm SVL); the solid line encloses records for snakes in the medium size-class (600–1100 mm SVL); the line of long dashes encloses records for snakes in the large size-class (>1100 mm SVL). For clarity, only peripheral points are shown for each size-class.

among the three size-classes, but large snakes especially used perches not exploited by the smaller size classes.

Treeboas were not uniformly distributed through the transects, and some portions of the transect received more use than others. At Westerhall, the contiguous segments of the transect that produced the most observations were 60–120 m in length and had contiguous crown vegetation, either 100% uncultivated or with a high incidence (75%–100%) of mango and breadfruit trees. Conversely, those segments that produced few or no observations were under sugarcane or pineapple cultivation or were open with vegetation cropped from grazing livestock. These areas sometimes contained mango or other fruit trees, but they were invariably solitary, lacking crown vegetation that was contiguous with other trees. The total number of observations of *Corallus grenadensis* from throughout the transect was positively correlated with occurrence of mango trees ($P = 0.0001$; Spearman Rank Correlation) and uncultivated woodlands ($P = 0.0002$, Spearman Rank Correlation). No correlation was detected between the number of observations and the occurrence of cultivated fruit trees exclusive of mangos ($P > 0.05$). Conversely, the total number of observations was negatively correlated with open (virtually treeless) transect segments on east and west sides of the transect (Spearman Rank Correlation, $P = 0.0001$). Isolated trees or bushes did not harbor snakes. For example, 200 of 201 (99.5%) observations were made while snakes were in trees or bushes that were contiguous with other trees or bushes.

There were no large expanses of treeless habitat at Mt. Hartman and virtually none of it was under cultivation. In all 140 observations, snakes were in vegetation that was contiguous with other vegetation (i.e., no snake was observed on vegetation that would require ground-level movements to reach other vegetation). The number of small snakes was negatively correlated with incidence of mangroves (r = -0.39348, $P = 0.0001$), but positively correlated with occurrence of scrub forest with a high incidence of legumes (r = 0.23324, $P = 0.0156$). The presence of large snakes was weakly correlated with the incidence of mangroves (r = 0.18354, $P = 0.0549$), but not incidence of scrubby thorn forest.

The three size-classes of *C. grenadensis* exhibited differential use of three habitat categories at each of the sites (Figs. 3.3 and 3.4). Small snakes were encountered mostly in scrub forest with a high incidence of thorn-laden trees; medium size snakes occurred in similar situations at both sites but also in fruit trees (18.4%) at Westerhall. At Westerhall, large snakes were most often encountered in mango trees and other cultivated trees (e.g., breadfruit, cacao, coconut palm, and banana), and less often in dry scrub woodlands. At Mt. Hartman, large snakes occurred most often in mangroves, but also regularly in dry scrub woodland, and large individuals moved back and forth between the two types of vegetation (either during a single night's foraging, or on different nights). No sexual differences in habitat selection (χ^2, $P > 0.05$) were found within each of the three size categories at either site.

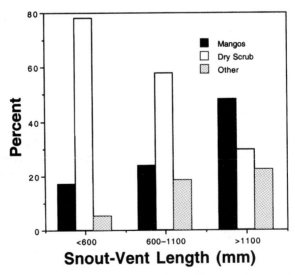

Figure 3.3. Habitat use by three size-classes of *Corallus grenadensis* at the Westerhall study site.

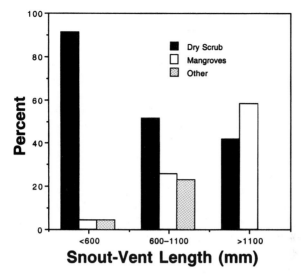

Figure 3.4. Habitat use by three size-classes of *Corallus grenadensis* at the Mt. Hartman Bay study site.

    Corallus grenadensis required only a narrow corridor of trees in which to move and forage. At Westerhall, concentrations of treeboas were observed in tree lines only one tree wide, usually with a high incidence of mango and breadfruit trees and contiguous with other trees (either native or introduced), and bordering small plots of sugarcane. Similarly, at Mt. Hartman, *C. grenadensis* occurred in a strip of mangroves often <5 m wide. At both sites, however, it was possible to use narrow avenues of vegetation to reach broad expanses of trees.

    At Mt. Hartman, a total of 98 anoles was counted on the forest (east) side of the transect, and 46 on the mangrove (west) side. Based on Spearman Rank Correlations, the number of anoles was negatively correlated with the occurrence of mangroves (r = −0.23319, *P* = 0.0142) and positively correlated with scrub forest with a high incidence of legumes (r = 0.23324, *P* = 0.0156).

Discussion

    I consider *Corallus grenadensis* a versatile (or persistent) species in that it has successfully adapted to a wide range of environmental modifications on Grenada (Henderson et al. 1996). It occurs in a wide range of habitats (including those severely altered by human activity) and climatic regimes. It exploits a food source (lizards) largely absent from the diet of the closely related *C.*

hortulanus and *C. ruschenbergerii* on the Neotropical mainland (Henderson 1993b, 1993c; Chapter 5). It has so far adapted to or eluded introduced predators (including humans) which have adversely affected other West Indian vertebrate species.

Contiguous crown vegetation is the single most important criterion in habitat selection by *Corallus grenadensis*, and perhaps in any arboreal snake (Plummer 1981; Tolson 1988). Not only does it provide arboreal habitat for foraging and other basic activities, but it also provides a corridor for movement between local populations. Absence of these arboreal corridors isolates *Corallus* demes, and probably accounts for some of the color pattern variation in *C. grenadensis* (Chapter 2).

Structural habitat (perch heights and dimensions) is important in habitat utilization, with perch diameter being the most critical factor. With increasing mass, snakes must select perches that can support their weight while foraging, causing only minimal disturbance of sleeping or active prey (i.e., remaining inconspicuous, cryptic), and while bridging gaps in the vegetation (i.e., not weighing down one branch thereby increasing the gap distance and making the bridge more difficult or impossible). Large snakes used perches of greater diameter than smaller snakes, and often chose perches that were higher in the vegetation (Figs. 3.5 and 3.6). Snakes in the largest size-class at Westerhall were considerably larger than those in the largest size-class at Mt. Hartman, and used higher perches. While in general sexual differences were not noted within and between sites, females attain larger size than males in *C. grenadensis* and therefore adult females may be encountered more often in situations different from smaller females and most males. As noted by Henderson (1993b), the very largest treeboas often assume ambush foraging postures very close to ground level, where rodents will more likely be encountered; we observed similar behavior during this study. Thus, large treeboas appear to exhibit both active and ambush foraging modes, with active foraging occurring relatively high in trees and ambush tactics close to ground level.

Treeboas routinely perched higher and used perches of greater diameter and attained a larger size at the Westerhall site. Although trees reached greater heights at Westerhall than they did at Mt. Hartman, thereby allowing snakes to attain greater heights in the vegetation, it does not explain why snakes in the smallest size-class, which perched lowest in the vegetation, also assumed a higher mean perch height (see Table 3.2). Perhaps the vertical range of habitat use is stretched to fill the entire vertical range available at a given site. Or the between-site disparities may reflect differences in prey distribution within the respective habitats, but the data preclude addressing that hypothesis. Mean SVL of treeboas at Westerhall (797.1 ± 51.8) was greater than at Mt. Hartman (699.9 ± 49.4), but not significantly so (*t*-test, $P = 0.1793$); mean mass of Westerhall treeboas (168.3 ± 36.6) was significantly greater than for those at Mt. Hartman

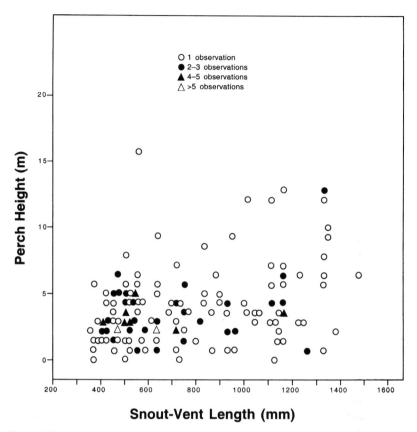

Figure 3.5. Relationship between snake size (SVL) and perch height at the Mt. Hartman Bay and Westerhall Estate sites combined (n = 219, r = 0.336, Pearson Correlation; *P* = 0.0001).

(86.1 ± 19.0) (*t*-test, *P* = 0.0523). Perhaps this indicates that Westerhall treeboas had more food available to them, and we have routinely encountered larger treeboas in agriculturally disturbed areas. Furthermore, the largest treeboas collected on Grenada to date have come from an agriculturally disturbed site (Beausejour Estate, St. George Parish). Although other factors may contribute to the size distribution of *Corallus grenadensis* on Grenada, areas of active fruit and vegetable cultivation may support rodent populations of higher density than other areas, thereby providing treeboas with more large prey items.

Perhaps the most interesting parallel between the two sites was the distribution of the three size classes in general habitat categories. Small snakes at

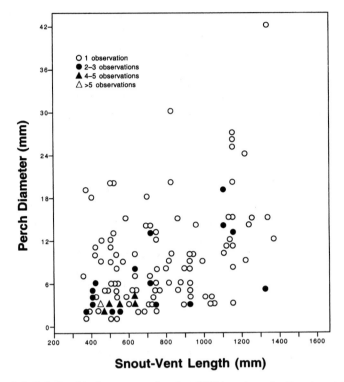

Figure 3.6. Relationship between snake size (SVL) and perch diameter at the Mt. Hartman Bay and Westerhall Estate sites combined (n = 192, r = 0.511, Pearson Correlation; *P* = 0.0001).

both sites were most often associated with scrub woodland with a high incidence of thorny legumes. At Mt. Hartman we found a correlation between anole abundance and this kind of habitat. Conversely, large snakes, for which anoles are not an important dietary element, were encountered less often in the thorn scrub. Whether this was because of prey distribution or because of the large acacia thorns (which might make movement difficult; small treeboas can crawl between the thorns, big ones cannot) is unknown. Snakes in the largest size category at Westerhall occurred most often in mango trees, but with relatively high proportions occurring in other fruit trees and in the dry scrub. At Mt. Hartman, the largest snakes occurred most often in mangroves, with an almost equal proportion in scrub woodlands with a high incidence of thorny legumes. Large marked snakes moved back and forth between the mangrove and scrub habitats. Although thorny scrub woodland is not altogether abandoned, there is an ontogenetic shift from that habitat to something quite different (i.e., cultivated fruit trees or mangroves) at both sites. This may be attributed to the following: 1) a shift in the prey species that are exploited by different size classes of treeboas; 2) the availability of more large branches; and/or 3) an antipredator strategy wherein thorn-laden branches provide protection to snakes too small to protect themselves in any other way. Since even the largest treeboas are slender and it is unlikely that they would have difficulty finding branches to support their mass in most habitats, the second hypothesis is unlikely. The third hypothesis may have some merit, but I have no evidence to support it, in part because so little is known about treeboa predators. I do not have data to adequately address the first hypothesis, but since food is such a critical resource, I feel that hypothesis is the most tenable. Ontogenetic shifts in diet are not uncommon among snakes, occurring across a broad taxonomic and phylogenetic spectrum, e.g., pythonids (Shine and Slip 1990), colubrids (Henderson et al. 1988), and viperids (McCoy and Censky 1992). Among Neotropical species, Sexton (1958) has described an ontogenetic habitat shift in *Bothrops venezuelensis* (his sample apparently included some *B. asper* as well: W.W. Lamar, in litt., April 2000) that is correlated with a shift in diet (from frogs to rodents), and similar to that which we have described for *C. grenadensis*.

   Corallus grenadensis exhibits an ontogenetic shift in diet from anoles to rodents: snakes <600 mm SVL prey exclusively on anoles, those 600–1110 mm SVL take anoles and endotherms, and snakes >1100 mm SVL prey exclusively on endotherms (primarily introduced rodents). This shift in diet corresponds with the shift in habitat at the two study sites. Small snakes favored scrub woodlands with a high incidence of thorny legumes, and we found a correlation between anole abundance and this kind of habitat at Mt. Hartman. The Mt. Hartman site is in one of the most xeric areas of the island, and *A. aeneus* and small treeboas were common at the margin of the thorn scrub. Structurally, mangrove foliage provides denser shade and probably is less desirable habitat for *A. aeneus*. A similar scenario may apply to Westerhall, where mango trees provide a canopy of dense shade that is not exploited as often by *A. aeneus* (the more numerous anole at that site, also), as is the scrub forest.

   Conversely, large snakes were encountered less often in the thorn scrub. Anoles are a less important element in their diet, there was a negative correlation between occurrence of anoles and the incidence of mangroves, and the incidence of treeboas in mangroves becomes greater as the snakes increase in size. Snakes in the middle size category overlapped in both habitat and diet with the two extreme size classes, and they are in ontogenetic transition between the extremes. In general, for a given snake species, larger individuals are more trophically versatile than smaller snakes in that they can exploit a wider taxonomic and size range of prey items (Arnold 1993), and it is true for West Indian *Corallus* (Henderson 1993b). In *C. grenadensis*, trophic versatility is apparently correlated with habitat versatility: small snakes are more restricted trophically (feeding exclusively on anoles) and spatially (i.e., confining activity to dry scrub habitat and using the narrowest range of structural habitat variables), than larger individuals.

CORALLUS HORTULANUS

Considering how widespread this species is, and how often it is encountered relative to other snake species in lowland South America, amazingly little is known about its habitat utilization. The widespread distribution of *Corallus hortulanus* in rainforest throughout Amazonia and the Guianas is well documented (e.g., Amaral 1976; Duellman 1978, 1989, 1990; Dixon 1979; Hoogmoed 1979, 1983; Moonen et al. 1979; Dixon and Soini 1977, 1986; Chippaux 1986; Fugler 1986; Zimmerman and Rodrigues 1990; Silva 1993; Henderson 1994, 1997a; Henderson et al. 1995; Martins and Oliveira 1998; Starace 1998), but it occurs in a variety of other habitats and morphoclimatic domains (*sensu* Ab'Saber 1977) as well. Starace (1998) considered it ubiquitous in French Guiana, occurring in a variety of situations, including primary and secondary forest, water courses bordered by *Montrichardia arborescens*, in the fronds of the palm *Mauritia flexuosa*, and at times in human habitations. He usually encountered them 1.0–4.0 m above ground level, but occasionally higher in large trees. Chippaux (1986) encountered *C. hortulanus* in essentially the same situations in French Guiana as Starace (1998), and also found it in human dwellings. William W. Lamar (in litt., April 2000) reports finding it routinely in the rafters of houses, and also in abandoned arboreal termite nests.

Based on the distribution map for this species (see Fig. 1.1; also Henderson 1997a) and the South American vegetation map in Campbell and Lamar (1989), *C. hortulanus* can be encountered in sclerophyllus woodland, Atlantic forest, montane deciduous scrub, cerrado, savanna/grassland with woody species, and caatinga (where it may be confined to gallery forests: see Puorto and Henderson 1994, and Henderson et al. 1995), as well as rainforest.

Based on 34 observations in Amazonian Brazil (at sites in Acre, Pará, and Rondônia), *C. hortulanus* was observed in upper and low primary forest, secondary forest, mixed forest, second growth, river forest, river forest swamp, forest edge, and palm forest. The snakes were found at perch heights ranging from 0.7–10.0 m ($\bar{x}$ = 2.8 ± 0.36 m; n = 28), and on perches with diameters of 2.0–50.0 mm ($\bar{x}$ = 15.9 ± 2.6 mm; n = 28) (L.J. Vitt, in litt., 5 Feb 1999). At several sites in Central Amazonia, Martins and Oliveira (1998) encountered *C. hortulanus* at heights of 0.5–25.0 m. By day, they found a treeboa coiled in a hollow trunk 1.5 m above water. Little is known about the use of rainforest canopy by arboreal snakes. Nevertheless, despite the potential for considerable vertical movement (from ground level to about 30 m) in lowland rainforest habitat, it appears that *C. hortulanus* spends most of its time foraging at heights <4.0 m. It is possible, however, that diurnal roosting sites for this species may be considerably higher, although this does not appear to be the case for the three other members of the complex. Many of the diurnal resting sites that I have observed in *C. cookii, C. grenadensis,* and *C. ruschenbergerii* have been under 5.0 m.

Corallus hortulanus is often encountered along the edges of bodies of water, including rivers (Lancini 1979; Martins and Oliveira 1998), swamps (Duellman and Mendelson 1995), mangroves (Starace 1998), streams (Dixon and Soini 1986), lakes (Martins and Oliveira 1998), and lagoons (W.W. Lamar, in litt., 1998). Although these treeboas do, indeed, frequent vegetation at water's edge, they also occur away from water. William W. Lamar (in litt., April 2000) has encountered *C. hortulanus* "in deep forest and not along streams." It is likely that they are so often associated with waterside vegetation because a water barrier creates a habitat edge, and it is easy to search for snakes and other reptiles from the water.

Although their activity is largely confined to arboreal situations, in rainforest habitat in Rondônia, Brazil, four of ten *C. hortulanus* collected were found coiled on the ground, and treeboas were observed crossing roads (Silva 1993). Martins and Oliveira (1998) found one crossing the road at a site in Central Amazonia (Amazônas, Brazil). At Iquitos, in Amazonian Peru, a 635 mm SVL treeboa was found DOR with a bird in its stomach (USNM 197249), Dixon and Soini (1986) report finding a DOR *C. hortulanus,* and Duellman and Mendelson (1995) found a juvenile crawling across a road at night in northern Departamento Loreto, also in Amazonian Peru.

CORALLUS RUSCHENBERGERII

Based on the vegetation and edaphic zone maps in Campbell and Lamar (1989), in Central America *Corallus ruschenbergerii* occurs in tropical moist forest and subtropical wet forest. On the South American mainland it occurs in lower montane dry forest, lower montane wet forest, rainforest, flooded grassland, lowland dry forest/thorn forest, and savanna/grassland with woody species.

In Panama, Sexton and Heatwole (1965) collected *C. ruschenbergerii* by day and night from branches overhanging the Río Canclón and the Río Chucunaque (Darien Province). In Colombia, W.W. Lamar (pers. comm.) found this species to be very common in coastal mangroves, and Pérez-Santos and Moreno (1988) also reported it as occurring in mangroves in Colombia. Roze (1964) described *C. ruschenbergerii* as abundant in the mangroves on Isla Margarita (off the coast of Venezuela). On the Venezuelan mainland it occurs in gallery forests, along rivers, and in mangroves (including situations near the sea: Roze 1966). In the llanos, Rivero-Blanco and Dixon (1979) record *C. ruschenbergerii* from mata, deciduous, and gallery forests, and morichales (areas dominated by the palm *Mauritia minor*). I have observed foraging *C. ruschenbergerii* in gallery forest along the Río Matiyure in the Venezuelan llanos (at Hato El Cedral, Apure), occasionally on branches overhanging the water, and W.W. Lamar (in litt., April 2000) has encountered it asleep by day on branches over gallery forest creeks in the Colombian llanos. Although often associated with water like *C. hortulanus*, it has also been encountered in deep forest and not along streams (W.W. Lamar, in litt., April 2000).

The species is widespread on Trinidad, from sea level to about 360 m asl, but most specimens have been taken in the northern one-half of the island (e.g., the Northern Range; Mt. Harris in the Central Range) in habitats ranging from relatively undisturbed forest edge to edificarian situations near Port-of-Spain (Henderson and Boos 1993). As elsewhere, *Corallus ruschenbergerii* is usually encountered along road cuts, the margins of rivers, lakes, reservoirs, and other edge situations. On three occasions Murphy (1997) encountered treeboas crossing roads in secondary forest at night, and USNM 306071 was collected DOR in Tobago. By day, Mole and Urich (1894) found them "rolled up in the loose folds among the twigs of a tree, the branches of which overhang a stream." Mole and Urich (1894) reported that they frequently were "found in bamboo clumps, and in bushes in the vicinity of or overhanging, streams," and when "they lie in the slender twigs at the furthest extremities of the thick branches of the tree partially screened by the leaves are singularly inconspicuous." *Corallus ruschenbergerii* has been observed in a tree overhanging the Caribbean Sea on the north coast of Trinidad (Hans Boos, pers. comm., 20 Mar 1999). I have observed *C. ruschenbergerii* foraging at water's edge at Hollis Reservoir (Quarre Dam) in the Northern Range, sometimes on branches that overhang the water by 4.0–5.0 m, and in mangrove (*Rhizophora*) edge in the Caroni Swamp. I have also found the species common in secondary forest along a road cut above the Arima River in the Northern Range at elevations of 100–200 m. A *Corallus ruschenbergerii* was collected in the branches of *Clusia*, which was growing on rocks on the northern coast of Trinidad (Boos 2001). One of several local names for *C. ruschenbergerii* in Trinidad is "mango snake" (Boos 2001), indicating, again, the proclivity of treeboas for mango trees.

In Costa Rica, *Corallus ruschenbergerii* is common in vegetation bordering and near the edge of rivers from Drake's Bay (Península de Osa) northward along the Pacific Coast. It also occurs in mangrove stands along the lower courses of rivers draining the mainland from at least Dominical southward (W.W. Lamar, in litt., April 2000).

Chapter 4

Activity

This boa is essentially arboreal and nocturnal.... Trust in immobility and their resemblance to branches and twigs seems reflected in the ease with which they can be approached in daylight and seized.

Beebe (1946) describing a member of the *Corallus hortulanus* complex

DIEL ACTIVITY

Surprisingly little is known about diel activity in snakes, perhaps in large part due to the difficulty in maintaining visual contact with such elusive animals. The brilliant eyeshine in *Corallus* has aided us in making and maintaining visual contact. Within the *Corallus hortulanus* complex, I have quantifiable data only for *Corallus grenadensis*. I suspect that the other members of the complex exhibit a similar activity pattern. Certainly other nocturnal snake species exhibit a similar pattern of activity (Table 4.1).

During the day, *Corallus grenadensis* usually (90% of observations) coiled on the distal ends of branches. Only their prehensile tails were wrapped under branches, and their bodies rested on top of the branches. The coils were more or less concentric, but often with some overlap (i.e., a portion of one coil resting on a portion of another), and the head resting on top of one of the coils (see photo of *C. hortulanus* in Moonen et al. 1979). Inactive snakes invariably had an umbrella of leaves shielding them from full sunlight; similar behavior has been observed in the Australian python, *Morelia spilota* (Shine and Fitzgerald 1996). For *C. grenadensis*, choosing situations such as this may provide protection from avian predators and minimize heat loading. The canopies were often just a small sprig of vegetation, but sufficient to conceal the snake and to create a sun-shade mosaic. Inactive snakes observed in mangrove habitat (usually *Rhizophora mangle*) invariably selected perches that were over water (as opposed to the land side of the narrow coastal strip of mangroves). Aside from slight changes in posture, no activity was observed during daylight

73

Table 4.1. Time and duration of activity and light levels in some tropical nocturnal snakes.

Species	Time of Activity	Light Intensity	Source
Boidae			
Corallus grenadensis	1800–0530 h, but peaks 1900–2200 h then gradually decreases; all has terminated by ca 0530 h	activity initiated and terminated at ca. 16 lux	present study
Corallus hortulanus	about 1800–0600 h, but most activity 1800–2400 h	?	Chippaux 1986
Epicrates monensis	starts early evening and declines before 2400 h	?	P.J. Tolson, pers. comm., 1997
Pythonidae			
Liasis fuscus	most occurred shortly after dusk	?	Shine and Madsen 1996
Colubridae			
Boiga irregularis	1800–0600 h, peaks 2200–0200 h	?	Fritts et al. 1987
Imantodes cenchoa[1]	?	some activity at <16 lux, foraging starts usually at <4.3 lux	Henderson and Nickerson 1976
Leptodeira annulata	1900–2300 h	?	Vitt 1996

Table 4.1. (*Continued*)

Species	Time of Activity	Light Intensity	Source
Viperidae			
Bothrops jararaca	1830–2130 h dusk–early night (1820–2030 h)	? ?	Sazima 1988 Sazima 1992
B. venezuelensis[2]	predominantly after 1800 h, but perhaps as early as 1600 h	<21.5 lux	Sexton 1958
Lachesis stenophrys	starts abruptly at dusk (ca 1800 h) and stops abruptly at dawn	?	H.W. Greene and M. Santana, pers. comm., 1997
Trimeresurus flavoviridis[1,3]	starts at 2000–2400 h	<10^{-3} lux	Yamagishi 1974

[1]Based on captive snakes
[2]Sample contained some *Bothrops asper* (W.W. Lamar, in litt., April 2000)
[3]Occurs slightly north of the Tropic of Cancer.

hours. Bartsch (in Cochran 1934) encountered *C. grenadensis* in a bunch of orchids and in a hollowed tree limb by day on Île à Quatre.

Activity in *Corallus grenadensis* began at dusk. The earliest time at which foraging behavior was observed was 1755 h. The onset of activity in *C. grenadensis* was associated with declining air temperature and light intensity. On six occasions (six different snakes) at the Mt. Hartman Bay site in October, it was possible to witness the onset of foraging and to monitor light level. During five of the six episodes, the snake initiated activity between 1809–1812 h; the sixth episode occurred at 1816 h. Light levels at the onset of activity were 1.1–40.9 lux ($\bar{x} \pm$ SE = 16.9 $\pm$ 5.3 lux, n = 6). Overall, the percentage of snakes observed that were active reached over 90% between 1900 and 2000 h and remained relatively constant through 2100–2200 h (Fig. 4.1). After 2200 h, activity generally declined, except for a resurgence between 0200 and 0300, which may have been an artifact of a small sample (n = 8). Activity ceased completely by 0535 h. Light intensity was ca. 16.0 lux at 0530. No activity was observed between 0535 and 1755 h.

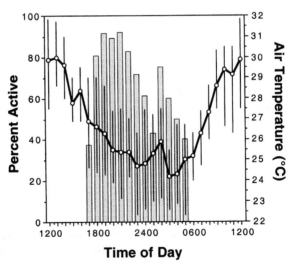

Figure 4.1. The relationship between activity and air temperature in *Corallus grenadensis* on Grenada. The gray vertical bars indicate the percentage of observed snakes that were active each hour (total number of observations = 528; the mean number $\pm$ SE of observations/hour = 22.0 $\pm$ 7.4 [1–118]). The solid black line indicates mean hourly air temperature, and the associated vertical lines indicate the temperature range at each hour (total number of air temperatures = 272; the mean number of air temperatures recorded/hour = 11.3 $\pm$ 1.1 [4–22]). Observations made between 1800 h and 1900 h appear at 1800 h on the graph; those made between 1900 and 2000 appear at 1900 on the graph, etc. Modified from Henderson and Winstel (1997).

Treeboa activity increased as air temperature dropped (Fig. 4.1). There was a negative correlation (Pearson) between hourly mean air temperature and the percentage of observed snakes that were active ($r = -0.69519$, $P = 0.0002$, $n = 24$). Air temperature continued to decline throughout the night, and did not begin to increase until the time (0500–0600 h) that all treeboa activity terminated. In a subset of 122 observations in which an air temperature was recorded for each observation, snakes were active at temperatures between 22 and 28°C, but 68% of the observations ($n = 93$) occurred at temperatures of 24–27°C. Of the snakes observed between 24 and 27°C, 89.2% were active, but of those snakes observed at 22–24°C ($n = 27$), only 66.7% were active. Inactive snakes were observed at temperatures of 28–32°C, but all of those observations occurred during daylight hours.

Activity Budget

In general, of every 24 hours, *Corallus grenadensis* may devote anywhere from about 25% to 45% of its time to foraging; nocturnal nonforaging activity may account for 0–25% of its time; and 50–55% of its time is spent in resting, sleeping, and thermoregulation (including prey assimilation) activities during daylight hours.

Discussion

Nonresting activity in *Corallus grenadensis* is strictly nocturnal and crepuscular. Initiation and termination of activity are strongly associated with light intensity and temperatures. Chippaux (1986: Table 5) indicated an activity pattern in *C. hortulanus* in French Guiana very similar to that described for *C. grenadensis*, i.e., most activity from dusk (about 1800 h) until midnight, and then tapering-off from midnight until dawn (0600 h), and he indicated a similar pattern for *C. caninus* (but with activity terminating well before dawn). Henderson and Winstel (1992) commented on the rapid onset of activity in *C. grenadensis* between 1800 and 1815 h at a site along the Beausejour River. The onset of activity may be endogenous (see review in Underwood 1992), although entrained by some extrinsic factor such as photoperiod, temperature, or an interaction between the two. Bustard (1968) determined that activity in an Australian nocturnal gekkonid initiated at sunset provided the temperature was within a certain range. Activity might continue until dawn if temperature remained above a certain level, but a drop in temperature would greatly curtail activity. Likewise, temperature may be a factor in determining the onset of activity at dusk in *C. grenadensis*, and in determining how long into the night a snake forages. At the Mt. Hartman Bay site, treeboas observed during the day usually were on perches that provided a western exposure, thereby permitting the sun's rays to hit them for as long as possible in the afternoon, just prior to the onset of nocturnal activity. A similar situation was noticed in *C. ruschen-bergerii* in Trinidad's Caroni Swamp. Possibly this strategy allows the snakes to attain and maintain a relatively high body temperature for as long as possible and start foraging soon after sundown. Regardless of ambient temperatures, however, activity stops at dawn.

Henderson and Henderson (1995) demonstrated altitudinal variation in foraging *C. grenadensis*, with snakes at higher elevations foraging at significantly lower body temperatures than those at lower elevations. We did not here include any of the few records available for treeboas at altitudes >400 m asl, but there *C. grenadensis* has been observed foraging with air temperature at 20°C.

On Grenada, *C. grenadensis* preys on scansorial lizards (*Anolis*) that sleep on trees and bushes during the night, and on nocturnal rodents (Henderson 1993b; Chapter 5). Less often it feeds on small birds (e.g., Bananaquits). We have observed it striking at bats investigating tree branches bearing fruit. Our observations indicate the following: 1) that foraging may terminate for the night long before dawn even if the snake has not been successful in obtaining food; and 2) that foraging may occur from dusk until dawn, but based on the percentage of snakes that are not active after midnight, this is probably not the usual pattern. Henderson and Henderson (1995) suggested that a treeboa that fed early in the evening would terminate foraging. However, several *C. grena-densis* have been found with two anoles in their gastrointestinal tract at the same approximate stage of digestion, indicating that they had been ingested within a short time of each other. In these instances foraging activity was not terminated after the capture and ingestion of one anole.

There are subtleties of *C. grenadensis* activity that we have observed but are as yet unable to interpret (e.g., loosely or partially coiled but with head extended; Fig. 4.2). However, based on other studies (see Table 4.1), our observations of *C. grenadensis* indicate a pattern of activity (and possibly activity budget) that is similar to other nocturnal tropical snakes. Although few data are available, activity in tropical nocturnal snakes generally begins early in the evening and the number of active snakes peaks before midnight or soon thereafter, and then the number of active snakes decreases until dawn, when all foraging activity stops. A similar pattern has also been observed in some nocturnal gekkonids (e.g., Bustard 1970; Vitt and Zani 1997) in the tropics.

Diurnal resting behavior in other members of the *Corallus hortulanus* complex is similar to that described for *C. grenadensis*. I have observed *C. cookii* resting on branches near the Chateaubelair River in St. David Parish. One was at 2.0 m on a shaded branch, its body resting on but not around the branch; another was coiled at 2.0–3.0 m in a mango tree along a road cut.

Moonen et al. (1979) provide a photograph of a diurnally resting *C. hortu-lanus* in Suriname, and it has assumed a position comparable to what I have observed in *C. grenadensis*. Similarly, Starace (1998) provides a photograph of a *C. hortulanus* coiled on the branch of a *Montrichardia arborescens*; the

Figure 4.2. *Corallus grenadensis* in a loose coil posture on a branch about 2.5 m above the Beausejour River. Photo by R.A. Winstel.

snake is coiled on the branch but not around it, and its head is completely exposed and resting on a coil. By day in Amazonian Brazil (Acre, Rondônia), L. J. Vitt (in litt., 5 Feb 1999) has encountered *C. hortulanus* under the bark of a tree at the edge of primary forest at 1359 h, and another coiled on a branch at 2.5 m in a clearing at 1420 h, and W.W. Lamar (in litt., April 2000) has encountered it in abandoned arboreal termite nests by day.

In the Caroni Swamp (Trinidad), I have observed *Corallus ruschenbergerii* during the day. Each of three large females was coiled tightly in the fork of a branch of a red mangrove tree (*Rhizophora*), 2.0–10.0 m above the water (1) or the ground (2). As in other members of the complex, the snakes were resting on the branches, rather than coiled around them. William W. Lamar (in litt., April 2000), however, has found *C. ruschenbergerii* in Costa Rica and Colombia tightly coiled around the branch on which it was resting.

FACTORS AFFECTING NOCTURNAL ACTIVITY

Moon Phase

It has been suggested for several species of snakes that brightly moonlit nights suppress activity (Klauber 1939; Madsen and Osterkamp 1982). Likewise, it is my perception that moon phase impacts the activity of *Corallus grenadensis*. However, since other factors are involved in snake activity, and since we have made no attempt to do controlled experiments on the effect of moon phase (such as those by Clarke et al. [1996] for *Crotalus v. viridis*) my observations are, with one exception, largely anecdotal. At Westerhall Estate in April 1993, we practiced a standard searching technique along a transect through an area of mixed agriculture. Two very thorough searches were conducted every night. Starting with a new moon, we observed a mean of 14.0 ± 0.6 snakes/night over 4 nights; at the quarter moon we were observing 11.3 ± 1.2 snakes/night over 3 nights, and at the one-half to three-quarter moon, we encountered only 8.0 ± 0.7 snakes/night over 5 nights. Treeboa activity could be depressed on brighter nights as they may be more visible to predators (e.g., owls). Alternatively, since there is evidence that rodent activity is depressed on bright nights (Longland and Price 1991) in order to minimize the risk of predation, activity in larger treeboas may be suppressed in response to the reduction of rodent activity. William W. Lamar (in litt., April 2000) has observed *C. hortulanus* foraging in deep shadow on moonlit nights in Amazonian Peru.

Rainfall

It is my perception that a hard rain curtails the foraging activity of *Corallus grenadensis*. It is difficult to make an intelligent assessment as rainfall during field work was intermittent and usually of short duration. On the few occasions that rainfall was very heavy in areas where treeboas were common (e.g., Westerhall Estate), we either stayed under cover until the rain abated, or we had difficulty seeing far enough to be able to find treeboas in the vegetation. In areas where rainfall is frequent and heavy (e.g., Grand Etang or Spring Gardens), *C. grenadensis* was rarely seen in any case. I have observed *C. grenadensis* active in moderately heavy rain, but whether the snake was still foraging or seeking shelter is unknown. If rainfall awakens sleeping *Anolis* and makes them more alert, active foraging by *C. grenadensis* while it is raining may not be energetically advantageous. Alternatively, as suggested by W.W. Lamar (in litt., April 2000), rainfall may eliminate scent trails leading to sleeping anoles, again making foraging energetically disadvantageous. In captivity, *C. grenadensis* that are sprayed with a fine mist of water become agitated and leave their perches. Rodda (1992) reported that the arboreal snake *Boiga irregularis* "bolted at the start of heavy rain."

SEASONAL ACTIVITY

Seasonal activity in temperate snakes has received considerable attention (e.g., Gibbons and Semlitsch 1987); tropical species have received less attention, but data are available documenting seasonal differences related to precipitation (Henderson et al. 1978; Rodda et al. 1999). More recently, Daltry et al. (1998) have documented that humidity influences snake activity in a tropical Asian pit viper.

At Mt. Hartman Bay, two Grenadian farmers working near the study site agreed that *Corallus grenadensis* was more common in mangroves (*Rhizophora mangle*) during the dry season. Similarly, at Balthazar Estate, I was told that *C. grenadensis* is more common in bamboo along the Balthazar River in the dry season. My data from Mt. Hartman Bay are equivocal: I made an equal number of observations of snakes in mangroves in the wet and dry seasons. However, for the only observations (n = 2) that I made of treeboas <600 mm SVL in *Rhizophora mangle*, both observations occurred in the dry season. As Henderson et al. (1978) found a positive correlation between rainfall and the seasonal incidence of arboreal edge species (including *C. hortulanus*) in the vicinity of Iquitos, Peru, and despite the paucity of additional evidence from Grenada, I believe that the observations/opinions shared with me by the Grenadians have merit and may prove accurate. It is unlikely, however, that rainfall is the only factor involved in determining seasonal activity in tropical snakes (Henderson et al. 1978).

MOVEMENTS

Short-term Movements

Data are available for 13 *Corallus grenadensis* at the Mt. Hartman Bay and Westerhall Estate sites for spans of 5–17 days (mean = 9.8 ± 1.1). The mean SVL of snakes for which we have data is 594 ± 55 mm (range = 400–1165 mm). Because we recorded only in which 10-m section a snake was captured and subsequently recaptured (or reobserved), a snake reobserved in the same section may have moved nearly 10 m. Likewise, a snake that was reobserved in an adjacent section may have moved anywhere from 1 m to nearly 20 m. For that reason I present data on potential mean minimum and maximum daily movements. Mean minimum movement was 3.3 ± 1.1 m/day (range 0.0–11.4 m) and mean maximum movement was 10.9 ± 1.7 m/day (range 2.9–22.5 m).

Other snakes were marked and subsequently reobserved, but the 13 used in the analysis were reobserved on two to ten occasions. Certainly we missed seeing marked snakes from night to night. Although the eyeshine of treeboas greatly facilitated locating them, if a snake's head was not positioned just right, or if the eye was hidden from the beam of a headlamp by a sprig of vegetation, we could easily miss the snake.

Only one snake in the sample was >750 mm SVL, and this may be a reason the mean daily movements are relatively short. Snakes <600 mm SVL ($\bar{x}$ = 484.3 ± 18.8 mm; n = 8) had mean daily minimum movements of 2.15 ±

1.4 m and mean daily maximum movements of 8.5 ± 1.6 m, whereas snakes >600 mm SVL ($\bar{x}$ = 770.4 ± 101.0 mm; n = 5) had mean daily minimum movements of 5.1 ± 1.7 m and mean daily maximum movements of 14.7 ± 3.0 m. Smaller snakes fed exclusively on anoles, and because anoles occurred at high densities, small snakes could stay in a more localized area to forage. Snakes in those size-classes that fed predominantly on rodent prey had to forage in larger areas in order to successfully find prey that occurred at, presumably, significantly lower population densities.

More limited data are available for *Corallus hortulanus*. A 1520 mm SVL female collected from a vine tangle on 28 Nov 1989 at Cuzco Amazonico (Madre de Dios, Peru), was marked and released at the capture site on 1 Dec; on 2 Dec she was observed in the same vine tangle about 10 m from the original capture site (W.E. Duellman, in litt., 17 May 1996). Starace (1998) observed an adult *C. hortulanus* utilize the false ceiling of a house as a daytime retreat for over 1 year. It would vacate the edifice in the evening in order to forage, and then return again before daybreak.

Long-term Movements

I have data for only three long-term movements (i.e., those movements that occurred over an interval of at least 100 days) for *C. grenadensis*, and all are from the Mt. Hartman Bay site. A subadult male originally captured on 8 Oct 1996 was recaptured on 2 Feb 1998 (482 days elapsed) 10–20 m from the original site and in the same stand of *Acacia nilotica*. An adult female originally captured on 4 Dec 1995 was recaptured on 17 April 1996 (134 days elapsed) along the same trail and 140–150 m from the original site. That same female was recaptured again on 30 Sept 1996 (166 days elapsed), again along the same trail and in the same stand of *Rhizophora mangle*, and 50–60 m from the April recapture site. She was within 100 m of where she was originally captured on 4 Dec 1995.

Plate 1. *Corallus cookii* from 3.2 km E of Layou, St. Patrick Parish, St. Vincent. Photograph by R.W. Henderson.

Plate 2. *Corallus cookii* from 3.2 km E of Layou, St. Patrick Parish, St. Vincent. Photograph ©R.A. Sajdak.

Plate 3. *Corallus cookii* from 3.2 km E of Layou, St. Patrick Parish, St. Vincent. Photograph ©R.A. Sajdak.

Plate 4. *Corallus grenadensis* from Pearls, St. Andrew Parish, Grenada. Photograph ©R.A. Sajdak.

Plate 5. *Corallus grenadensis* from Pearls, St. Andrew Parish, Grenada. Photograph ©R.A. Sajdak.

Plate 6. *Corallus grenadensis* from the eastern edge of Mt. Hartman Bay, St. George Parish, Grenada. Photograph by R.W. Henderson.

Plate 7. *Corallus grenadensis* from Pearls, St. Andrew Parish, Grenada. Photograph ©Ky Henderson.

Plate 8. *Corallus grenadensis* from Calvigny Estate, St. George Parish, Grenada. The treeboa is exhibiting typical balling-posture. Photograph by R.A. Winstel.

Plate 9. *Corallus grenadensis* from Pearls, St. Andrew Parish, Grenada. The snake is killing an *Anolis aeneus* in a staged situation. Photograph ©R.A. Sajdak.

Plate 10. *Corallus grenadensis* from Spring Gardens Estate, St. Andrew Parish, Grenada. Photograph by R.W. Henderson.

Plate 11. *Corallus hortulanus* from Iwokrama, Rupununi, Guyana.
Photograph ©M. O'Shea.

Plate 12. *Corallus hortulanus* from Iwokrama, Rupununi, Guyana.
Photograph ©M. O'Shea.

Plate 13. *Corallus hortulanus* from Karanambo, Rupununi, Guyana. Photograph ©M. O'Shea.

Plate 14. *Corallus hortulanus* (Laurie J. Vitt [LJV] 4795) from Cuyabeno, Sucumbios, Ecuador. Photograph ©L.J. Vitt.

Plate 15. *Corallus hortulanus* (LJV 4745) from Cuyabeno, Sucumbios, Ecuador. Photograph ©L.J. Vitt.

Plate 16. *Corallus hortulanus* from Garza Cocha, near Anyañgu, Sucumbios, Ecuador. Photograph ©P.J. DeVries.

Plate 17. *Corallus hortulanus* from Momoncillo, Loreto, Peru. Photograph ©W.W. Lamar.

Plate 18. *Corallus hortulanus* (LJV 6438) from Porto Walter, Acre, Brazil. Photograph ©L.J. Vitt.

Plate 19. *Corallus hortulanus* (LJV 8698) from Rio Ituxi, Amazonas, Brazil. Photograph ©L.J. Vitt.

Plate 20. *Corallus hortulanus* (LJV 6789) from Rio Ituxi, Amazonas, Brazil. Photograph ©L.J. Vitt.

Plate 21. *Corallus hortulanus* (LJV 5628) from 101 km S Santarem, Pará, Brazil.
Photograph ©J.P. Caldwell.

Plate 22. *Corallus hortulanus* from Acampamento Juruá (Rio Xingu), Pará, Brazil.
Photograph ©L.J. Vitt.

Plate 23. *Corallus hortulanus*
Peru: Loreto:
lower Río Nanay
Photograph ©W.W. Lamar.

Plate 24. *Corallus hortulanus* from Marcílio Dias, Santa Catarina, Brazil (26° 08' S).
Photograph by G. Puorto.

Plate 25. *Corallus hortulanus* from Estação Ecológica Juréia-Itatins, Iguape, São Paulo, Brazil. Photograph by I. Sazima.

Plate 26. *Corallus ruschenbergerii* (juvenile) from the Arima Valley, Northern Range, Trinidad. Photograph ©R.A. Sajdak.

Plate 27. *Corallus ruschenbergerii* from Caroni Swamp, Trinidad. Photograph ©M. O'Shea.

Plate 28. *Corallus ruschenbergerii* from Caroni Swamp, Trinidad. Photograph ©R.A. Sajdak.

Plate 29. *Corallus ruschenbergerii* from Caroni Swamp, Trinidad. The snake is in an ambush posture typical of large *C. ruschenbergerii*. Photograph ©R.A. Sajdak.

Plate 30. *Corallus ruschenbergerii* from Caroni Swamp, Trinidad. The snake is in a diurnal resting posture typical of *C. ruschenbergerii*. Photograph ©R.A. Sajdak.

Plate 31. *Corallus ruschenbergerii* from Rincón, Puntarenas, Osa Peninsula, Costa Rica. Photograph by A. Solórzano.

Plate 32. *Corallus ruschenbergerii* from Río Matiyure, Apure, Venezuela. Photograph ©W.F. Holmstrom.

Chapter 5

Food and Foraging

The snake reared, struck and caught the bat on the wing, constricting it at the same time. All this was done with such rapidity that it could not be followed by the eye.

Wehekind (1974) describing *Corallus ruschenbergerii*

As the motorboat putt-putted and belched out small clouds of smoke, Rich Sajdak, Joel Friesch, and I entered a labyrinth of mangroves in Trinidad's Caroni Swamp. Our headlamps provided the only illumination under the *Rhizophora* canopy on the moonless night that was hard upon us. The setting was almost perfect and, as we scanned the trees with our lights, the only thing that could make it better would be the red-orange eyeshine of *Corallus ruschenbergerii*, largest of the *C. hortulanus* complex treeboas. Twenty minutes into the hunt we saw a large brilliant eyeshine dangling from the mangrove canopy. Within seconds we were able to make out the body of a huge treeboa suspended over the water and 3.0–4.0 meters above it. It had assumed a sit-and-wait ambush posture that I had seen used by large treeboas many times. Considering its position relative to the water and trees, I believed it was hunting for bats that used the watery maze as a flyway while foraging. Now everything was perfect: a spectacular snake in an incredible setting. What more could anyone ask for?

* * *

As in other members of the family Boidae, snakes of the *Corallus hortulanus* complex prey exclusively on vertebrates (Greene 1983a; Henderson et al. 1987, 1995; Henderson 1993b; Rodríguez-Robles and Greene 1996; Murphy and Henderson 1997). Within the complex, however, there are interspecific differences in diet composition, with an especially dramatic dichotomy between the mainland and West Indian species. The mainland taxa take a high percentage of birds and mammals and very few lizards; in contrast, the West Indian species consume a large number of lizards and mammals and very few birds (Fig. 5.1). The lizard-bird dichotomy is even more pronounced when diets

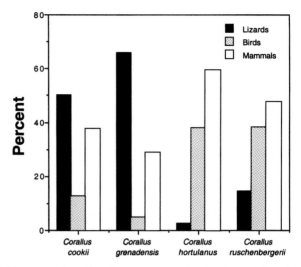

Figure 5.1. Representation of major prey groups in the diets of *Corallus hortulanus* complex treeboas.

are examined ontogenetically (Fig. 5.2). I have recovered only lizards, birds, and mammals from the stomachs of *C. hortulanus* complex treeboas. Beebe (1946), Cunha and Nascimento (1978), and Martins and Oliveira (1998) reported anurans in the stomachs of treeboas. Figure 5.3 presents a tree diagram based on a cluster analysis using diet composition, i.e., frequency of occurrence of four prey groups (lizards, birds, bats, rodents), largest prey taken, and maximum SVL. *Corallus hortulanus* and *C. ruschenbergerii* form one cluster, with *C. grenadensis* and *C. cookii* in separate clusters, with the latter species

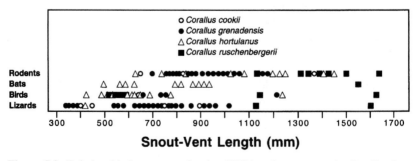

Figure 5.2. Relationship between snake size (SVL) and prey group in *Corallus hortulanus* complex treeboas.

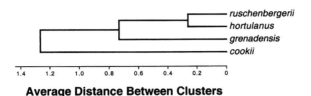

Figure 5.3. Tree diagram based on a cluster analysis. Variables utilized were frequency of occurrence of prey groups (lizards, birds, bats, rodents) in the diet, size (cm^3) of largest prey item recorded, and maximum SVL of the species of *Corallus*.

more removed from the other three (but this may be, in part, due to the limited amount of diet data).

Little is known about foraging behavior in members of the complex, although both active and sit-and-wait modes are employed (e.g., Henderson 1993b; Duellman and Mendelson 1995). Use of these two modes in the West Indies is largely coincident with the ontogenetic shift in diet from *Anolis* lizards to rodents (Henderson 1993b; Henderson et al. 1996). Active foraging appears to be restricted to the distal ends of branches. Prey location by boines is determined by several kinds of sensory information—mechanoreception, visual reception, chemoreception, and thermoreception—and these various sensory modes are hierarchal depending on ecological context (Cock Buning 1983). All species of *Corallus* have well-developed labial pits along the posterior margins of both jaws, with each sensory area lying between two adjacent scales (Maderson in Barrett 1970). According to Maderson (in Barrett 1970), in *Corallus* all of the specialized scales (supralabials and infralabials) "tend to lie in a groove, which gets deeper posteriorly." The labial pits are sensitive to radiant heat and to rapid changes that may be as subtle as 0.026°C (Bullock and Barrett 1968; Barrett 1970). It is significant that, according to Bullock and Barrett (1968), "boids would be able to detect prey (warmer or cooler than background) ..." Based on experiments by Noble and Schmidt (1937) using a member of the *Corallus hortulanus* complex (most likely *C. hortulanus*), blindfolded snakes (eight adults, ten neonates) could distinguish a moving warm object (warm electric light bulb vs. cold light bulb) from as far away as 48.5 cm. The treeboas would strike at the warm bulbs at distances of 16.0, 18.0, and 25.0 cm, but they had difficulty discriminating between the two bulbs at distances greater than 30.0 cm (the temperature difference between the two bulbs was 0.2°C or less). "Many blindfolded boas showed an obvious interest in the swinging bulb when over 40 cm. away but did not strike until it was brought 37, 34, or fewer centimeters from them." Experiments in which 1) the nostrils of the snakes were plugged, 2) the tongue was removed, or 3) "Covering the entire upper surfaces and sides of the snake's head with adhesive tape leaving only the pits on upper and lower labials exposed ..." did not affect a snake's ability to discriminate between the two bulbs. However, "filling the [labial] pits with a ten per cent solution of collodion stops the blindfolded snakes from striking at the swinging bulbs." Furthermore, "If the pits on one side of the head are closed with collodion and the bulbs swung at the usual distance of 16 to 25 cm. from that side of the head there is no response but the snake strikes at once when the warm bulb is swung over to the other side of the head." The young *C. hortulanus* struck more frequently at the warm bulb than did the adults, and two adult *C. caninus* responded to the warm, moving bulb "exactly" as did the *C. hortulanus*.

Based on observations of treeboas in captivity, the prehensile tail is invariably wrapped on a branch during prey capture (Willard, 1977; RWH pers. obs.). Prey is initially grasped in the snake's mouth. According to Deufel and Cundall (1999), at least two species of *Corallus* (*C. caninus* and *C. hortulanus*) exhibit a reduction of maxillary tooth tip angles (i.e., the tooth tips are bent back more sharply than in other booids). Treeboas (as well as other booids) snare prey with their maxillary teeth, and the "prey ultimately becomes wedged between the upper and lower jaws ..." The recurved shape of the teeth in concert "with the direction of travel of the upper jaw at prey contact cause the teeth to slide over the prey. Maxillary tooth penetration normally occurs as the prey recoils against the tooth tips" (Deufel and Cundall 1999). Coil application during constriction by species of *Corallus* is typical of that found in other species of boids: wound anterior, usually horizontal coils with an initial twist (Greene 1977; Greene and Burghardt 1978). Furthermore, the two species of *Corallus* studied by Greene (1977), *C. caninus* and a member of the *C. hortulanus* complex, exhibited a very high stereotypy value, indicating little variation in coil application pattern. The long anterior maxillary and mandibular teeth help treeboas maintain a secure grasp of prey objects during all phases of capture, killing, and deglutition.

CORALLUS COOKII

Diet

Based on only eight prey items (four *Anolis*, one bird, three mammals), it is difficult to get an accurate picture of diet composition (Table 5.1) or a possible ontogenetic shift in diet. Anoles (*Anolis griseus* and *A. trinitatis*) were taken by snakes 396–910 mm SVL, rodents were taken by snakes 655–1374 mm SVL, and the bird was recovered from a snake that was 655 mm SVL (Table 5.2). The anole taken by the 910-mm *C. cookii* was an *A. griseus* with a SVL of 110 mm; all other anoles were taken by snakes 396–752 mm SVL. It is likely that *C.*

Table 5.1. Prey recorded from members of the *Corallus hortulanus* complex. A plus sign (+) indicates that the prey has been recorded for that species of *Corallus*. See footnotes for explanations of (?).

Prey	C. cookii	C. grenadensis	C. hortulanus	C. ruschenbergerii
Fishes[1]			?	
Frogs				
Microhylidae				
Elachistocleis ovalis[2]			+?	+?
Hylidae unidentified			+	
Lizards				
Polychrotidae				
Anolis sp.			+	
Anolis aeneus		+		
Anolis griseus	+			
Anolis richardi		+		
Anolis trinitatis	+			
Corytophanidae				
Basiliscus basiliscus				+
Iguanidae				
Iguana iguana		+		

Table 5.1. (*Continued*)

Prey	*C. cookii*	*C. grenadensis*	*C. hortulanus*	*C. ruschenbergerii*
Birds				
Unidentified	+	+	+	+
Psittacidae unidentified			+	
Caprimulgidae unidentified			+	
Chordeiles rupestris			+	
Emberizidae				
Coereba flaveola		+		
Alcedinidae				
Ceryle torquata			+	
Chloroceryle inda			+	
Tyrannidae unidentified			+	
Elaenia			+	
Pipridae				
Manacus manacus			+	
Mammals				
Marmosidae				
Marmosa robinsoni				+

Table 5.1. (*Continued*)

Prey	C. cookii	C. grendensis	C. hortulanus	C. ruschenbergerii
Mammals (*cont.*)				
Phyllostomidae				
Artibeus jamaicensis			+	
Phyllostomus discolor			+	
Uroderma bilobatum				+
Vespertillionidae				
Myotis sp.			+	+
Herpestidae				
Herpestes javanicus				+
Sciuridae[3]				?
Echimyidae unidentified			+	
Muridae				
Akodon urichi	+			+
Mus musculus	+	+	+	+
Rattus rattus	+	+	+	+

[1]Based on Chippaux (1986), but I have not recovered fishes from stomachs, nor have I witnessed foraging behavior that suggests treeboas were foraging for fishes.

[2]Based on a record in Beebe (1946); it could apply to either C. hortulanus or C. ruschenbergerii.

[3]Based on Mole (1924), but I have not recovered any squirrels from digestive tracts.

Table 5.2. Sizes (SVL in mm) of treeboas that prey on various prey classes. Sample size is followed by mean ± SE and range.

Species	Lizards	Birds	Bats	Rodents
C. cookii	4 627.3 ± 122.5 396–910	1 655.0	0	3 954.3 ± 216.1 655–1374
C. grenadensis	40 637.7 ± 29.6 347–1025	3 878.3 ± 173.5 655–1220	0	19 914.4 ± 31.7 705–1170
C. hortulanus	1 398.0	14 669.9 ± 53.5 431–1240	8 739.1 ± 62.9 503–927	14 1029.0 ± 66.6 620–1410
C. ruschenbergerii	2 1371.0 ± 239.0 1132–1610	8 793.5 ± 141.8 520–1630	1 1560.0	8 1329.8 ± 85.5 852–1645

cookii undergoes an ontogenetic shift in diet similar to that exhibited by *C. grenadensis* (see Fig. 5.2). Prey size (n = 3) ranged from 1 cm^3 (*Anolis trinitatis*) to 31 cm^3 (the large *A. griseus* mentioned above); a rodent (*Mus musculus*) had a volume of 11 cm^3.

Prior to the introduction of *Mus* and *Rattus*, which arrived with Europeans, the primary endothermic prey for *Corallus cookii* was probably a recently extinct species of rice rat (*Oryzomys*) (Morgan and Woods 1986).

Foraging

Corallus cookii has been observed foraging at heights from ground level to more than 20 m. Based on a sample of only 21 observations, most foraging occurred at heights under 5 m. Although the number of observations available is much smaller than for *C. grenadensis*, most *C. cookii* were seen actively foraging on the distal ends of tree branches in a manner similar to that observed in *C. grenadensis*. This is the only member of the complex for which I have no documentation of them foraging over water, but it is likely that it exhibits the same strategy.

CORALLUS GRENADENSIS

Diet

Lizards (the polychrotids *Anolis aeneus* and *A. richardi*, and the iguanid *Iguana iguana*), small passerine birds (Bananaquit, *Coereba flaveola*), and introduced murid rodents (*Mus musculus* and *Rattus rattus*) are known to comprise the diet (see Table 5.1). Records are available for 78 prey items based on my research (62 records) and that of Pendlebury (1974; 16 records from Carriacou). Of those 78 prey items, 53 (67.9%) were lizards, 21 (27.0%) were mammals, and 4 (5.1%) were birds. Of the lizards, one was an *I. iguana* and the other 52 were anoles (98.1%).

Like *Corallus cookii* on St. Vincent, prior to the introduction of *Mus* and *Rattus* with Europeans, the principal endothermic prey of *C. grenadensis* was probably rice rats (Oryzomyini: Lippold 1991; Pregill et al. 1994). Osteological evidence of two species of rice rats has been recovered on Grenada, and they possibly co-occurred with, and were out-competed by, the alien *Mus* and *Rattus* (but see MacPhee et al. 1999).

Corallus grenadensis exhibits an ontogenetic shift in diet from *Anolis* lizards to rodents (see Fig. 5.2). Up to about 750 mm SVL, prey was almost exclusively anoles (94.1% by frequency); in the size range 750–950 mm SVL, snake predation had made a strong shift to rodents (75.0%); at over 1000 mm SVL, anoles were virtually absent from the diet of *C. grenadensis*. Birds were taken rarely and did not appear in the diet until a SVL of 650 mm was reached. Mean SVL of snakes that ate lizards was 637.7 ± 29.6 mm (range 347–1025 mm), and 914.4 ± 31.7 (range 705–1170 mm) for those that ate mammals.

The importance of lizards in the diets of *Corallus cookii* and *C. grenadensis* is typical of West Indian macrostomatan snakes in general (Henderson and Crother 1989; Rodríguez-Robles and Greene 1996; Table 5.3). The ontogenetic shift exhibited by these boids occurs in other West Indian boids as well (*Epicrates* spp.: Henderson et al. 1987; Rodríguez-Robles and Greene 1996).

Prey size (volume) ranged from 0.5 cm^3 to 55 cm^3 ($\bar{x}$ = 8.9 ± 2.4 cm^3). It was correlated (Pearson) with SVL (r = 0.57352, P = 0.0011, n = 30), midbody circumference (r = 0.71631, P = 0.0001, n = 29), and head width (r = 0.60957, P = 0.0004, n = 29). Mean mass ratio (prey mass/snake mass; MR) was 0.11 ± 0.02 (range = 0.01–0.30; n = 22). Although one would expect larger snakes to take larger prey items, one would not necessarily expect prey mass to increase relative to snake mass. Therefore it is not surprising that mass ratio was not correlated with SVL (r = −0.00506, P = 0.9822, n = 22), midbody circumference (r = 0.16263, P = 0.4696, n = 22), or head width (r = 0.04990, P = 0.8255, n = 22). Figure 5.4 presents a plot of the first and second principal components using SVL, midbody circumference, head width, and mass ratio. The morphological variables showed high loadings on the first principal com-

Table 5.3. Major islands of the Lesser Antilles and their macrostomatan snake faunas. The islands are listed approximately north to south.

Island (area in km²)	Maximum SVL¹ (in mm)	Adaptive Zone	Primary Prey Group
Anguilla (91)			
Alsophis rijgersmaei	790	ground	lizards
St. Martin (91)			
Alsophis rijgersmaei	790	ground	lizards
St. Barthélémy (22)			
Alsophis rijgersmaei	790	ground	lizards
Saba (13)			
Alsophis rufiventris	920	ground	frogs, lizards
St. Eustatius (20)			
Alsophis rufiventris	920	ground	frogs, lizards
St. Christopher (176)			
Alsophis rufiventris	920	ground	frogs, lizards
Nevis (93)			
Alsophis rufiventris	920	ground	frogs, lizards
Barbuda (162)			
Alsophis antiguae*	660	ground	lizards
Antigua (282)			
Boa sp.*	?	ground?	?
Alsophis antiguae	660	ground	lizards
Montserrat (101)			
Alsophis antillensis	930	ground	frog, lizards
Guadeloupe (1510)			
Alsophis antillensis	930	ground	frogs, lizards
Liophis juliae	458	ground	frogs, lizards
Dominica (790)			
Boa constrictor	3000	ground	mammals
Alsophis antillensis	930	ground	frogs, lizards
Liophis juliae	458	ground	frogs, lizards

Table 5.3. (*Continued*)

Island (area in km²)	Maximum SVL[1] (in mm)	Adaptive Zone	Primary Prey Group
Martinique (1106)			
Liophis cursor	671	ground	frogs, lizards
Bothrops lanceolata	1580	ground	mammals
St. Lucia (604)			
Boa constrictor	3000	ground	mammals
Clelia errabunda	1380[2]	ground	snakes, mammals
Liophis ornatus	1235	ground	frogs?, lizards?
Bothrops caribbaea	1300	ground	mammals
Barbados (430)			
Liophis perfuscus	797	ground	frogs?, lizards?
St. Vincent (345)			
Corallus cookii	1374	trees	lizards, mammals
Chironius vincenti	1260	ground, trees	frogs
Mastigodryas bruesi	830	ground, trees	frogs, lizards
Grenada (311)			
Corallus grenadensis	1625	trees	lizards, mammals
Clelia clelia	2000	ground	snakes?, mammals
Mastigodryas bruesi	830	ground, trees	frogs, lizards

*known only from fossil record.
[1]From Schwartz and Henderson 1991.
[2]From Underwood 1993.

ponent, and mass ratio had a high loading on the second. Whether the prey was an anole or a rodent had little impact on mass ratio. Figures 5.5 and 5.6 plot the relationships between snake SVL and prey volume and SVL and MR, respectively, for all four members of the complex.

It is interesting that I have not recovered any gekkonids from the stomachs of *Corallus grenadensis*, or from any member of the *C. hortulanus* complex for that matter (although I have taken a gecko, probably *Thecadactylus rapicauda*, from the stomach of a small *C. caninus*). *Hemidactylus mabouia* and *T.*

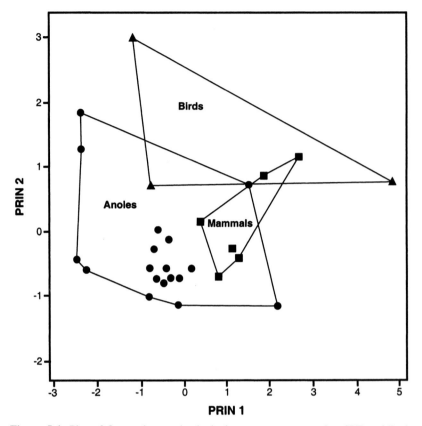

Figure 5.4. Plot of first and second principal component axes using SVL, midbody circumference, head width, and mass ratio (prey mass/snake mass) for *Corallus grenadensis*.

rapicauda are not uncommon on Grenada, and are often observed in areas where treeboas are encountered. Perhaps nocturnally active gekkonids (in contrast to nocturnally quiescent *Anolis*) are too alert for active foraging treeboas to capture, or perhaps the foraging strategies of *C. cookii* and *C. grenadensis* are adapted for the lizard prey that is most often encountered, i.e., anoles.

Foraging

More is known about foraging and diet in this member of the complex than any other, but there is still much to learn, especially about how nocturnally

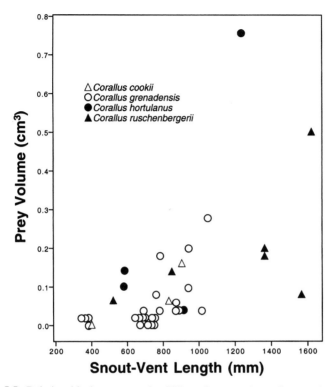

Figure 5.5. Relationship between snake SVL and prey volume for members of the *Corallus hortulanus* complex.

quiescent anoles are located. In a sample of 443 observations made at four localities, 72.6% of the treeboas were foraging at heights <5.0 m, and 40.8% were at heights between 2.0 and 3.9 m (Fig. 5.7). Only 7.2% of the observations were of snakes foraging <1.0 m, 12.2% were observed at heights over 6.9 m, and only 0.7% were at heights >20.0 m. Foraging heights differed between localities (see Fig. 5.7). For example, at Westerhall Estate, most foraging occurred at heights between 3.0 m and 6.9 m, while at Mt. Hartman Bay foraging was concentrated between 1.0 m and 3.9 m. In a sample of 23 observations made on four of the Grenadine islands (Mustique, Canouan, Union, Carriacou), 20 *C. grenadensis* were seen foraging at heights of 1.0–2.9 m. It is noteworthy that the vegetation on the Grenadines more closely resembles that at Mt. Hartman Bay than that at Westerhall Estate, thereby offering a possible explanation of the low foraging heights.

Although large (>1.0 m) *Corallus grenadensis* may occur anywhere in

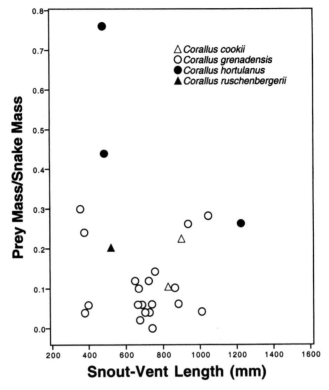

Figure 5.6. Relationship between prey mass/snake mass and snake SVL in members of the *Corallus hortulanus* complex of treeboas.

the vertical structure at a given site, they frequently occur close to ground level, employing an ambush foraging mode to capture nocturnally active rodents. Henderson (1993b), in a sample of 33 observations lumping both West Indian taxa (then both under the umbrella of *C. enydris*), found that the mean SVL of treeboas foraging <1.0 m was 940 ± 95 mm, while that of treeboas foraging between 1.0 and 2.9 m was 662 ± 51 mm (P < 0.01, t-test). At the Mt. Hartman site, mean SVL for treeboas foraging <1.0 m was 815.7 mm (range = 375–1332 mm SVL), 603.7 mm at 1.0–1.9 m (range = 389–1150 mm), 582.0 mm at 2.0–2.9 m (350–1150 mm SVL), and 680.0 mm at 3.0–3.9 m (range = 400–1130 mm SVL)

Active foraging occurs on the distal portions of branches on the periphery of trees and bushes. *Corallus grenadensis* will often investigate most thoroughly those branches and leaf surfaces below the branch on which they are supported, presumably because they are less likely to disturb a sleeping anole if

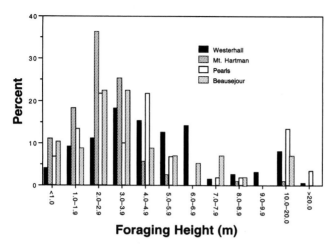

Figure 5.7. Foraging heights of *Corallus grenadensis* at four localities on Grenada.

they are not actually on the same branch. The snakes move slowly and almost constantly with frequent tongue-flicking on the surfaces of leaves and branches. Snakes have been observed to stop and press their snout against a branch surface. It seems likely that active foraging *C. grenadensis* are attempting to locate the scent trail of an anole that has gone to roost on the distal end of a branch (sleeping either on a leaf surface or on the branch itself). I assume that if a scent trail is detected, it is followed until either the anole is encountered or until the trail is lost. This strategy probably leads to many unsuccessful trials, as the scent trail of an anole that was merely moving across a branch or leaf hours before going to roost may lead the snake on the proverbial "wild goose (or lizard) chase." It is possible, of course, that foraging treeboas are able to discriminate the chemical intensity of a trail, thereby discounting many scent trails that were made long before anoles would be seeking roosting sites. Nevertheless, unless a "good" trail is encountered only after several days of searching, it seems likely that most trail-following (if, indeed, that is what the anole hunters do) does not terminate with a feeding episode. Short-term observations suggest that the snakes are thorough in their searches for the scent trails, tongue-flicking many branch and leaf surfaces, and covering an area of 1–2 m^2 in 1–2 hours. It has been suggested that brown tree snakes (*Boiga irregularis*) may choose sites for ambushing geckos or other prey items based on odor trails left by the lizards (Rodda 1992). Based on captive observations, Chiszar et al. (1988) found evidence of chemical trail-following behavior in *B. irregularis*, suggesting that "non-volatile chemicals are most important in guiding choice behavior."

There is another possible consideration for locating lizard prey, and that is thermoreception. Most foraging activity occurs early in the night (i.e., before midnight; Henderson and Winstel [1997]; Chapter 4), and Bullock and Barrett (1968) have demonstrated that prey must merely have a temperature different from its background (substrate) in order for it to be detected by the thermoreceptors in the labial scales of boid snakes. By foraging early in the night, before lizard and substrate temperatures have had time to equalize, treeboas may increase their chances of finding anoles. The only predation I have witnessed, however, occurred at about 0200 h, and the prey was an anole.

Although I do not have extensive data on movements, and virtually none for durations of more than 17 days, what data I do have may provide insight into foraging strategies. On 43 occasions at Westerhall Estate, paint-marked snakes were observed after their initial capture and marking. Snakes were studied along a transect marked in 10-m increments, and when snakes were reobserved it was merely noted if they were in the same 10-m section or another. So a snake reobserved in the same section could have moved nearly 10 m and still have been recorded in the same section; a snake that was reobserved in a section adjacent to the one where it was originally captured could have moved nearly 20 m or less than 1.0 m. Based on snakes that were reobserved at least twice, those observed within 24 hours of their original capture had moved a mean of 1.0 section (range = 0.0–4.0; n = 25). Snakes reobserved after 2 days had moved a mean of 0.5 section (0.0–2.0; n = 12), and those reobserved after 3 or 4 days had moved a mean of 0.83 section (0.0–2.0; n = 6). At Mt. Hartman, snakes reobserved from 1–6 days after original release were observed to have moved a mean distance of 0.43 section (0.0–8.0; n = 10). In addition, at Westerhall, 13 of 35 snakes were observed at least once after capture, marking, and release. These data—slow thorough searching on leaves and branches, high incidence of snakes reobserved, and snakes reobserved within close proximity of previous observations over periods of several days—suggest that *Corallus grenadensis* may forage in a fairly localized area for several days. Since snakes "disappeared" after several days, it seems likely that they may have moved to a different foraging area. This strategy parallels that observed in *Boa constrictor*. Montgomery and Rand (1978) followed a radio-marked *B. constrictor* and found that it moved from burrow to burrow every 3–4 days, apparently waiting in anticipation for the return of the burrows' residents. Although the treeboas were active foragers, they, like *B. constrictor*, appear to stay in an area for only a few days before trying a new foraging area.

Miscellaneous Observations

1) On Carriacou, 17 Oct 1989, a treeboa repeatedly stuck its head into an apparently empty bird's nest on a tree branch at about 7.0 m above ground level. I disturbed the snake, moving it away from the nest, but 15–20 min later it had

returned to the nest; 2) On 26 April 1993 between 2000 h and 2100 h, at Westerhall Estate, a 742-mm treeboa lingered near a Bananaquit (*Coereba flaveola*) nest for more than 15 min while an adult bird was in the nest; 47 min later, the snake was very close to the nest opening and the bird was still present; 5 min later, the bird was gone and the snake was ascending into the vegetation without having consumed the bird; 3) At Mt. Pleasant Estate (St. Andrew Parish; 290 m asl), on 19 Oct 1989, a 978-mm snake hung by its tail from the stalk of a banana plant; the forepart of its body was in a typical prestrike posture. Several bats of undetermined species were observed flying up to the pendulous stalks of banana trees during the night; 4) At Westerhall Estate, on 18 April 1993, a *C. grenadensis* at 4.0 m on the distal end of tree limb, struck (unsuccessfully) at a bat that fluttered close to the tree presumably to investigate fruit on the tree; 5) At 0100 h on 14 October (my birthday) 1991, a small (<500 mm SVL) treeboa was sprawled at 2.2 m in a bush along the Beausejour River at Beausejour Estate; at 0200 h, still in the same bush, it was constricting a still-moving *Anolis aeneus*. It started swallowing the anole headfirst at 0209 h, while hanging with head downward. It completed ingestion at 0217 h. The next night (still 14 Oct), the snake was in the same bush. On 15 Oct at 1300 h, the snake was still in the same bush, coiled at the top and sandwiched between leafy foliage. On 16 Oct, at 1912 h, it was in precisely the same spot as when it captured the anole. It tongue-flicked leaves very thoroughly, almost as if licking the surfaces, with its snout in contact, or nearly in contact, with the leaf surfaces; 6) At 2045 h at Beausejour Estate, a 1057-mm SVL female was first observed perched in a small bush 0.5 m above ground with her head positioned downward in a typical ambush posture. She was still in that position at 2245 h, but at approximately 2330 h (estimated) she captured and ingested a *Rattus*; at 2350 h the snake was observed crawling into a small thorny palm; 7) A radio-marked treeboa at Beausejour Estate that was originally captured at 2245 h shortly after it had consumed a mammal (presumably *Rattus*) was not seen for 6 days after it was released. When seen again, there was no visible sign of the large meal it had consumed 6 days before, and we then observed the snake all night. Activity started at about 1810 h and was intermittent throughout the night; movement through the vegetation stopped at 2355 h; time was then spent in a loose coil, which continued until 0525 h when the snake started moving up into the leafy cover of a tree. Thus some activity occurred over a period of 11.25 hours, but movement (foraging) lasted for only 5.75 hours. I suspect that this amount of time is close to the maximum duration of any kind of activity in which *C. grenadensis* will engage on any night.

At Mt. Hartman Bay in an acacia-mangrove interface, *C. grenadensis* was observed foraging in acacia trees that were virtually devoid of foliage. *Anolis aeneus* slept on and between spines up to 5.5 cm long, and *C. grenadensis* foraged among the spines (see photo in Henderson 1996). Also at Mt. Hartman, in the mangroves at the periphery of Mt. Hartman Bay, it was not unusual to encounter treeboas foraging on branches over water.

Feeding Frequency

One of the most intriguing statistics gleaned from field work with *Corallus grenadensis* is the virtual absence of observations of acts of predation by the snakes. I have observed several hundred treeboas on 700–800 occasions; I have witnessed feeding once. I interpret this to mean that *C. grenadensis*, including snakes in those size-classes that feed exclusively or predominantly on anoles, feeds infrequently. But how infrequently? Secor (1995) calculated a prey capture rate (= number of field observations of predation/snake observation days) of 3.0% for active foraging *Masticophis flagellum*, and a rate of 1.5%, for sit-and-wait *Crotalus cerastes*. My single observation of predation by *Corallus grenadensis* over 170 nights gives a value of 0.6%, one much lower than that for the sit-and-wait forager *Crotalus cerastes*. Even if I included another observation in which I encountered the treeboa minutes after it had fed (observation 6, above), the value would have been only 1.2%.

I recovered 62 prey items from the examination of 194 snakes, but only a small percentage of those prey items was captured and ingested on the day that the snake was captured and preserved. Although I do not have a record of the state of digestion at which I recovered each prey item, I estimate that not more than 25% of the prey items were eaten on the day the snake was captured and preserved (and that is, if anything, a high estimate). Because *Corallus grenadensis* actively forages for anoles when young and then shifts to a diet of primarily rodents (probably captured, for the most part, by sit-and-wait foraging), I divided the 194 snakes into three size-classes (Table 5.4). Snakes in the smallest size-class fed predominantly on anoles (94.1% by frequency), had the highest percentage with food in their stomachs, had the shortest elapsed time between feeding episodes (8.9 days), and had the most feeding episodes on an annual basis (41). Snakes in the two larger size-classes preyed more often on endotherms (75.0–80.0%), and fed less frequently (15–25 feeding episodes/ year) than those in the smallest size-class. Greene (1997) felt "Generally snakes must ingest about six to thirty meals per year ..." Shine and Madsen (1997) found that juvenile water pythons (*Liasis fuscus*) in tropical Australia fed more frequently than did adults, even at equivalent prey densities.

In an attempt to get an index of treeboa to anole numbers, I used data collected on 3 nights at Mt. Hartman Bay. On the 3 nights I recorded 38, 49, and 57 anoles ($\bar{x}$ = 48.0 ± 5.5). Extrapolated to anoles/ha, the mean of the three samples was 87.3 ± 10.0/ha; range 69.1–103.6. Compared to published densities of 1760–3310/ha (Roughgarden et al. 1983), my numbers were very low. On the nights I recorded the anole numbers, I recorded, 3, 2, and 0 treeboas along

Table 5.4. Feeding rates in *Corallus grenadensis*. I estimated that only 25% of the recovered prey items were the result of an act of predation on the day the snake was collected. Therefore, for the size-class <750 mm SVL, only 25% of the 34 snakes with food in their stomachs, or 8.5, are used in subsequent calculations. The number of days between predation episodes was calculated by dividing the number of snakes in the size-class by the number of snakes that had just eaten (e.g., 76/8.5). The number of predation acts/year was determined by dividing 365 days by the number of days between feeding episodes (e.g., 365/8.9).

	Size-Class (SVL in mm)		
	<750	**750–950**	**>950**
No. in size-class	76	59	59
Percent with food in stomach	44.7	27.1	16.9
No. of snakes with lizards/No. of snakes with endotherms (percentages)	32/2 94.1/5.9	4/12 25/75	2/8 20/80
Number with food in stomach	34	16	10
No. of days between predation episodes	8.9	14.8	23.6
No. of predation episodes/year	41.0	24.7	15.5

the same transect (which extrapolates to 0.0–5.5/ha; $\bar{x} = 3.0 \pm 1.6$). Furthermore, during the month of field work (Oct 1996) at Mt. Hartman Bay when these counts were made, I recorded the lowest overall density of treeboas (ca. 4.0/ha) I have recorded at any of four localities. Still, based on the means, there were 29.1 anoles for every treeboa.

For still another index of treeboa-anole numbers, I used published numbers of anole densities compared to an average treeboa density. Roughgarden et al. (1983) recorded densities for *Anolis aeneus* and *A. richardi* at three sites on Grenada, and densities ranged from 1760–3310/ha (juveniles and adults, both species combined); $\bar{x} = 2650.0 \pm 461.9$ anoles/ha. I recorded treeboa densities (see Chapter 8) at four localities (none the same as Roughgarden et al.), and determined a mean of 29.3 ± 7.7 snakes/ha. Using the means for anoles and that for treeboas (and acknowledging the many flaws in this index), there were 91.1 anoles for every treeboa.

In short, it is difficult to imagine *Corallus grenadensis* as food-limited. Of course, not all size-classes of treeboas on Grenada eat anoles, but I doubt that *Rattus* is in short supply. I suspect the value calculated with Secor's formula is quite low, and that my numbers based on the incidence of undigested prey items in preserved snakes are more realistic, albeit rough estimates.

Body Temperature and Foraging

Body temperatures (T_b) and adjacent ambient (air, usually within 1 m of snake) temperatures (T_a) were recorded for *Corallus grenadensis* at six localities on Grenada: Mt. Hartman Estate (sea level), Pearls Estate (30 m), Westerhall Estate (65 m), Balthazar Estate (75 m), Spring Gardens Estate (455 m), and Grand Etang National Park (525 m). Three altitudinal categories were arbitrarily determined (sample sizes in parentheses): low = below 50 m (44), moderate = 50–400 m (12), and high = above 400 m (7).

Data were recorded between 1900 h and 2400 h in April 1988, 1989, and 1994, and October 1990 (high elevations only). All of the snakes were foraging (i.e., crawling slowly through vegetation above ground level: Henderson 1993b). Temperatures were taken cloacally with a quick-reading mercury thermometer (Miller & Weber, Queens, NY). Usually, foraging snakes were grasped by the tail and allowed to stay on the vegetation in which they had been foraging while the T_b was taken. Snakes that were higher in the vegetation were induced to crawl onto long sticks and then brought down closer to ground level; T_b was then recorded while the snake was still on the long stick. Data were analyzed using SAS (Pearson Correlation Coefficient, one-way ANOVA, Duncan's Multiple Range Test [DMRT], and chi-square). Sixty-three body temperatures were recorded. Mean T_b was 25.6 ± 1.66 (20.8–28.6); mean T_a was 24.9 ± 1.49 (20.0–27.1). Temperature data for the three altitudinal categories are summarized in Table 5.5. Figure 5.8 illustrates the relationship between T_b and T_a in each of the three altitudinal categories. Body temperature and T_a were correlated (Pearson Correlation Coefficient, r = 0.805, $P < 0.0001$, n = 63), but the number of snakes with T_b above T_a is significant ($\chi^2 = 8.09$, 1 df, $P < 0.01$). Analysis of variance indicated significant differences among the three altitudinal categories ($P < 0.0001$, F = 106.61), and the DMRT indicated significant differences between each altitudinal category ($P < 0.05$, df = 59). *Corallus grenadensis* in populations occurring at higher elevations forage with significantly lower T_bs than do those in populations at lower elevations.

Many potential factors are involved in body temperature variation (Peterson et al. 1993), and the data currently available for *Corallus grenadensis* allow only speculation as to which factors it is responding to (e.g., temperature, radiation) and how (dorsal ground color). We know that, regardless of altitude, *C. grenadensis* preys primarily on nocturnally quiescent lizards (*Anolis*) and

Table 5.5. Summary of temperature data (°C) for *Corallus grenadensis* at three altitudinal ranges on Grenada. T_b = body temperature and T_a = ambient (air) temperature.

	Low (<50 m)	Moderate (50–400 m)	High (>400 m)
T_b ± S.E.	26.7 ± 0.10	24.1 ± 0.29	22.8 ± 0.46
T_b Range	25.4–28.6	22.8–25.8	20.4–24.3
T_a ± S.E.	25.6 ± 0.15	23.9 ±0.22	22.3 ± 0.47
T_a Range	23.2–27.1	22.4–24.7	20.0–23.5
$(T_b - T_a)$	1.14	0.20	0.43

active rodents (*Mus* and *Rattus*), although sleeping birds and, probably, active bats are also eaten. We have evidence that *C. grenadensis* attains a larger size at moderate elevations (50–100 m) in areas of mixed agriculture.

Although *C. grenadensis* is distributed from sea level to at least 520 m on Grenada, it is rare at the highest elevations (based on the number of snakes

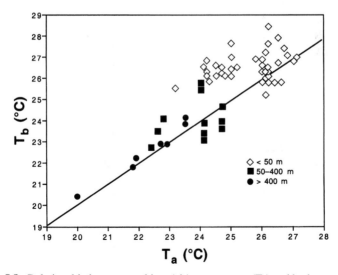

Figure 5.8. Relationship between ambient (air) temperature (T_a) and body temperature (T_b) in foraging *Corallus grenadensis* at three elevational ranges.

encountered/man-hour at elevations over 400 m; Chapter 8), suggesting that the higher elevations are suboptimal and probably close to the altitudinal limit for the species on Grenada. Fieldwork on Grenada, which is close to the northern limit of the range for members of the complex, has demonstrated that *C. grenadensis* is most common at elevations below 100 m, and in disturbed habitats (e.g., mixed agriculture; Chapter 3). Increasing altitude is correlated with decreasing ambient temperature and increasing precipitation and cloud cover. Correspondingly, on Grenada the incidence of the predominant dorsal ground color in *C. grenadensis* also changes (Chapter 2; see also Henderson 1990b, 1996): there is a high incidence of "yellow" (= tan, khaki, yellow-brown, brownish yellow, pale orange: Henderson 1993a: Fig. 3) snakes at low elevations; with increasing elevation, the incidence of yellow snakes decreases, and I am unaware of yellow specimens from localities over 300 m. Conversely, dark brown snakes (Henderson 1990b: Fig. 2; Henderson 1993a: Fig. 2—Note: the captions for Figures 2 and 3 in Henderson 1993a are reversed) predominate at elevations over 400 m, but they are virtually absent from lower elevations. At moderate elevations, the predominant dorsal ground color is taupe (gray-brown).

Corallus grenadensis may have made an evolutionary response to the suboptimum conditions of high altitude habitats on Grenada. Presumably, a dark dorsal ground color would confer some thermoregulatory advantage (e.g., less reflective, faster heating rate: Forsman 1993; Peterson et al. 1993) to a snake living in an area of depressed ambient temperature and amount of possible insolation, coupled with increased rainfall and cloud cover, and dense, lush vegetation. Conversely, a pale (e.g., yellow) dorsal ground color may similarly confer some advantage (high reflectivity) to *C. grenadensis* inhabiting areas where ambient temperature is high, the incidence of cloud cover is low, and the vegetation is often sparse and open; at Mt. Hartman, snakes were often found foraging on branches devoid of foliage, but armed with spines up to 5.5 cm in length.

Since *Corallus grenadensis* is a nocturnal forager, a correlation between T_a and T_b should not be surprising; once the sun has set, there may be little opportunity for behavioral modification of T_b by a snake that is an active forager; thus, it is forced to thermoconformity. However, T_b in *C. grenadensis* was consistently higher than T_a, indicating that the snakes may have retained heat from the day and T_b had not yet equilibrated with falling ambient temperatures. Alternatively, the snakes may have been thermoregulating behaviorally on heat-retaining substrates (branches, foliage), and T_bs may have more closely matched substrate temperatures (which were not recorded) than air temperatures. Preliminary evidence indicates that during the day *C. grenadensis* does actively thermoregulate, at least during a portion of daylight hours (Henderson and Winstel 1992): maximum daytime temperature recorded for *C. grenadensis* is 34.4°C for a snake digesting a meal on the distal end of a branch overhanging a river, at a site at 55 m asl (adjacent air was 28.6°C). We have no daytime body temperatures for *C. grenadensis* at altitudes above 55 m. Although the known activity range of body temperatures for *C. grenadensis* on Grenada is approximately 20–35°C (the approximate range of many temperate and tropical species: Lillywhite 1987; Peterson et al. 1993), the snakes are active (i.e., foraging) in a much narrower range of T_bs (20.4–28.6°C) regardless of altitude. The range of T_bs at a given altitude and climatic regime are even narrower, and the standard errors for each mean are small (see Table 5.5). Determining preferred T_b range for a nocturnal snake is complicated, as the snake is more dependent on ambient temperature while it is active. Is preferred T_b achieved during the day when the snake is sedentary, or is it reached at night during the height of activity, i.e., akin to the nocturnality hypothesis (e.g., Autumn et al. 1997)? Most likely there is a preferred daytime temperature for prey assimilation and maximal growth (e.g., Autumn and De Nardo 1995), and *C. grenadensis* exhibits behavioral thermoregulation (Henderson and Winstel 1992; see also Huey et al. 1989) to achieve it. At night duration of foraging activity by *C. grenadensis* may become dependent on the thermal environment. We have observed that foraging often ceases near midnight regardless of whether or not a snake was successful in securing prey, and this may be a response to decreasing ambient temperatures (Chapter 4).

Drinking

It is assumed that treeboas obtain most of their drinking water from rain that accumulates in depressions in trees, and also water that beads up on the surfaces of leaves. In addition, in captivity several species of arboreal snakes have been observed to drink droplets of water from their bodies (RWH, pers. obs.; Chiras, 1998). It is likely that this occurs under natural situations, also. *Corallus grenadensis* was observed drinking water in the field only once. At the Mt. Hartman study site toward the end of the dry season (late April), about 10 min after a light rain started, a 630 mm SVL female drank water that collected in irregularities in the bark surface of an unidentified species of tree.

CORALLUS HORTULANUS

Diet

I have recovered only a lizard, birds, and mammals (bats and rodents) from the stomachs of *Corallus hortulanus*. Chippaux (1986: Table 6) lists fishes as occasional prey of *C. hortulanus* in French Guiana. Cunha and Nascimento (1978) reported anurans in the stomach of at least 1 *Corallus hortulanus* from the lower Amazon, Martins and Oliveira (1998) found the remains of a frog in a treeboa from Central Amazonia, and Chippaux (1986) lists frogs as important prey for *C. hortulanus* in French Guiana. The 37 prey items I personally recovered included 1 lizard (2.7%), 14 birds (37.8%), and 22 mammals (59.5%). The lizard was recovered from a treeboa that was 398 mm SVL; it is probably an anole, but a positive identification was impossible due to advanced digestion. Several of the birds were flycatchers (Tyrannidae), and Martins and Oliveira (1998) reported a passerine and an alcedinid (*Chloroceryle inda*), Astor et al. (1998) recovered a piprid, and W.W. Lamar (in litt., April 2000) has taken an alcedinid (*Ceryle torquata*) and a caprimulgid (*Chordeiles rupestris*) from Peruvian *C. hortulanus*. Of the mammals, at least eight were bats—Dixon and Soini (1986) found a *Myotis albescens*, and W.W. Lamar (in litt., April 2000) recovered an *Artibeus jamaicensis* from a Peruvian specimen taken from the roof of a house—and the rest were rodents (murids and echimyids). Like other members of the complex, *C. hortulanus* undergoes an ontogenetic shift in diet. Unlike the West Indian species, where the shift was from lizards to rodents, in *C. hortulanus* the shift was from birds (and to a lesser degree bats), to rodents. Up to about 750 mm SVL, birds and bats constitute most of the diet, although rodents are sometimes taken by small treeboas. Fully fledged birds were recovered from treeboas 431–1240 mm SVL ($\bar{x}$ = 669.8 = 53.5), and bats from snakes 503–927 mm SVL ($\bar{x}$ = 739.1 ± 62.9). At about 750 mm SVL, avian prey became less important and mammals were the dietary mainstay (see Fig. 5.2). Rodents were recovered from snakes 620–1410 mm SVL ($\bar{x}$ = 1029.0 ± 66.6). Prey volumes ranged from 6.5–150 cm^3 (n = 4). I was able to calculate only two prey mass/snake mass ratios (MR), both for birds: 0.24 and 0.44. Astor et al. (1998) recovered a 17-g white-bearded manakin (Passeriformes: Pipridae: *Manacus manacus*) from a small (22.5 g, 498 mm SVL) *C. hortulanus* at a site ca. 130 km northeast of Rio de Janiero; the MR was 0.76. Martins and Oliveira (1998) calculated MR for two *C. hortulanus* from Rio Jau in Central Amazonia: one (1495 mm SVL, 365 g) consumed a 7-g bat and MR was 0.02; another (855 mm SVL, 125 g) ingested an 21-g echimyid rodent and MR was 0.17.

Six of the eight bat records (75.0%) came from treeboas collected in Bolivia, and six of nine prey records (66.7%) for Bolivia were chiropterans. No other geographic (or political) area exhibited such a disproportionate frequency of prey exploitation, and I assume that it is merely an artifact of collecting.

Miller (1983) observed a captive female *Corallus hortulanus* ingest her own freshly deposited egg masses. She grasped, constricted, and swallowed each of seven masses in a normal feeding sequence. Six additional masses were removed from the enclosure and determined to be infertile; it is assumed that those ingested were also infertile. Similarly, Jes (1984) observed a member of the *C. hortulanus* complex consume four of seven undeveloped eggs. Starace (1998) observed cannibalism under captive conditions. In the Georgetown (Guyana) Zoo, a newborn anaconda (*Eunectes murinus*) was swallowed by a *Corallus hortulanus* (Roth 1960).

Foraging

I have observed only one *Corallus hortulanus* foraging (at Yanamono, Loreto, Peru). Like other species of the complex, it was actively foraging on the distal end of a branch at about 2.5 m. William W. Lamar (pers. comm.) has observed many *C. hortulanus* in the Upper Amazon (especially Peru), and describes the species as an active forager, as does Starace (1998). Duellman and Mendelson (1995) described two large adults (1510 mm SVL and 1280 mm SVL) as "in hunting postures on vines 0.4–0.5 m above the ground at night," and Duellman (pers. comm.) felt that large adults waited in ambush close to ground level along mammal trails. Martins and Oliveira (1998) reported *C. hortulanus* "hanging on the vegetation facing the ground, apparently in a sit-and-wait posture" ... and "one individual from a primary forest at Ilha de Maracá, Roraima, was also hanging on the vegetation, probably foraging for bats that used the trail as a flying corridor." Those observations are consistent with mine for large *C. grenadensis*.

Hopkins and Hopkins (1982) described the capture of a bat (probably *Phyllostomus discolor*) by a *Corallus hortulanus* at a site about 60 km north of Manaus, Brazil. Bats were observed visiting the capitula of the tree *Parkia nitida* (Leguminosae: Mimosoideae), and at 2115 h the boa was observed at the base of a flower-bearing branch and moving toward the group of capitula. "During the next ten minutes [the snake] made several unsuccessful attempts to catch bats visiting and flying past one capitulum. It then moved to a different capitulum and successfully caught a bat at its first attempt." Similarly, I have observed a *C. grenadensis* unsuccessfully strike at a bat coming into a fruiting tree on Grenada.

Several species of neotropical boids have been observed foraging for bats in three different contexts. The first context is via active foraging. On St. Lucia, Arendt and Anthony (1986) observed a *Boa constrictor* with a total length of 1100 mm (396.9 g) capture a roosting bat (*Brachyphylla cavernarum*, 67.0 g) from a tree hollow at 7.2 m above ground level in the late afternoon (1640 h). In addition, the authors found bat remains in feces passed by the *B. constrictor* taken at the bat roost, suggesting that the snake was a regular visitor to the roost site. Although Arendt and Anthony (1986) interpreted this behavior as ambush foraging, I regard it as active foraging. The second context is that described for *C. hortulanus* and *C. grenadensis* (i.e., capturing bats that are attracted to flowers or fruit on a tree). The third context is in caves which harbor bats, and the boas wait in ambush for the bats at the mouth of the cave as they exit at dusk, or at a constricted opening within the cave through which the bats must fly in order to get to the mouth. This has been described in three species of *Epicrates* in the West Indies, *E. cenchria* on the South American mainland, and in *Boa constrictor* in Mexico, Central America, and South America (Table 5.6).

Table 5.6. The context of bat predation by neotropical boines.

Species	Where	Predation Context	Source
Boa constrictor	Mexico	Cave	Villa and Lopez 1966
	Costa Rica	Cave	W.W. Lamar, in litt., April 2000
	Colombia	Cave mouth	W.W. Lamar, in litt., April 2000
	Isla Providencia	Cave	Thomas 1974
	St. Lucia, W.I.	Tree hollow	Arendt and Anthony 1986
Corallus grenadensis	Grenada, W.I.	Bats attracted to fruit or flowers in a tree	RWH, pers. obs.
Corallus hortulanus	Brazil	Bats attracted to flowering tree	Hopkins and Hopkins 1982
Corallus ruschenbergerii	Panama	Ambushed from tree?	Smith and Grant 1958
	Colombia	Ambushed from tree?	W.W. Lamar, in litt., April 2000
Epicrates angulifer	Cuba, W.I.	Cave mouth and interior	Miller 1904; Hardy 1957; Silva-Taboada 1979
Epicrates cenchria	Colombia	Cave	Lemke 1978
	Peru	Ambushed in tree?	W.W. Lamar, in litt., April 2000
Epicrates inornatus	Puerto Rico	Cave mouth	Rodríguez and Reagan 1984; Rodríguez-Duran 1996
Epicrates subflavus	Jamaica	Cave mouth	Prior and Gibson 1997

Because of the patchy distribution of this trophic resource (bats in caves), it is unlikely that many individuals of each species are able to exploit it. Nevertheless, the observations by Hardy (1957), Rodríguez-Duran (1996) and Prior and Gibson (1997) indicate that individuals may remain in the vicinity of the caves for prolonged periods. Although bat-catching may seem energetically suspect (i.e., >200 unsuccessful capture attempts by a single *E. subflavus* in one night: Prior and Gibson 1997), the caves do provide a potentially abundant and reliable source of food. I suspect, however, that bat predation in the context of that described for *Corallus hortulanus* is much more prevalent and geographically widespread.

Drinking

W.W. Lamar (in litt., April 2000), observed "an adult *C. hortulanus* in deep rainforest in Vaupés, Colombia, as it gracefully drank water from a palm sheaf on the forest floor. The snake was hanging in a sinuous shape by its tail, delicately drinking the accumulated rainwater."

CORALLUS RUSCHENBERGERII

Diet

As in other members of the complex, the diet comprised lizards, birds, and mammals (see Table 5.1 and Fig. 5.2). The mammals included one opossum, one bat, one mongoose, and the rest murid rodents. The diet of *Corallus ruschenbergerii* appears to parallel its mainland congener *C. hortulanus* in exhibiting an ontogenetic shift in diet from birds to mammals (especially murid rodents). Twenty-two prey items were recovered: 3 lizards (13.6%), 8 birds (36.4%), and 11 mammals (50.0%). Birds were taken by snakes 520–1630 mm SVL ($\bar{x}$ = 793.5 ± 141.8 mm) and mammals by snakes 852 mm to 1645 mm SVL ($\bar{x}$ = 1355.3 ± 79.6 mm, n = 11). Two lizards were taken from snakes 1132–1610 mm SVL. In both cases, the snakes were from Panama and the prey was *Basiliscus*; I recovered one, and the other was reported by Sexton and Heatwole (1965). One of the basilisks was the largest prey item I personally recovered (100 cm³) from this species. Prey size ranged from 10 cm³ to 100 cm³ ($\bar{x}$ = 37.8 ± 13.3 cm³ for all prey items and 34.3 ± 3.5 cm³ for three rodents). Only one MR was determined: 0.2 for a 522-mm SVL snake from Panama that had consumed a bird.

In addition to data that I gleaned from examining stomachs, Hans Boos (pers. comm., Sept. 1992) collected a *C. ruschenbergerii* in Trinidad that regurgitated an unidentified species of bat, and Smith and Grant (1958) recovered one of the tent-making bats (*Uroderma bilobatum*) from a young treeboa (655 mm total length). William W. Lamar (in litt., April 2000) found an unidentified bat in a treeboa taken in mangroves in Colombia. Three *C.*

ruschenbergerii taken by W.W. Lamar and A. Solórzano in mangroves along the Río Sierpe in Costa Rica contained two *Basiliscus basiliscus* and one unidentified bird (A. Solórzano, in litt., 11 July 2000). The four records of *Basiliscus* consumed by *C. ruschenbergerii* in Costa Rica and Panama are intriguing. Likely the frequent association of basilisks and treeboas with bodies of water increases the likelihood of *Basiliscus-Corallus* encounters.

 Corallus ruschenbergerii takes larger prey species than other members of the complex. A 1510-mm SVL female (FMNH 49915) took a mouse opossum (Marsupialia: Marmosidae: *Marmosa robinsoni*), FMNH 49925 (SVL 1360 mm) contained at least two *Akodon* (Rodentia: Muridae), and Urich (1933) reported a mongoose (Carnivora: Herpestidae: *Herpestes javanicus*) in the stomach of a "full-grown specimen (6 ft. in length)" of *C. ruschenbergerii*. All of these records are from Trinidad, where the species attains larger size than elsewhere in its range.

Foraging

Like other members of the complex, *Corallus ruschenbergerii* forages on the distal portions of branches, and frequently over water. At Hollis Reservoir (Quarre Dam) in Trinidad's Northern Range, *C. ruschenbergerii* was observed crawling slowly on the periphery of trees at heights of 3.0–7.0 m at water's edge or over the water. One snake was in a *Cecropia* tree, and another was in a *Philodendron* tangle. Several snakes were on branches that extended up to 5.0 m over the water. Crawling out on branches over water, or assuming an ambush strategy on those same branches, would appear to limit the number of prey encounters. Those isolated foraging sites could, however, be ideal for preying on bats foraging along the periphery of the reservoir. An alternative hypothesis is that the snakes explore many of these overwater branches on a given night, on the chance they will encounter roosting birds. Indeed, we saw several flycatchers (Tyrannidae) sleeping on the distal ends of overwater branches at Hollis Reservoir, and flycatchers have been recovered from the stomachs of *C. hortulanus*. Similarly, in gallery forest along the Río Matiyure in the Venezuelan llanos, *C. ruschenbergerii* was observed moving slowly on the distal ends of branches at heights of 2.0–3.0 m above ground at water's edge or over the water. In Trinidad, a *Corallus ruschenbergerii* was collected in a birdcage (in which it had consumed the former occupant) (Boos 2001), illustrating the active foraging exhibited by this species.

 Three large (1425–1700 mm SVL) female *Corallus ruschenbergerii* that I observed in Trinidad's Northern Range and Caroni Swamp during March 1999, exhibited an ambush foraging posture. Two of the snakes were in *Rhizophora* either at water's edge or over the water, and both were postured with their heads oriented downward. The third was in vegetation (at 0.7 m) along a road cut, and it, too, was motionless with its head oriented down. Of 15 other *C. ruschenbergerii* that were observed foraging, the largest was 1020 mm SVL, and all were actively crawling through the vegetation; air temperatures ranged from 21.8–23.0°C. Foraging height for the snakes regardless of size (n = 19) ranged from 0.5–20.0 m ($\bar{x}$ = 6.9 ± 1.2 m). Mean foraging height for the three largest snakes was 2.3 ± 1.0 m (0.7–4.0 m); mean foraging height for all others (n = 16) was 7.7 ± 1.4 m (0.5–20.0 m). Daytime body temperatures of two large females were 31.3°C and 31.7°C between 1445 h and 1615 h in the Caroni Swamp. Both were in sun-shade mosaics in *Rhizophora* trees.

Chapter 6

Predators and Defensive Behavior

Their teeth are numerous, long, and sharp, and when disturbed the snakes are always ready to bite, throwing their heads forward with a ferocious lunge, which is very formidable to those unused to snakes' ways.... They rarely if ever retreat when threatened.

Mole and Urich (1894) describing Corallus ruschenbergerii in Trinidad

* * *

The writer does not hesitate in branding them among the most mean-tempered of the non-venomous serpents.

Ditmars (1941) describing species of Corallus

* * *

The numerous rather long teeth can make unpleasant lacerations.

Underwood (1962) describing one of the West Indian species of Corallus

Working late in my office at the museum one night, I decided to take a break from typing and change the water in the enclosure in which I kept the largest live *Corallus ruschenbergerii* I had ever seen. From snout to tail tip it reached 2311 mm; I had seen one preserved specimen that was slightly larger. The snake had been collected at Hollis Reservoir in Trinidad's Northern Range, and had been carried to the U.S. by Allen Young (an insect ecologist). When he handed the snake over to me, he warned me to be careful as it was big and vicious.

I slid open the plexiglass door of the treeboa's enclosure. The snake was immediately alert: its head was raised and its neck was in a typical prestrike S-posture. Having successfully avoided strikes during hundreds of treeboa encounters, I was confident that I could remove the water bowl without suffering a puncture from the long teeth at the front region of its mouth. For a reason that eludes me, I hesitated for only the blink of an eye, and in that instant the snake sank its fanglike teeth into my hand. But, atypical for treeboas, she did not withdraw from the bite immediately. Instead, she coiled around my hand with her head buried in the coils. I found that with only one hand I was helpless to remove her from my other hand. Blood was already dripping on the floor. I was not in any great discomfort, but I knew it would be difficult to continue typing with the boa adhered to my hand.

There was one other person working that night on my floor of the museum. With the snake balled on my hand, and leaving a trail of blood, I marched down the corridor and asked Greg Septon if he would mind removing the snake from my hand. Thankfully, Greg is not uncomfortable about snakes, and he immediately unwrapped the treeboa. I returned her to the enclosure (with fresh water), grabbed some paper towels, and retraced my trail to Greg's office, wiping up my blood along the way.

PREDATORS

Little is known about predators of treeboas. Mole (1924) reported a secondhand observation of the colubrid snake *Clelia clelia* preying on *Corallus ruschenbergerii* in Trinidad, and Henderson et al. (1996) reported a small *C. grenadensis* being found in the stomach of an opossum (*Didelphis marsupialis*) on Grenada. By night, at the edge of an oxbow lake in Amazonian Peru, W.W. Lamar (in litt., April 2000) collected a smooth-fronted caiman (*Paleosuchus trigonatus*) that had a freshly killed *C. hortulanus* (about 700 mm total length) in its mouth.

Two encounters with subhuman primates have been reported. Bartecki and Heymann (1987) witnessed "mobbing" by saddle-back tamarins (*Saguinus fuscicollis nigrifrons*) of what was presumably a mating pair of *Corallus hortulanus* in rainforest habitat in northeastern Peru. Two individuals of the group of six tamarins approached to within 1.5–2.0 m of the snakes. While the tamarins emitted excitement calls, the two *C. hortulanus* slowly retreated into the liana's interior. There was never any physical contact between the snakes and the tamarins, and it is unlikely that the snakes were in any danger of being injured or killed. The mobbing behavior of the tamarins did interrupt mating, however, and the snakes did choose to retreat.

The African monkey *Cercopithecus mona* (Cercopithecidae) was introduced to Grenada (probably during the slave trade: Groome 1970), and it has been observed molesting *Corallus grenadensis* at Grand Etang National Park. Because of the elevation (>500 m), treeboas are rare at Grand Etang, and it seems unlikely that there are many treeboa-monkey encounters there.

Similarly, Hopkins and Hopkins (1982) witnessed a *Corallus hortulanus* capture and kill a bat (probably *Phyllostomus discolor*) at a site about 60 km north of Manaus, Brazil. They reported that "The caught bat squawked loudly for about 30 seconds before becoming silent and during this period other bats mobbed the snake. The intensity of mobbing gradually declined, but continued for at least 30 minutes ..." In Trinidad, a pair of channel-billed toucans (*Ramphastos vitellinus*) was observed "mobbing" a "6-ft-long" *C. ruschenbergerii* on the ground near their nest, and ffrench (1973) suggested the "snake may well be a predator of the toucans' eggs or young."

The paucity of data regarding predation on treeboas does not imply that their lives are not fraught with danger. Although there are no supporting data, it seems likely that raptors are the most important predators of *Corallus*. For example, laughing falcons (*Herpetotheres cachinnans*) inhabiting primary forests in Guatemala prey exclusively upon snakes, of which a "large proportion" are said to be arboreal species (Parker 1990). Likewise, also in Guatemala, great black hawks (*Buteogallus urubitinga*), preyed more often on *Boa constrictor* than any other snake species (with snakes and lizards comprising 60% of the diet by frequency), and it preyed frequently on arboreal species (Gerhardt et al. 1993). More significantly, Bierregaard (1984) reported that, of six snakes found in the nest of a Guiana crested eagle (*Morphnus guianensis*), three were *Corallus caninus*, the most massive member of the genus (rivaled only by *C. ruschenbergerii*); it also included at least one *Epicrates cenchria*. If *M. guianensis* can prey on *C. caninus*, it can certainly prey on sympatric members of the *C. hortulanus* complex (all of which are less massive than *C. caninus*). On Grenada, the broad-winged hawk (*Buteo platypterus*), hook-billed kite (*Chondrohierax uncinatus*), and merlin (*Falco columbarius*) were often seen flying over *Corallus* habitat by day, and barn owls (*Tyto alba*) were observed hunting in the same habitats at night.

It would be remiss to not include the introduced mongoose (*Herpestes javanicus*) among those species that are potential predators of treeboas, especially in the West Indies. At Mt. Hartman Bay I have observed *Herpestes* foraging by day at 5–10 m above ground level in trees in which I have seen *C. grenadensis* foraging at night. One tree in particular in which I witnessed a mongoose foraging supported many bromeliads. I do not know if *C. grenadensis* ever spends daylight hours coiled in bromeliads, but I would not be surprised if they did. Similarly, the tayra (*Eira barbara*) is a likely predator of treeboas. William W. Lamar (in litt., April 2000) has observed this mustelid carnivore kill and eat a *Boa constrictor* that was lying in ambush for monkeys (*Cebus albifrons*), and he has observed them hunting in trees along oxbows in Peru.

Although I have dissected hundreds of treeboas, I have seen no obvious evidence of internal parasites; I stress, however, that I have not made a thorough or systematic search for them. I have found unidentified species of ticks (Acarina: Ixodides) on the heads of all species in the complex except *C. cookii*, and on the bodies of *C. grenadensis* and *C. hortulanus* as well. None of the snakes with ticks was heavily infested, and none seemed to be debilitated (i.e., emaciated) due to the infestation. The ectoparasites *Eutrombicula alfreddugesi* and *E. goldii* were recorded by Brennan and Jones (1960) on *Corallus ruschenbergerii* from Trinidad. The protozoan *Haemogregarina* sp. and the nematode *Dracunculus* sp. were recovered from *C. ruschenbergerii* on Trinidad by Everard (1975).

DEFENSIVE BEHAVIOR

Corallus hortulanus complex treeboas exhibit several antipredator behaviors: retreat and hiding, tail-vibrating, balling-posture, emitting an offensive odor, biting, body rotation, and confusion rendered by color pattern polymorphism.

Crypsis

By day, treeboas sleep coiled on branches, with only the prehensile tail wrapped around the branch (see Chapter 4). I have been remarkably unsuccessful in finding *Corallus grenadensis* during the day, despite hundreds of hours of searching. Even with the aid of radio-telemetry, *C. grenadensis* is difficult to locate by day. This is due to three factors: 1) treeboas assume a very compact posture during daylight hours, often on the distal ends of branches; 2) they are often shielded by leafy vegetation; and 3) their coloration is not garish and it allows the snake to meld with its surroundings. The predominant dorsal coloration of treeboas is a shade of brown or gray (taupe is the most common), even those that can be described as "yellow" are in reality closer to tan or khaki. Coiled on a tree limb, also invariably a shade of brown or gray, treeboas are remarkably inconspicuous. A spray of leafy vegetation adds additional protection as follows: 1) it may completely hide the snake; or 2) it produces a mosaic of light and shade (dappling) which breaks up the outline of the snake and makes accurate discernment by a predator difficult or impossible. Approaching my study site in late November-early December (dry season) at Mt. Hartman Bay, where 71.1% of the 38 *Corallus grenadensis* observed were yellowish, I noticed that in excess of 50% of the canopy foliage was yellow. In addition to variable dorsal color and pattern, members of the *C. hortulanus* complex are invariably counter-shaded (i.e., venter paler than dorsum), thereby making it more difficult to discern treeboas from below.

Apostatic Selection

Because of the color and pattern polymorphism in *Corallus grenadensis* and *C. hortulanus*, potential predators of treeboas that have color vision may be unable to develop a search image for these snakes, especially when they are inactive during the day. Although at a given locality one color pattern will often predominate (at least on the Grenada Bank), a wide-ranging predator such as a raptor does not hunt intensively enough in a single localized area, thereby precluding the chance for learning what color object (i.e., treeboa coiled on a branch) to search for. Even if a predator successfully captures a treeboa, this prior experience will be of minimal benefit in subsequent foraging because of the tremendous amount of color and pattern variation in *C. grenadensis* and *C. hortulanus*. Color pattern polymorphism may be especially advantageous to species that occur at high densities (Owen 1963).

Retreat and Hiding

When disturbed during the day, *Corallus grenadensis* is quick to flee, and will usually ascend to higher vegetation and/or move into the interior of a tree crown. Even a slight disturbance of a branch supporting a treeboa is enough to get it moving. At night, when active, *C. cookii*, *C. grenadensis*, and *C. ruschen-bergerii* are remarkably tolerant of disturbances to the perches they are using, if the disturbance is caused by another "branch" (i.e., a long pole that is used to pull or entice the snakes from their perches). Once aware of a human (i.e., a potential predator), they will attempt to ascend and/or penetrate deeper into the tree's crown. We observed *C. grenadensis* at Westerhall Estate enter a hollowed cacao branch after being captured and then released. It is possible that the snake had spent the day in the hollow (or perhaps used it routinely over days or weeks), and knew its position in case of danger.

Tail-Vibrating

Beebe (1946) described a young treeboa, presumably *Corallus hortulanus* at Kartabo, Guyana, that vibrated its tail against twigs at the same time that it was biting him. Beebe noted that he "… was startled by the rattling." In several hundred encounters with *C. grenadensis* and considerably fewer with other members of the complex, I have never observed this behavior.

Balling-Posture

Kreutz (1989) described balling behavior in *Corallus hortulanus*, based on the photograph that appears in the article; see also Kirschner and Seufer (1995), Martins (1996), and Martins and Oliveira (1998, including Plate 11), and I have observed this behavior many times in *Corallus grenadensis* (see Plate 8) and occasionally in *C. cookii* and *C. ruschenbergerii*; it has been documented in other boines as well (*Epicrates cenchria*: Murphy 1997; see also Plate 9 in Kornacker 1999; *Eunectes*: Dirksen et al. 1998; Mole and Urich 1894). The snake coils its body into a tight spheroid, with the head buried in the coils. It is possible to play catch with a treeboa when it assumes this posture. Although *C. grenadensis* will occasionally exhibit this behavior upon capture, it is most often observed when removed from a cloth bag.

Emitting an Offensive Odor

When captured and initially handled in the field, all members of the complex will void the contents of their cloacae, including uric acid, feces, and musk. Although I would not recommend marketing the scent as perfume, I have smelled more unpleasant odors emitted from other snake species (e.g., *Epicrates striatus*). Besides, if you smell like *Corallus* at the end of the night, you know it has been a good one. It would be interesting to learn what impact this habit has, if any, on a potential predator.

Biting

I have been struck at by captive treeboas only when they are "cornered," or by wild treeboas when physical contact has been made. Treeboas are not aggressive in that if given the opportunity to flee they will do that rather than attack. Certainly unprovoked attack is unknown. With the exception of a bite from a large female (1857 mm SVL) *Corallus ruschenbergerii*, bites that I have suffered have resulted in only temporary discomfort and superficial injury. On a number of occasions I have observed captive *C. grenadensis* kill small *Mus musculus* with a single bite and release, the long anterior teeth apparently having penetrated a vital organ. On these occasions the snakes did not retain a grip on the mouse, and ultimately did not ingest the mouse after it died. I believe these were defensive bites delivered by a snake that was not hungry, but felt annoyed or threatened by the mouse. Martins' (1996) S-coil often precedes a bite.

Body Rotation

I have observed *Corallus cookii*, *C. grenadensis*, and *C. ruschenbergerii* rotate their bodies along their longitudinal planes when just captured by hand. This behavior presumably is employed to break the grip of the animal that has captured it and to facilitate escape. Martins (1996) has documented this antipredator tactic in *C. hortulanus*.

Chapter 7

Reproduction

The young [tree boas], which are very small and thin with enormous heads, immediately display all the habits of the adult snake, coiling in the branches and being ever ready to bite fiercely.

Mole and Urich (1891) describing *Corallus ruschenbergerii*

Considering how geographically widespread members of the *Corallus hortulanus* complex are, and how relatively abundant members are in their respective ophidiofaunas, we know remarkably little about reproduction in this complex of species. I have had to rely heavily on observations of snakes held in captivity for information regarding reproduction. Oxtoby (1989) reported a successful mating in a 2-year-old treeboa of the *C. hortulanus* complex, but first reproduction is apparently more common in their third or fourth year (Ross and Marzec 1990).

CORALLUS COOKII

I have no data regarding reproduction in this species, aside from those fortuitously accumulated via collecting. Based on the collecting dates of specimens <500 mm SVL, births occur between October and March. I have personally collected *C. cookii* <500 mm SVL in October (451 mm SVL), November (337–375 mm SVL) and March (372–492 mm SVL). October and November are wet season months, but rainfall is diminished in December and January–March births coincide with the dry season in St. Vincent. Appropriate size prey (*Anolis*) for small treeboas is available throughout the year.

CORALLUS GRENADENSIS

Virtually nothing is known about social behavior in species of *Corallus* (including chemical communication, e.g., Mason 1992), but there is some evidence of aggregating behavior in *C. grenadensis*. At the Westerhall site, over several nights in 1993 we observed multiple snakes utilizing the same trees: 19 April: three snakes in a mango tree; 20 April: three snakes (at least one of which was a male) were in contact in a nutmeg tree; 21 April: four snakes active in a mango tree (one of which was a male from 19–20 April); 22 April: three snakes in a mango tree, all within 1.0 m of each other; 23 April: four snakes in close proximity; 24 April: four snakes in same mango tree; 25 April: three snakes in contact in same mango tree. These aggregations seem similar to that reported for the Neotropical tree snake *Imantodes cenchoa* in the Peruvian Amazon (Doan and Arriaga 1999). If these were, indeed, courtship/mating aggregations in *C. grenadensis*, I would expect births to occur late in the year or very early the next calendar year. Based on appearance of young snakes, both are reasonable possibilities.

A local farmer I met at Concord Falls (St. John Parish) told me that he and his son encountered eight *C. grenadensis* in the hollow of a mango tree, but he could not recall at what time of year he made the observation. A similar aggregation was reported in *Boiga irregularis* (Pendleton, 1947). A fisherman I met at Mt. Hartman Bay (who led me by boat during the day to several treeboas), told me that he saw many treeboas mating in the mangroves at Mt. Hartman Bay; he thought that occurred in June, but he was not positive. At La Sagesse Estate (St. David Parish), I was told that seven *C. grenadensis* were observed in a single tree at the edge of La Sagesse Bay in mid-March.

Ross and Marzec (1990) determined that mating in captive *C. enydris cookii* (= *C. cookii*, *C. grenadensis*, or *C. ruschenbergerii*) peaks in January and February and that births occur May–August. Al Winstel (in litt., 7 June 1997) had births occur on 8 September and 10 October with snakes from Grenada. Gravid *Corallus grenadensis* were collected on Grenada 9 (UF 73145), 13 (ASFS X7005), and 16 (ASFS X7044) May; all had undeveloped eggs. Museum of Comparative Zoology (MCZ) specimen 79762 contained 17 nearly full-term young (300–330 mm SVL) on 18 June. Based on snakes that I or my field associates collected, all snakes <400 mm SVL (n = 14) were collected October–December, and of 42 snakes <500 mm SVL, 83.3% were collected October–December. Of snakes 500–599 mm SVL (n = 14), 64.3% were collected in April–May (Fig. 7.1). In February 1998, I collected snakes with SVLs of 330 mm (at Petit Etang, St. David Parish, ca. 365 m) , 425 mm and 430 mm (at Westerhall), and 437 mm (at Mt. Hartman Bay). The snake from Petit Etang is of a size that makes me suspect it was born either very late or very early in the calendar year. It is important to note that I have not done field work in Grenada during June–September, so it is possible (and likely) that young appear prior to October. On Grenada, the wet season occurs June–November (see Fig. 2.1), and it is likely that is when most litters appear. Those months are also the warmest (see Fig. 2.2). Appropriate size prey (*Anolis*) is available throughout the year for small treeboas.

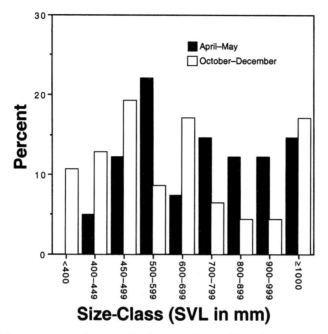

Figure 7.1. Percent of snakes taken in nine size-classes of *Corallus grenadensis* during two sampling periods.

Little is known concerning litter size. A 1587 mm SVL snake had 29 undeveloped eggs (ASFS X7005; A. Schwartz field notes); a 1562 mm SVL snake had 40 undeveloped eggs (ASFS X7044; A. Schwartz field notes); a 1400 mm SVL snake had 17 nearly full-term young (MCZ 79762). BMNH 97.7.23.28–48 constitute what I consider to be a litter of 21 snakes. The snake with the 40 undeveloped eggs had the potential for the largest litter for which I am aware. Of course, not all of those 40 eggs would necessarily develop and reach full term. In 1698 Pére Labat (in Mole 1926) noted 74 unborn young in either *Corallus grenadensis* or *C. ruschenbergerii*. Regardless of the species, the potential litter size seems unlikely.

CORALLUS HORTULANUS

In a sample of 24 *Corallus hortulanus* collected in Amazonian Brazil (Acre, Rondônia), Laurie Vitt (in litt., 5 Feb 1999) found the largest immature female was 1058 mm SVL, and the smallest mature female was 960 mm SVL.

Starace (1998) reported that male *Corallus hortulanus* engage in violent fighting during the mating season. Whether these observations are based on captive snakes or those observed in the field is unknown. Vergner (1993) reported fighting between captive male *C. hortulanus*; the context of the fighting is unknown.

Bartecki and Heymann (1987) reported what they thought to be copulation by *Corallus hortulanus* during daylight hours on 9 July in Amazonian Peru. If their observations were accurately interpreted, birth would occur in December or January. Based on data from the Instituto Butantan, *C. hortulanus* <400 mm SVL from the Brazilian state of Amazonas (n = 2) were collected in January and April.

I plotted the monthly size distribution of 145 specimens of *Corallus hortulanus* that came into the Instituto Butantan from localities in southeastern Brazil (i.e., the states of Espírito Santo, Minas Gerais, Paraná, Rio de Janiero, Santa Catarina, and São Paulo). Few very small snakes (<500 mm SVL) were included in the sample, and they were collected June to November (which bridges wet and dry seasons in southeastern Brazil; Ratisbona 1976), with the highest concentration appearing in October (Fig. 7.2). This is in agreement with the mating-birth schedule presented by Ross and Marzec (1990) for *C. hortulanus* (= their *C. enydris enydris*).

A treeboa that I purchased in 1965 from a reptile dealer based at Leticia, Amazonas, Colombia, arrived at my home on 1 April. It refused all food, and

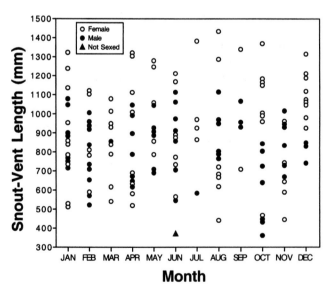

Figure 7.2. Monthly incidence of *Corallus hortulanus* collected in southeastern Brazil and based on size (SVL). Data courtesy of Giuseppe Puorto and Instituto Butantan.

gave birth to 15 live and 4 stillborn babies on 3 July (wet season in the Colombian Amazon: Snow, 1976). Al Winstel (in litt., 7 June 1997) observed the births of nine litters of captive-bred *C. hortulanus* between 10 August and 13 January. Abuys (1990) recorded litters of 8–14 based on captive breedings. William W. Lamar (pers. comm.) encountered a pregnant *C. hortulanus* (2020 mm total length) in a termite nest on 1 November (wet season: Johnson 1976) at Momoncillo, Loreto, Peru. Peter J. Tolson (pers. comm.) has likewise encountered gravid *Epicrates monensis* in termite nests on the Puerto Rico Bank.

CORALLUS RUSCHENBERGERII

In Trinidad, Mole and Urich (1891, 1894) reported mating in February, March, and April, and birth of 20–30 young in August and September (wet season: Portig 1976); they reported a secondhand observation of copulation in February with birth the following August. Emsley (1977), also in Trinidad, reported mating January–May, and birth in July and August. With gestation at about 180–210 days, a female that was mated in April would give birth in October or November, and one that mated in May would not give birth until the following November or December. Hans Boos (pers. comm., 20 March 1999) recalled observing a large female and two male *C. ruschenbergerii* coiled together at Hollis Reservoir.

Hans Boos showed me a litter of *Corallus ruschenbergerii* that had been born in September (wet season). They were bred in captivity and the parents came from Hollis Reservoir (Quarre Dam) in the Northern Range (Trinidad). On 2 October, six members of the litter had SVLs 415–455 mm. They had not been fed since birth. Murphy (1997) reported a female from Trinidad with 15 oviductal eggs from Trinidad.

The apparent pattern among all four members of the *Corallus hortulanus* complex is to breed February–May and to produce litters during the second half of the calendar year, and almost invariably during months of high precipitation.

Chapter 8

Populations

It is a fairly common arboreal snake ...

Groome (1970) describing *Corallus grenadensis*

* * *

It was so common that the mangroves lit up like a small city owing to all the treeboa eyes reflecting back at me.

W.W. Lamar (in litt., April 2000) describing *Corallus ruschenbergerii* on Isla de Salamanca, Colombia

* * *

During the five-year period there seems to have been a steady increase in the incidence of Bothrops atrox [= B. asper] *..., and a similarly steady decrease in the incidence of* [Corallus ruschenbergerii] *...*

Dunn (1949) commenting on the relative abundance of some Panamanian snakes

Little is known about population structure and densities in tropical snakes in general, and the Neotropics in particular. The reason for this is simple: few attempts have been made at studying snake populations in the tropics. Why? At least seemingly, and probably in reality, populations of snakes in the tropics (especially in rainforest habitat) occur at much lower densities than in temperate areas. Of course, it is possible that snake-herpetologist encounter rates are lower just because we are not looking in the right place at the right time. Whatever the reason, we know little about tropical snake populations.

Virtually all of the available data for Neotropical snake populations has come from habitats other than rainforest, and this includes the available data on treeboas of the *hortulanus* complex. Almost from the start of my *Corallus* work in the West Indies, I recorded the number of treeboas observed, how much time was spent searching for the snakes, and how many people were involved in the searches. Although we have density estimates from only a few sites, we do have encounter rates (number of snakes observed/man-hour [m-h] of searching) from more sites. Data on distribution of size-classes in *C. grenadensis* from several localities on Grenada are also available. In addition, the literature provides some additional insights into the relative abundance of *Corallus* at various sites or areas throughout the range of the complex.

ABUNDANCE, DENSITIES, AND ENCOUNTER RATES

Encounter rates and population densities are summarized in Table 8.1.

Corallus cookii

Although Barbour (1937) suggested that *Corallus* had been eliminated from St. Vincent (reiterated by Westermann 1953), and Albert Schwartz considered it rare, certainly in 1987 it was locally abundant at several sites. It is the most commonly encountered snake on St. Vincent. The only encounter rate I have is 4–6 treeboas/m-h of searching at a site 3.2 km east of Layou (St. Patrick Parish). This is from along a narrow paved road in a heavily disturbed area of mixed agriculture. This encounter rate is comparable to those from the Grenada Bank. But this St. Vincent site was the best I found, whereas there are many sites on the Grenada Bank that yielded similar (or better) encounter rates.

Corallus grenadensis

We have more information about this species than any of the other members of the complex, and it is likely that *Corallus grenadensis* attains higher population densities than any member of the complex. About 35 years ago (in 1964), J.D. Lazell collected at Beausejour, and a notation in his field notes of 19 June regarding two specimens of *C. grenadensis* that he collected and preserved read, "Both together in a ball in tree ca. 150 ft up (very large tree). Many other balls too difficult to bother with. Ca. 20 Boas [= *Corallus*] around." In my own experience, driving into new collecting sites on Grenada, it was not unusual to find the first treeboa on a branch above the parked vehicle. On Grenada, nightly encounter rates ranged from <1.0/m-h to >10.0/m-h. The lowest encounter rates occurred at higher elevations (>400 m asl), and in very xeric areas (Mt. Hartman Bay). The highest encounter rates occurred in areas of mixed agriculture and moderate rainfall at elevations <100 m asl. Many of the encounter rates fell between five and six snakes/m-h, including that for one of The Grenadines.

Density estimates were determined by one or the other of the following methods: 1) direct counts of snakes in a known area; 2) Lincoln Index based on short-term mark-and-recapture studies. The direct counts were often done along a narrow strip (e.g., 10 m × 600 m) of edge habitat. The counts were then extrapolated to a 1-hectare area. All of the density estimates were made in disturbed areas with some agricultural activity (although it was minor at Mt. Hartman Bay), and the estimates ranged from about four (Mt. Hartman Bay) to 69 (Pearls) *C. grenadensis*/hectare. I anticipate that densities would be lower at elevations >100 m, and that they might fall to <1/ha at elevations >400 m asl in some habitats.

My data, in general, do not support the notion among many Grenadians that treeboas are not as common as they once were. Declines were observed at Mt. Hartman Bay and at Westerhall Estate from 1993 and 1994 to 1998, both sites at which treeboas were captured and released. However, a decline was also observed at Beausejour Estate, a site at which the snakes were not part of a mark-recapture project. Recent field work (February 1998 and April 2000) was productive at all sites visited except Mt. Hartman Bay. Figure 8.1 illustrates changes in encounter rates at five sites on Grenada. Mt. Hartman showed a steady decline between 1994 and 2000, and the numbers at Pearls increased with each sampling (four samples between 1988 and 2000). The other three sites exhibited fluctuations. Many variables can affect nightly encounter rates (e.g., rainfall, moon phase), so vacillations are to be anticipated. It is important, also, to note my perspective versus that of someone who has spent their entire life on Grenada. My experience with *Corallus grenadensis* spans a relatively short period of time (1988–2000), whereas a Grenadian may have a perspective going back 30, 50, or more years. Therefore, it is certainly possible that treeboas were more common 30–50 years ago than they are today (2000), but it is also possible that the Grenadian's perspective has a cumulative aspect. That is, cumulatively over 30 years or 50 years the Grenadian has encountered many treeboas, but not necessarily more at any one time than we are currently encountering at some sites.

Corallus hortulanus

This is a commonly encountered snake species throughout much of its wide range. In Suriname, M.S. Hoogmoed (in litt., 26 Jan 1990) described *C. hortulanus* as "rather common in the area around Paramaribo, in roadside vegetation." Rodriguez and Cadle (1990) considered the *C. hortulanus* population at Cocha Cashu (in Manu National Park, Amazonian Peru) "large." William W. Lamar (in litt., 25 Mar 1997), working from boats in Amazonian Peru, has encountered up to six treeboas in 30 min, but three to six *C. hortulanus* per hour by boat is more typical. Dixon and Soini (1986), working at a number of sites in the Iquitos region of Amazonian Peru, collected 18 *C. hortulanus*, more than any other boid, and the only other snakes that were collected more

Table 8.1. Encounter rates and densities of treeboas in the *Corallus hortulanus* complex. Unless otherwise stated, encounter rates (snakes/man-hour) were determined during searches made on foot.

Species	Locality (elevation in m)	Encounter Rate and/or Density (no. of sampling periods)	Source
C. cookii	St. Vincent: St. Patrick: 3.2 km E Layou	ca. 4-6/man-hour (3)	R. Henderson, Oct 1987
C. grenadensis	Grenada: St. Andrew: Pearls (30 m)	2.9 ± 0.3/man-hour (2)	R. Henderson, May 1988
		3.8/man-hour (1)	R. Henderson, Oct 1991
		8.4 ± 1.8/man-hour (3)	R. Henderson, Feb 1998
		55–69/hectare	R. Henderson, Feb 1998
		8.3 ± 3.0/man-hour (2)	R. Henderson, Apr 2000
	Grenada: St. Andrew: Balthazar Estate (75 m)	5.7/man-hour (1)	R. Henderson, Apr 1996
		3.3/man-hour (1)	R. Henderson, Feb 1998
		3.8/man-hour (1)	R. Henderson, Apr 2000
	Grenada: St. Andrew: Grand Etang (525 m)	<1/man-hour (22)	R. Henderson, 1988–1995
	Grenada: St. Andrew: Spring Gardens Estate (460 m)	0.2 ± 0.1/man-hour (10)	R. Henderson, 1988–1998
	Grenada: St. David: Westerhall Estate (65 m)	6.0/man-hour (1)	R. Henderson, Oct 1991
		16–25/hectare	R. Henderson, Apr 1993
		1.3 ± 0.5/man-hour (3)	R. Henderson, Feb 1998
		4.1 ± 0.8/man-hour (2)	R. Henderson, Apr 2000

Table 8.1. (*Continued*)

Species	Locality (elevation in m)	Encounter Rate and/or Density (no. of sampling periods)	Source
C. grenadensis (cont.)	Grenada: St. David: B Bacolet (30 m)	5.2/man-hour (1)	R. Henderson, Oct 1991
	Grenada: St. George: Beausejour (55 m)	4.2 ± 0.6/man-hour (3) 19–27/hectare	R. Henderson, Oct 1991 Henderson and Winstel 1992
	Grenada: St. George: Mt. Hartman Bay (sea level)	2.4 ± 0.1/man-hour (9) 19/hectare 1.3 ± 0.3 (13) 0.5 ± 0.1/man-hour (23) ca. 4/hectare 0.2 ± 0.2/man-hour (6) 0.3 ± 0.3/man-hour (2)	R. Henderson, Apr 1994 R. Henderson, Apr 1994 R. Henderson, Apr 1996 R. Henderson, Oct 1996 R. Henderson, Oct 1996 R. Henderson, Feb 1998 R. Henderson, Apr 2000
	St. Vincent: Grenadines: Canouan	5.0/man-hour (1)	R. Henderson, Oct 1990
C. hortulanus	Amazonian Peru	3–6/hour (by boat)	W.W. Lamar, in litt., 1997
C. ruschenbergerii	Venezuela: Delta Amacuro: Orinoco Delta	12–15 along 3 km (in boat)	G.R. Fuenmayor, in litt., 1996
	Trinidad: Northern Range	0.7/man-hour	R. Henderson, Mar 1999

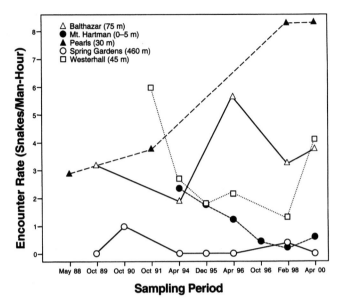

Figure 8.1. Mean rates (snakes/man-hour) at which *Corallus grenadensis* was encountered at five sites on Grenada from 1988 to 2000.

often and that fed predominantly on endotherms were the colubrid *Pseustes poecilonotus* (n = 20) and the viperid *Bothrops atrox* (n = 86). At Tumi Chucua, a site in Amazonian Bolivia, Fugler (1986) found *C. hortulanus* to be the most common snake species. In contrast, Duellman (1978) collected only one specimen at Santa Cecilia in Amazonian Ecuador, but that site is situated at 340 m, an elevation that is suboptimum for the species.

Corallus ruschenbergerii

At Hollis Reservoir (Quarre Dam) in October 1992, in Trinidad's Northern Range, I encountered one *C. ruschenbergerii* about every 15 minutes by boat. In March 1999, working along Blanchisseuse Road (also in the Northern Range), we encountered treeboas at a rate of up to 0.7/m-h; based on previous work in Trinidad, I considered this excellent. Dunn (1949) provides some indication of the relative abundance of *C. ruschenbergerii* based on collections made in Panama. Of the total 10,690 specimens, 372 (3.5%) were *C. ruschenbergerii* and virtually all were from the Darien region. Two other boids were represented by similar numbers: *Boa constrictor* (388 specimens, 3.6%) and *Epicrates cenchria* (385 specimens, 3.6%). *Boa constrictor* and *E. cenchria* occurred more commonly throughout the entire sample regardless of locality, but where *C. ruschenbergerii* was common (i.e., the Darien area), it was far more so than the other two boids. The Darien collection consisted of 3044 specimens representing 44 species; *C. ruschenbergerii* was represented by 346 specimens (the third most common species). In contrast *Corallus annulatus* was represented by only one specimen. Similarly, the Yavisa sample—a sub-sample of the Darien collection made "on the Río Chucunaque a few miles above its junction with the [Río] Tuira" and entirely from lowland banana and plantain farms—taken in the years 1933–1937, consisted of 2321 snakes of which 171 were *C. ruschenbergerii* but only one *C. annulatus*, a species that, although fairly wide-ranging, would seem to be nowhere common. In the Yavisa collection, *C. ruschenbergerii* was the fourth most common snake (behind *Bothrops asper*, *Leptodeira rhombifera*, and *Chironius carinatus*), and accounted for a minimum of 4.4% of the yearly snake catch (*B. asper* accounted for 10%, *L. rhombifera* 8.2%, and *C. carinatus* 8.0%).

In northwestern Colombia, near Barranquilla, W.W. Lamar (pers. comm., April 2000) noted that *C. ruschenbergerii* was very common in the coastal mangroves on Isla de Salamanca. In Venezuela, along a 3-km stretch in the Orinoco Delta, G.R. Fuenmayor (in litt., 12 Sept 1996), observed 12–15 *C. ruschenbergerii*, of which "… 90% eran adultos muy grandes …"

Discussion

Lillywhite and Henderson (1993) summarized what little was known about population densities in arboreal snakes. Densities ranged from <1 snake/ha (*Elaphe obsoleta*) to >400 snakes/ha (*Opheodrys aestivus*); both are temperate species. Plummer (1997) has since calculated a maximum population density of about 800/ha in *O. aestivus*, an invertebrate predator. Data are available for only one other arboreal West Indian boid, *Epicrates monensis*, and it feeds predominantly on *Anolis*; Tolson (1988) calculated a density of >100/ha on Cayo Diablo (Puerto Rico Bank). The densities calculated for *Corallus grenadensis* are, among arboreal vertebrate-eating snakes, relatively high. In comparison, at a site in Amazonian Peru, Schulte (1988) estimated that the population density of *Corallus caninus* was about one per 2.7 km^2 (or 0.004 snake/ha), but he was not confident of the reliability of that value.

Members of the *Corallus hortulanus* complex are often commonly encountered by humans in lowland snake communities. Among snake species that prey on endothermic vertebrates, there are few that are encountered more frequently. There are three reasons why members of the complex are so often encountered and, therefore, well represented in collections: 1) they are all edge species, and probably more conspicuous than those snake species that routinely occur in forest interiors; 2) at night they are easily found by their telltale red-orange eyeshine. When searching for members of the complex at night, it is not necessary to develop a search image of the snake, but rather to look for the eyeshine and be able to discern it from the eyeshine of other animals; and 3) members of the complex appear to be genuinely common relative to other sympatric snake species.

When comparing the encounter rates for *C. grenadensis* against those for *C. hortulanus* and *C. ruschenbergerii*, it is critical to remember that all of the Grenada censuses were done on foot, whereas the others were done by boat. If the Grenada rates had been based on censuses conducted from a boat or other moving conveyance, the hourly encounter rates would likely have been many times higher. It is likely that treeboa densities are higher in the West Indies than on the mainland because of dietary differences. On the mainland, *C. hortulanus* and *C. ruschenbergerii* prey predominantly on endothermic vertebrates throughout their entire lives. In the West Indies, *C. cookii* and *C. grenadensis* prey on *Anolis* for the first several years of their lives. Anoles are a ubiquitous and superabundant vertebrate food source in the West Indies, but not so on the Neotropical mainland (Henderson and Powell 1999). For example, population densities of *Anolis aeneus* on Grenada have been calculated at 130–1080/ha (Roughgarden et al. 1983), *A. richardi* on Grenada at 1630–1800/ha (Roughgarden et al. 1983), and *A. trinitatis* and *A. griseus* on St. Vincent at 5000/ha and 5500/ha, respectively (Roughgarden et al. 1983). In contrast, the population density of *A. fuscoauratus* in Amazonian Peru was calculated at 18.1/ha (Duellman 1987), that of *A. humilis* in Costa Rica at 91/ha (Scott 1976), and that of *A. polylepis* in Costa Rica at 224/ha (Scott 1976). Duellman (1987) presented biomass data for a lizard community at a rainforest locality in the Upper Amazon Basin of Peru. Twenty-one species accounted for 1040 g/ha. The only comparable data for the West Indies are those presented by Bullock and Evans (1990) for three widespread lizard species (*Anolis oculatus*, *Mabuya mabouya*, and *Ameiva fuscata*) on Dominica, where the maximum biomass occurred in coastal woodlands and was recorded as 44,700 g/ha. In lowland rainforest habitat on Dominica, the highest recorded biomass was 950 g/ha for *A. oculatus* alone; in comparison, in Amazonian Peru, *A. fuscoauratus* accounted for only 20.3 g/ha. Similarly, *Ameiva ameiva* accounted for 193.4 g/ha in Peruvian rainforest (in clearings) (Duellman 1987), but *A. fuscata* accounted for up to 25,070 g/h in coastal woodland habitat on Dominica (Bullock and Evans 1990).

Lizards provide an abundant food resource in the West Indies, including the Lesser Antilles, and most macrostomatan snakes exploit them as prey (see Table 5.2; Henderson and Crother 1989; Rodríguez-Robles and Greene 1996). It would be surprising if *Corallus* in the Lesser Antilles did not prey on *Anolis*, and high densities of anoles undoubtedly contribute to the high densities attained by treeboas; that is, trophically, the West Indian environment can sustain high populations of vertebrates able to exploit a superabundant lizard population.

POPULATION CHARACTERISTICS

Sex Ratio

I am confident of the sex ratio data only for the Mt. Hartman Bay site *Corallus grenadensis*, as that is the only site at which we were able to collect nearly every snake we saw. (I am aware of only a single instance in which we were unable to capture a snake.) At Mt. Hartman Bay the sex ratio was a perfect 1:1.

Laurie J. Vitt (in litt., 2 Feb 1999) and associates, working in Amazonian Brazil and Ecuador, collected every *Corallus hortulanus* they could. Of 46 treeboas collected, nine were males and 37 were females (providing a male:female sex ratio of 1:4). The snakes were collected at several localities in two countries, therefore the 1:4 sex ratio is not for a local population. Nevertheless, the preponderance of females is intriguing. Females of *C. hortulanus* are larger than males, and it has been suggested (Parker and Plummer 1987) that "being larger, although possibly increasing exposure to predation, also increases survivorship."

Size-Class Distribution

Figure 8.2 presents size-class distribution for *Corallus grenadensis* at Mt. Hartman Bay and Westerhall Estate. Snakes in the 400–499 mm SVL size-class comprise the highest percentage in each of the two samples. The percentages representing larger size-classes drop sharply starting at 500 mm SVL. I interpret the sharp decline between the 400–499 and 500–599 mm size-classes as an indication of first-year mortality. The sharp decline in numbers is expected as small (= young) snakes are eliminated from the population, most likely due to predation.

Growth

Few data are available, and all are from the Mt. Hartman Bay site. A 1050-mm (mass 168 g) female *Corallus grenadensis* originally collected 4 Dec 1995 was recaptured on 17 April 1996 (134 days elapsed); her SVL was 1060 mm (mass 228 g); her growth rate was 0.08 mm/day. This same female was collected again on 30 Sept 1996 (166 days elapsed), and her SVL was 1110 mm (mass 257 g), indicating a growth rate of 0.24 mm/day. A male 530 mm SVL

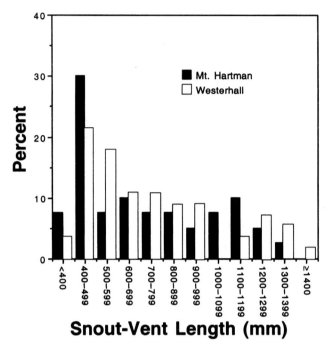

Figure 8.2. Incidence of snakes in 12 size-classes of *Corallus grenadensis* collected at two sites on Grenada.

(mass 19.5 g) *C. grenadensis* was first captured on 8 Oct 1996; it was recaptured on 2 Feb 1998 (482 days elapsed) and its SVL was 830 mm (mass 71 g); growth rate was 0.62 mm/day. Not surprisingly, growth rate is higher in the smaller/younger snake. The differences in the two growth rates determined for the adult female may be attributed to seasonal differences: the slower growth rate occurred during the dry season, whereas the higher rate occurred during the rainy season. I do not have data regarding the relative seasonal abundance of rodent prey on Grenada, but it is possible that *Rattus* densities are higher in the wet season.

Chapter 9

Ecological Relationships
with Other Boids

With ... the long neck looped fantastically in support of the villainous head, an enraged Tree Boa appears far removed from its ponderous allies.

Ditmars 1941

Twenty-two species of boines are known to inhabit the American tropics from northern Mexico to southern South America, on many islands in the West Indies, and on islands on the continental shelf of Central and South America (Table 9.1). In order to get a better ecological perspective of the treeboas of the *Corallus hortulanus* complex, I here present information concerning other members of the neotropical boine fauna.

DISTRIBUTION

Latitude

As a group on the mainland, neotropical boines occur from about 30°N to 36°S. From north to south, boine diversity increases from one to seven species (not necessarily in sympatry) between 30°N and 6°N; there is a general decline in diversity from seven to one species between 3°S and 31°S. *Boa constrictor* has, by far, the widest latitudinal range of any species (ca. 66°), and *Corallus cropanii* has by far the smallest (<1°). The latitudinal range of *B. constrictor* is nearly twice as extensive as any other New World boine. Only the range of *Boa constrictor* extends north of the Tropic of Cancer in Mexico, but six species have ranges that extend south of the Tropic of Capricorn in southern South America—but at least three (*C. cropanii, C. hortulanus, Eunectes murinus*) occur that far south only in the coastal Atlantic rainforest. The ranges of several

Table 9.1. Summary of distribution, size, habitat, and diet in neotropical boines. Unless otherwise cited, the data for snakes outside the *Corallus hortulanus* complex are from Henderson et al. 1995. Max. size refers to SVL.

Species	Range	Max. Size	Habitat	Diet
Boa constrictor	Mexico to southern South America	ca. 5.0 m	desert to rainforest; largely ground-dwelling	fishes, lizards, birds, mammals
Corallus annulatus	Central America, northwestern South America	1.447 m	wet forest; arboreal	mammals?
Corallus blombergi	Pacific lowlands of Ecuador and southern Colombia	1.433 m	wet forest; arboreal	mammals?
Corallus caninus	Amazonia, Guianas	1.53 m	rainforest; arboreal	mammals
Corallus cookii	St. Vincent	1.374 m	orchards to rainforest; arboreal	lizards (anoles) and mammals
Corallus cropanii	southeastern Brazil	1.34 m	forest? arboreal	mammals[1]
Corallus grenadensis	Grenada Bank	1.625 m	xeric scrub to rainforest; arboreal	lizards (anoles) and mammals
Corallus hortulanus	Amazonia and Guianas southeastern Brazil	1.78 m	scrub forest to rainforest; arboreal	birds and mammals

Table 9.1. (*Continued*)

Species	Range	Max. Size	Habitat	Diet
Corallus ruschenbergerii	southern Central America and northern South America	1.87 m	plantations to rainforest; arboreal	lizards, birds, mammals
Epicrates angulifer	Cuba	ca. 4.0 m	wooded areas; largely ground-dwelling[2]	lizards, birds, mammals[2]
Epicrates cenchria	southern Central America to southern South America	ca. 2.0 m	near desert to rainforest	lizards, birds, mammals
Epicrates chrysogaster	southern Bahama Islands	1.3 m	xeric to mesic; barren to wooded; largely ground-dwelling[2]	lizards? and mammals[2]
Epicrates exsul	northern Bahama Islands	0.81 m	pinewoods; largely ground-dwelling	lizards (anoles)[3]
Epicrates fordii	Hispaniola	0.86 m	xeric to mesic scrub; ground-dwelling to arboreal[2]	lizards (anoles), mammals[4]
Epicrates gracilis	Hispaniola	0.9 m	lowland wooded areas; arboreal[2]	lizards (anoles)[4]

Table 9.1. (*Continued*)

Species	Range	Max. Size	Habitat	Diet
Epicrates inornatus	Puerto Rico	1.86 m	rainforest, karst forest; disturbed areas; largely ground-dwelling[2]	mammals[2]
Epicrates monensis	Puerto Rico Bank	1.01 m	xeric woodland and scrub; arboreal[2]	lizards (anoles)[2]
Epicrates striatus	Bahama Islands and Hispaniola	2.33 m	xeric to mesic forested areas; active on the ground and in trees[2]	lizards (anoles), birds, mammals[4]
Epicrates subflavus	Jamaica	2.0 m	moist limestone forests; active on the ground and in trees[2]	lizards(?), birds (?), mammals[2]
Eunectes deschauenseei	northeastern South America	ca. 3.0 m	largely aquatic	mammals?
Eunectes murinus	Amazonia, Guianas and llanos to southeastern Brazil	ca. 8.0 m	llanos to rainforest; largely aquatic	fishes, reptiles birds, mammals
Eunectes notaeus	southern South America; pantanal	3.54 m	open flooded areas; largely aquatic	fishes, reptiles, birds, mammals[5]

[1]Marques and Cavalheiro (1998); [2]Tolson and Henderson (1993); [3]Rodríguez-Robles and Greene (1996); [4]Henderson et al. (1987); [5]Strüssmann (1997).

widespread species plus the entire range of *C. cropanii* terminate in southeastern Brazil at about 24°–28°S. That roughly corresponds to the 1500 mm isohyet and the southern limit of the Atlantic forest. Not surprisingly, the size of the latitudinal range of boines on the mainland is correlated (Pearson Rank Correlation Procedure) with the number of described subspecies (range = 0–9) for each species on the South American mainland (r = 0.69021, $P < 0.03$) and the number of morphoclimatic domains inhabited by each species (range = 1–11); r = 0.88760, $P < 0.0006$).

Eleven species of boines (two species of *Corallus* and nine species of *Epicrates*) are endemic to the West Indies. With the exception of the Cuban endemic *Epicrates angulifer* (maximum SVL about 4.0 m), none attains a SVL in excess of 2.5 m. *Boa constrictor* occurs on Dominica and St. Lucia, with each island having an endemic subspecies. The latitudinal range of the West Indian boine fauna extends from about 26°53′N (*E. striatus* is the northernmost species) south to about 12°N (*C. grenadensis* is the southernmost species). *Epicrates striatus* has the widest latitudinal range among West Indian boines (<10°), and it is the only West Indian endemic that occurs on more than one island bank. *Corallus cookii* has a latitudinal range of about 15′, and that of *C. grenadensis* is about 1°.

Vegetation

Table 9.2 summarizes the distribution of boines in South America in regard to the distribution of vegetation. Rainforest harbors more species than any other category of vegetation, and areas that are dry and/or largely treeless harbor the fewest. *Boa constrictor* occurs in more categories than any other species, followed by *E. cenchria*, *C. hortulanus*, *E. murinus*, and *C. ruschenbergerii*. The other five species appear to have narrower habitat requirements. The number of purported subspecies described for each species on the South American mainland is positively correlated with the number of vegetation zones (n = 1–15) in which that species occurs (Pearson Correlation Procedure, r = 0.85940, $P < 0.0014$). It is difficult to make valid comparisons between mainland and West Indian taxa without comparable vegetation classifications. Nevertheless, on Grenada *C. grenadensis* has an almost ubiquitous distribution from sea level to about 300 m asl, occurring in habitats ranging from xeric scrub to rainforest (see Table 3.1).

Climate

Effects of temperature in regard to the mainland boine fauna are critical only when examining the northern and southern boundaries of the latitudinally wide ranging species *B. constrictor*, where mean winter temperature of 10°C

Table 9.2. Distribution of boines in South American vegetation/edaphic zones (based on a map in Campell and Lamar 1989).

Vegetation Zone	Boa[1]	Corallus annulatus	Corallus blombergi	Corallus caninus	Corallus cropanii
Subhumid deciduous forest	×				
Lower montane wet forest	×				
Sclerophyllus woodland	×				
Evergreen shrubland	×				
Rainforest	×	×	×	×	
Atlantic forest	×				×
Pantanal	×				
Wet palm grassland	×				
Montane deciduous scrub	×				
Flooded grassland	×[2]				
Cerrado	×			×	
Lowland dry forest/ thorn forest	×				
Savanna/grassland with woody species	×				
Caatinga	×				
Chaco	×				
Desert/deciduous thicket	×				

[1]*Boa* = *Boa constrictor*.

[2]Although locality records for *B. constrictor* and *E. cenchria* occur in the flooded grasslands, I feel the species occur only in gallery forest or forest remnants associated with this vegetation class.

Eunectes notaeus has been omitted as its distribution is not sympatric with any species of *Corallus*.

Corallus hortulanus	*Corallus ruschenbergerii*	*Epicrates cenchria*	*Eunectes deschauenseei*	*Eunectes murinus*
		×		
		×		
×	×	×		×
×		×		×
		×		×
		×		×
	×	×		
		$×^2$	×	×
×		×		×
	×	×		
×	×	×		×
$×^3$		×		
		×		

[3]Although *C. hortulanus* occurs within the boundaries of the area generally designated as caatinga, it does not occur in typical caatinga vegetation (Puorto and Henderson 1994).

appears to determine the northern and southern geographic limits for the species. Conversely, patterns of rainfall bear strong influence on the distribution of reptiles, including boine snakes. Mainland boines occur in areas with annual rainfall regimes that range from <100 mm to >3000 mm. Most occur in regimes that average 1500–3000 mm annually. Only *Boa, C. hortulanus, C. ruschenbergerii*, and *E. cenchria* occur in areas where annual rainfall is <1500 mm annually, but they also occur in areas that receive in excess of 3000 mm annually. On Venezuela's Península de Paraguaná, *Boa constrictor* and *E. cenchria* occur in areas that receive <500 mm of rainfall annually (A. Markezich, pers. comm.). More dramatically, *B. constrictor occidentalis* inhabits evergreen shrubland in western Argentina that receives only 100–200 mm of precipitation annually. *Epicrates cenchria alvarezi* occurs in areas that receive 300–400 mm annually. In western Peru, *B. c. ortoni* inhabits an area that receives <100 mm of rainfall annually. Although both annual precipitation and boine ranges exhibit irregular distributions in South America, in general I found a positive correlation between rainfall and boine species density (Spearman Rank Correlation Procedure, $r = 0.9750$, $P < 0.05$).

Morphoclimatic Domains

As an index of ecological versatility, I determined the number of morphoclimatic domains (Ab'Saber 1977) included within the ranges of each boine in South America. Three species (*B. constrictor, C. hortulanus*, and *E. cenchria*) utilize more domains than any other species (Table 9.3). Five species (*Boa, C. caninus, C. hortulanus, E. cenchria, E. murinus*) have the broadest ranges and are widely sympatric with each other; all five occur throughout the Equatorial Amazonian Domain (Henderson 1994; Henderson et al. 1995). The range of *C. caninus* is the fifth largest among the mainland boines, but it exhibits narrow ecological breadth.

Not surprisingly, species with more limited distributions do not occur in as many domains. *Corallus annulatus* and *C. blombergi* have only limited South American distributions (Henderson et al. 2001). The combined ranges of the two species encompasses about 125,000 km² (in contrast to, for example, *C. hortulanus* which has a range in excess of 3.3 million km²), but where they do occur they are found in tropical wet forest with annual precipitation often in excess of 2500 mm. Similarly, *Eunectes deschauenseei* has a limited distribution in inundated savanna (Campo de Várzea) in northeastern Brazil (including Ilha de Marajó) and coastal French Guiana. *Corallus cropanii* is, based on the three specimens known in museum collections, limited to an area of about 600 km² on the coastal plain of southeastern Brazil in what was formerly Atlantic rainforest in the Tropical Atlantic Domain.

Table 9.3. Latitudinal and altitudinal range and number of morphoclimatic domains (Ab'Saber 1977) within the ranges of boines on the neotropical mainland.

Species	Total Degrees of Latitude	Subspecies[1]	Altitudinal Range	Morphoclimatic Domains[2]
Boa constrictor	ca 66	10/7	0–1500	11
Corallus annulatus	19	0	0–400	2
Corallus blombergi	3.5	0	0–200	1
Corallus caninus	24	0	0–1000	2
Corallus cropanii	1	0	0–50	1
Corallus hortulanus	34	0	0–1000	5–6
Corallus ruschenbergerii	10.5	0	0–600	3
Epicrates cenchria	38	9	0–1000	10
Eunectes deschauenseei	7.5	0	0–100	2
Eunectes murinus	35	0	0–850	4
Eunectes notaeus	15	0	0–250	3

[1]Total number of subspecies/number of subspecies on the South American mainland.
[2]South America only; species with ranges extending into Central America, Mexico, and/or the West Indies (*Boa, C. annulatus, C. ruschenbergerii, E. cenchria*) may demonstrate even greater ecological versatility.

Species in Sympatry

From two to possibly six boine species occur sympatrically in South America and two to three in Central America; north of about 17°N on the mainland *Boa constrictor* is the only boine. Potentially six species occur in a limited area through the narrow range of *Eunectes deschauenseei* in northeastern Brazil and French Guiana. The widest area of sympatry is in the Equatorial Amazon Domain, where five species are widely sympatric (Henderson 1994; Henderson et al. 1995). In the West Indies, only Hispaniola harbors more than one species of boine (*E. fordi, E. gracilis*, and *E. striatus*), where *E. striatus* is widely sympatric with either *E. fordi* or *E. gracilis* (which have more limited distributions), and all three species are sympatric at several sites; see maps in Schwartz and Henderson (1991) and Tolson and Henderson (1993).

Among members of the *Corallus hortulanus* complex, only *C. hortulanus* and *C. ruschenbergerii* occur in sympatry (or syntopy) with other boines. *Corallus hortulanus* is widely sympatric and probably syntopic with *Boa, C. caninus, E. cenchria*, and *E. murinus*. *Corallus ruschenbergerii* is widely sympatric—and probably often syntopic—with *Boa* and *E. cenchria*, moderately sympatric with *E. murinus*, and perhaps narrowly sympatric with *C. hortulanus*.

Insular Distributions of Mainland Taxa

Besides the West Indian taxa, two predominantly mainland species (*Boa* and *C. ruschenbergerii*) have insular distributions (Table 9.4). Not surprisingly, both are species that occur in diverse habitats, and display considerable ecological versatility, i.e., good qualities for colonizing species. Fishermen have reported seeing live *Boa constrictor* floating in the Caribbean between small islands off Belize (B. Sears, in litt., April 1991). They co-occur on several large (>300.0 km²) islands (Trinidad, Tobago, Isla Margarita). Only Trinidad, the largest island which harbors mainland boines and which at one time was connected to the mainland, has four species; Isla Margarita and Tobago each harbor three species. *Boa constrictor* inhabits islands <0.5 km² and *C. ruschenbergerii* occurs on islands as small as 5.0 km² . Besides the endemic species of *Corallus*, only *Boa constrictor* has invaded the Lesser Antilles.

DIETS

Diet provides an informative ecological dimension by which to analyze distributions, especially those that are sympatric/syntopic; size differences in syntopic boines alleviate potential competition for food resources. Mainland boines exploit every vertebrate class, although predation on amphibians is rare and routine crocodilian predation is limited to anacondas. None of the mainland boines are lizard specialists—although juveniles of *Boa constrictor* and *Epicrates cenchria* may regularly include lizards in their diets—and they probably constitute a relatively small proportion (by frequency of occurrence and prey mass) of their diets, in sharp contrast to boines in the West Indies (Henderson et al. 1987; Chapter 5) and Australasian pythons (Shine and Slip 1990). Birds and mammals are the principal prey groups of adult mainland boines. They exploit a taxonomically diverse array of prey that is equally diverse in size, from flycatchers to storks and from small rodents to capybara and deer (Table 9.5). Species representing more than 60 families of vertebrates are consumed by boines on the Neotropical mainland, and I believe that this number will increase when the diets of *Corallus annulatus*, *C. blombergi*, *Eunectes deschauenseei*, and especially *E. cenchria* are studied in detail. Virtually nothing is known about the first three species (all with relatively small geographic ranges), and we know next to nothing about the geographically and ecologically widespread *E. cenchria*. Species that are ground-dwelling and/or large take a broader array of prey types and sizes than arboreal and/or small species. Prey items representing 30 vertebrate families have been recorded from *B. constrictor*, and the anacondas appear also to be prey generalists. *Corallus hortulanus*, the most geographically widespread treeboa, exploits at least ten vertebrate families, but certainly takes prey from others as well (e.g., Didelphidae, Marmosidae).

Prey mass ratios (prey mass/snake mass) in mainland boines range from under 0.10 to more than 0.80 (Greene 1983a; Henderson et al. 1995). In general, larger species prey on a wider array of prey taxa than do smaller species. Because the maximum size prey a snake can consume is limited by its gape, larger snakes are physically capable of ingesting a wider range of prey sizes than are smaller snakes.

DISCUSSION

In general, the neotropical mainland boine fauna occurs at elevations <1000 m asl in a variety of habitats. Plant cover (open or forest) is a critical factor and all species, except for two largely aquatic species (*E. deschauenseei* and *E. notaeus*) with limited distributions, occur in tropical wet forest. Although primarily forest-inhabiting species (*B. constrictor*, *E. cenchria*, *C. ruschenbergerii*) have invaded largely treeless habitats (e.g., llanos), they usually occur in gallery forests or forest remnants associated with otherwise treeless areas.

An obvious but interesting distribution pattern emerged among congenerics. *Eunectes murinus* is very widespread, but its two congenerics have more limited distributions and each at the periphery of the range of *E. murinus*,

Table 9.4. Insular records of neotropical boines with largely mainland distributions. We do not know if breeding populations of the designated boines occur on each of these islands. This table updated from Henderson et al. (1995), and expanded based on information in Porras (1999).

Island	*Boa constrictor*	*Corallus hortulanus*	*Corallus ruschenbergerii*	*Epicrates cenchria*	*Eunectes murinus*
Mexico					
Islas Tres Marías					
I. María Magdalena	x				
I. María Madre	x				
I. María Cleofas	x				
Ensenada del Pabellón (Sinaloa)					
I. de las Iguanas	x				
I. de Bahía las Varas (Nayarit)	x				
Isla Mujeres	x				
Isla Cozumel	x				
Belize					
Turneffe Is.	x				
Ambergris Cay	x				
Cay Caulker	x				
Crawl Cay	x				
Wee Wee Cay	x				
Coco Plum Cay	x				

Table 9.4. (*Continued*)

Island	Boa constrictor	Corallus hortulanus	Corallus ruschenbergerii	Epicrates cenchria	Eunectes murinus
Honduras					
Cayos Cochinos	×				
Islas de la Bahía					
I. Roatán	×				
I. Elena	×				
I. de Guanaja	×				
Isla Zacate Grande	×				
Nicaragua					
Islas del Maíz					
I. de Maíz Grande	×				
I. de Maíz Pequeña	×				
Costa Rica					
Isla de Caño	×				

Table 9.4. (*Continued*)

Island	Boa constrictor	Corallus hortulanus	Corallus ruschenbergerii	Epicrates cenchria	Eunectes murinus
Panama					
Arch. Bocas del Toro					
I. Bastimientos	×				
I. Pastores	×				
San Blas Islands					
I. Suscantupu			×		
Golfo de los Mosquitos					
I. Escudo de Veraguas	×				
I. Taboga	×				
I. Cébaco			×		
Arch. de las Perlas					
I. del Rey (San Miguel)			×		
I. Contadora			×		
I. San José	×				
I. Saboga	×				
I. Perico	×				
Colombia					
San Andrés	×				
Providencia	×				
Santa Catalina	×				
I. Gorgona	×				
I. Gorgonilla	×				

Table 9.4. (*Continued*)

Island	Boa constrictor	Corallus hortulanus	Corallus ruschenbergerii	Epicrates cenchria	Eunectes murinus
Venezuela					
Isla Margarita	×		×	×	
Trinidad					
Gasparee I.	×		×	×	×
Isla Monos	×				
Tobago	×		×	×	
Brazil					
Ilha Grande		×			
West Indies					
Antigua[1]	×				
Dominica	×				
St. Lucia	×				

[1]This is an extinct population with no historic record (Pregill et al. 1994).

Table 9.5. Diets of boids on the neotropical mainland. A plus sign ($+$) indicates that a member of the family has been recorded in the diet of that species; a ($-$) indicates that the family has not been recorded, and a (?) indicates 1) uncertainty as whether or not the family is exploited by a species for which no detailed diet data are available (e.g., *Eunectes deschauenseei*), or 2) uncertainty as to from which snake species the prey item was recovered (*Corallus hortulanus* or *C. ruschenbergerii*).

Prey[1]	Boa	*Corallus annulatus*	*Corallus blombergi*	*Corallus caninus*	*Corallus cropanii*
Fishes	+	−	−	−	−
Cichlidae	−	−	−	−	−
Characidae	−	−	−	−	−
Serrasalmidae	−	−	−	−	−
Doradidae?	−	−	−	−	−
Amphibians					
Frog	−	−	−	−	−
Microhylidae	−	−	−	−	−
Hylidae	−	−	−	−	−
Reptiles					
Turtles					
Chelidae	−	−	−	−	−
Pelomedusidae	−	−	−	−	−
Lizards					
Gekkonidae	−	−	−	+	−
Polychrotidae	−	−	−	−	−
Corytophanidae	−	−	−	−	−
Iguanidae	+	−	−	−	−
Teiidae	+	−	−	−	−
Snakes					
Boidae	−	−	−	−	−
Crocodilians					
Alligatoridae	−	−	−	−	−
Crocodylidae	−	−	−	−	−

Corallus hortulanus	Corallus ruschenbergerii	Epicrates cenchria	Eunectes deschauenseei	Eunectes murinus	Eunectes notaeus
−	−	−	?	+	+
−	−	−	−	−	+
−	−	−	−	−	+
−	−	−	−	−	+
−	−	−	−	−	+
−	−	+	−	+	−
?	?	−	−	−	−
+	−	−	−	−	−
			?		
−	−	−	−	+	+
−	−	−	−	+	−
−	−	−	−	−	−
+	−	−	−	−	−
−	+	−	−	−	−
−	−	−	−	+	−
−	−	+	−	+	+
−	−	−	−	+	−
−	−	−	?	+	+
−	−	−	−	+	−

Table 9.5. (*Continued*)

Prey[1]	Boa	Corallus annulatus	Corallus blombergi	Corallus caninus	Corallus cropanii
Birds					
Thraupidae	+	−	−	−	−
Psittacidae	+	−	−	−	−
Caprimulgidae	−	−	−	−	−
Formicariidae	+	−	−	−	−
Phalacrocoracidae	−	−	−	−	−
Ardeidae	−	−	−	−	−
Threskiornithidae	−	−	−	−	−
Tinamidae	+	−	−	−	−
Rheidae	+	−	−	−	−
Phasianidae	+	−	−	−	−
Columbidae	+	−	−	−	−
Aramidae	−	−	−	−	−
Jacanidae	−	−	−	−	−
Charadriidae	−	−	−	−	−
Ciconiidae	−	−	−	−	−
Anhimidae	−	−	−	−	−
Emberizidae	+	−	−	−	−
Alcedinidae	−	−	−	−	−
Tyrannidae	+	−	−	−	−
Pipridae	−	−	−	−	−
Icteridae	−	−	−	−	−
Mammals					
Marsupials					
Didelphidae	+	−	−	−	−
Marmosidae	−	−	−	+	+
Edentates					
Myrmecophagidae	+	−	−	−	−
Dasypodidae	+	−	−	−	−
Chiroptera	+				
Phyllostomidae	−	−	−	−	−
Vespertillionidae	−	−	−	−	−
Primates					
Callitrichidae	+	−	−	−	−
Cebidae	+	−	−	−	−
Hominidae	−	−	−	−	−

Corallus *hortulanus*	*Corallus* *ruschenbergerii*	*Epicrates* *cenchria*	*Eunectes* *deschauenseei*	*Eunectes* *murinus*	*Eunectes* *notaeus*
	+		?		
−	−	−	−	−	−
+	−	−	−	−	−
+	−	−	−	−	−
−	−	+	−	−	−
−	−	−	−	+	+
−	−	−	−	−	+
−	−	−	−	−	+
−	−	−	−	−	−
−	−	−	−	−	−
−	−	−	−	−	−
−	−	−	−	−	−
−	−	−	−	−	+
−	−	−	−	+	−
−	−	−	−	−	+
−	−	−	−	+	+
−	−	−	−	+	+
−	−	−	−	−	−
+	−	−	−	−	−
+	−	−	−	+	−
+	−	−	−	−	−
−	−	−	−	−	+
−	−	−	−	−	+
−	+	−	−	−	−
−	−	−	−	+	−
−	−	−	−	−	−
+	+	+	−	−	−
+	−	−	−	−	−
−	−	−	−	−	−
−	−	−	−	−	−
−	−	−	−	+	−

Table 9.5. (*Continued*)

Prey[1]	Boa	Corallus annulatus	Corallus blombergi	Corallus caninus	Corallus cropanii
Mammals (*cont.*)					
Carnivores					
Procyonidae	+	−	−	−	−
Herpestidae	+	−	−	−	−
Canidae	+	−	−	−	−
Felidae	+	−	−	−	−
Perissodactyls					
Tapiridae	−	−	−	−	−
Artiodactyls					
Tayassuidae	−	−	−	−	−
Cervidae	+	−	−	−	−
Bovidae	+	−	−	−	−
Rodents			?		?
Sciuridae	+	−	−	−	−
Muridae	+	+	−	+	−
Erethizontidae	+	−	−	−	−
Hydrochaeridae	−	−	−	−	−
Caviidae	+	−	−	−	−
Chinchillidae	+	−	−	−	−
Agoutidae	+	−	−	−	−
Dasyproctidae	+	−	−	−	−
Echimyidae	+	−	−	−	−
Lagomorphs					
Leporidae	+	−	−	−	−

[1]Sources of information on prey: *Boa* (Beebe 1946; Greene 1983b; Henderson et al. 1995; Martins and Oliveira 1998; Boback et al. 2000; Sironi et al. 2000); *Corallus annulatus* (Henderson et al. 1995); *C. caninus* (Henderson 1993c; Pough et al. 1998: Fig. 8–19); *C. cropanii* (Marques and Cavalheiro 1998); *C. hortulanus* (Chapter 5); *C. ruschenbergerii* (Chapter 5); *Epicrates cenchria* (Vitt and Vangilder

one at the northeastern edge (*E. deschauenseei*) and the other at the southern edge (*E. notaeus*). Apparently *E. deschauenseei* and *E. murinus* occur syntopically (e.g., on Ilha de Marajó), but in the Pantanal *E. notaeus* occurs in the central swampy regions and *E. murinus* is restricted to peripheral streams (Henderson et al. 1995). Similarly, the widespread species *Corallus hortulanus* has a congener (*C. cropanii*) with a limited distribution at the southeastern

Corallus hortulanus	*Corallus ruschenbergerii*	*Epicrates cenchria*	*Eunectes deschauenseei*	*Eunectes murinus*	*Eunectes notaeus*
−	−	−	−	−	+
−	+	−	−	−	−
−	−	−	−	−	+
−	−	−	−	−	−
−	−	−	−	+	−
−	−	−	−	+	−
−	−	−	−	+	−
−	−	−	−	−	−
+	+	+	−	+	+
−	−	−	−	−	−
−	−	−	−	+	+
−	−	+	−	−	+
−	−	−	−	−	−
−	−	−	−	+	−
−	−	−	−	+	+
+	−	+	−	−	−
−	−	−	−	−	

1983; Martins and Oliveira 1998); *E. murinus* (Strimple 1993; Henderson et al. 1995; Martins and Oliveira 1998; W.W. Lamar, in litt., April 2000; Valderrama and Thorbjarnarson 2001); *E. notaeus* (Strüssmann and Sazima 1991; Strüssmann 1997; Waller et al. 2001).

boundary of its range. Although *Corallus hortulanus* and *C. caninus* are widely sympatric, *C. hortulanus* exhibits much greater ecological versatility than does *C. caninus*, occurring in a wider variety of habitats and rainfall regimes and exploiting a wider taxonomic range of prey species (Henderson 1993c; Stafford and Henderson 1996). Where this pattern occurs, the species with more limited distributions occur outside of, or at the periphery of, the Equatorial Amazon Domain.

Boa constrictor has a broader geographic, altitudinal, climatic, and ecological (e.g., habitat, diet) range than any other New World boine; it is comparable to one of Vanzolini's (1988) "patternless" lizard distributions. It is a habitat (see Tables 9.1 and 9.2) and diet (see Table 9.5) generalist that has successfully colonized many islands and remains common in human-disturbed habitats. It is likely, however, that *B. constrictor* actually comprises several species. Beside *B. constrictor*, three other species (*C. hortulanus, C. ruschenbergerii, E. cenchria*) demonstrate considerable ecological versatility. Besides occurring in a wide range of natural situations, these three species, like *B. constrictor*, thrive in drastically modified habitats. But among neotropical boines, adaptation to an altered environment is best exemplified by *C. grenadensis* on Grenada: it is abundant in fruit orchards, living in tree species that did not occur on the island 300 years ago, preying on rodents that did not occur on the island 500 years ago, and avoiding predators that arrived within the last century (Henderson et al. 1996).

At the other end of the spectrum are the species with what appear to be more specialized requirements. Although the anacondas are trophic generalists, they are restricted to aquatic habitats, and *E. deschauenseei* and *E. notaeus* have restricted distributions. *Eunectes murinus* is geographically widespread, restricted to aquatic habitats, and a trophic generalist. Its habitat requirements and ability to subdue and swallow very large prey items make it complementary to the boines with which it is widely sympatric. The ecological versatility of mainland species ranges from stenoecious to euryoecious, but it is important to note that, although all euryoecious species are geographically widespread, not all widespread species are euryoecious. *Corallus caninus*, for example, has a broad geographic range, but it is limited largely to one morphoclimatic domain. Its sister species *Corallus cropanii* (*fide* Kluge 1991) is similarly narrowly restricted, both geographically and ecologically.

Chapter 10

Treeboas and Humans

These reptiles possess a somewhat special interest for residents of tropical America, seeing that they are at once a pest and a pest-destroyer in the general economy of nature.

Quelch (1897) referring to boine snakes in Guyana

* * *

Could agriculturalists be persuaded not to slaughter these useful allies?

Urich (1933) referring to *Corallus ruschenbergerii* on Trinidad

* * *

The impact of European man on islands made the changes due to aboriginal man seem minor by comparison.

Fosberg 1983

The impact of humans on the distribution, abundance, and ecology of reptiles, especially on islands, has been well documented in recent years, e.g., Case and Bolger (1991); Case et al. (1992); Henderson (1992); Rodda et al. (1997). There is no reason to believe that human-treeboa encounters in the pre-Columbian West Indies or on the neotropical mainland were not common. Whether involved in subsistence hunting or farming, indigenous peoples had the potential of encountering species of *Corallus* on a daily basis. Today, members of the *Corallus hortulanus* complex have ecologies that are often closely associated with humans: they live in human-disturbed habitats—even entering human dwellings in search of food and shelter—eat prey species introduced into their ranges by humans, and try to avoid predators introduced into their ranges by humans. At most, treeboas and humans have had a shared history of 15,000–20,000 years. For the vast majority of that time, the impact of humans on treeboas has probably been negligible. The past five centuries, however, have witnessed a human population explosion within portions of the range of the *Corallus hortulanus* complex, coupled with rampant habitat destruction or alteration. Today it is difficult, if not virtually impossible, to study the ecology of species of *Corallus* without taking into account human influence. As alluded to in previous chapters, human generated alterations of tree-boa ecology have not always had detrimental ramifications, but in the long run, members of the *C. hortulanus* complex would have been better off without us.

HUMAN HISTORY AND *CORALLUS* IN THE WEST INDIES

Members of the *Corallus hortulanus* complex have demonstrated ecological plasticity in habitat, climatic regimes, and diet. Successful colonization of oceanic islands and persistence in human-disturbed habitats is testimony to their adaptability. During the past 500 years on Grenada, *Corallus grenadensis* has had to 1) change its diet since its probable pre-Columbian rodent prey (*Oryzomys* spp.) is now extinct; 2) exploit tree species and habitat types that were not on the island previously; and 3) avoid potential predators that were introduced from the Old World or from the neotropical mainland (Table 10.1).

Mitochondrial DNA sequences suggest that West Indian populations of *Corallus* are more closely aligned to *Corallus* populations in northeastern South America (Guianas; northeastern Amazonia) rather than the geographically proximal Trinidad and Venezuela (Henderson and Hedges 1995). The strong South American influence in the Grenada Bank-St. Vincent fauna is well documented, but Trinidad or northern Venezuela (e.g., the Orinoco Delta), possibly via Trinidad, have been assumed to be the origin (e.g., Lescure 1987). Trinidad had a direct land connection to South America during the late Pleistocene low sea level stand (Eshelman and Morgan 1985), and is now separated from Venezuela by about 10.5 km of water. There is no geological evidence to indicate that the Grenada Bank ever had a continental connection (Maury et al. 1990). Although the Grenada Bank is situated closer to Venezuela and Trinidad (ca. 145 km) than to the Guyana coast (ca. 650 km), there is evidence for the potential overwater dispersal of treeboas to the southern Lesser Antilles from the South American mainland. Based on Hedges (1996), treeboas dispersed to the West Indies during the Quaternary. Proto-West Indian *Corallus* may have originated in the Guianas (e.g., the mouth of the Essequibo River in Guyana) or northeastern Brazil and reached the West Indies via the Guiana Current (Guppy 1917; Henderson and Hedges 1995; Hedges 1996; but see also Iturralde-Vinent and MacPhee 1999). Thus, *Corallus* had a long history in the West Indies prior to the arrival of humans.

According to Rouse (1989), Ortoiroid peoples (Amerindians) expanded from South America (the coastal regions of northeast South America and

Table 10.1. Summary of critical aspects of the ecology of *Corallus grenadensis* in pre- and post-Columbian Grenada.

	Pre-Columbian	Post-Columbian
Habitat	natural vegetation, native to the Neotropics in general and the West Indies in particular	natural vegetation, but with huge tracts of introduced cultivated orchards (bananas, cacao, citrus, mango, breadfruit, coconuts, nutmeg) and acacia
Diet	presumably predominantly native *Anolis* lizards and rodents of the murid genus *Oryzomys*; occasionally birds and bats	predominantly native *Anolis* lizards and introduced rodents of the murid genera *Mus* and *Rattus*; occasionally birds and bats
Potential predators	presumably native raptors	presumably native raptors; an introduced marsupial (*Didelphis marsupialis*); possibly an introduced carnivore (*Herpestes javanicus*); potentially an introduced primate (*Cercopithecus mona*)

Trinidad, areas inhabited by *Corallus hortulanus* and/or *C. ruschenbergerii*) into the Lesser Antilles about 5000 years before present (yBP). Habitat alteration undoubtedly occurred with their arrival in the region. Archaic Age cultural sites were usually coastal and often near mangroves (Pregill et al. 1994), habitat in which *Corallus* is encountered today. The Lesser Antilles were repeopled by Saladoid peoples from the Guianas about 2000 yBP, and between 1000 and 1400 yBP they split into two groups with the Troumassoids in the Windward Islands. Carib warriors invaded the Windward Islands from the Guianas after 1000 C.E. At the time of Columbus, ancestors of the Island-Caribs (distinct from that group of Caribs on the mainland) peopled the Windward Islands. A human population density estimate for the Lesser Antilles at the time of discovery is 500 per 100 km^2 (Newson 1976), but by the late 1700s "most aboriginal peoples had been extirpated through warfare, disease, enslavement, and interbreeding ..." (Pregill et al. 1994).

The history of agricultural exploitation on Grenada goes back at least 2000 yBP (Bullen 1964, 1965). A similar chronology exists for St. Vincent and the Grenadines. St. Vincent has been recognized as the primary Carib island during the Colonial period, occupying the island from around 1200 C.E. to the mid-1600s (Bullen and Bullen 1972). The first attempt to establish a settlement on Grenada by the British in 1609 was a failure. The first successful attempt was by the French in 1650 (Brizan 1984).

The plantation system ushered in the era of mass clearing of forests for sugarcane. On both St. Vincent and Grenada most cultivable areas were cleared of forests. "In the interior [of Grenada], practically all of the land right to the mountain tops was originally sold to estates, and cultivations were pushed to the highest practicable limit in most cases" (Beard 1949). Between 1700 and 1750, sugar, indigo, cotton, cacao, and coffee were cultivated, with the latter crop the most important. In 1700 there were only three sugar plantations on Grenada, but by 1763 there were 81, in addition to 208 coffee plantations (Brizan 1984). In 1772 there were 334 estates on Grenada, and 125 of them devoted 12,955 ha to sugarcane (Brizan 1984). Grenada, however, did not rely on a monoculture economy, and in the last half of the eighteenth century, it was the leading producer of coffee, cotton, sugar, and cacao in the Windward Islands. Therefore, although considerable land was cleared of trees for sugarcane, other land was planted in trees, albeit for other crops. By 1852, only 2581 ha were planted in sugarcane and, in 1982, 200 years after sugar had reached its economic apex, only 534 ha were devoted to sugar (Anonymous 1982). In the meantime, cacao, bananas, and nutmeg became economically important (2821 ha were planted in bananas and bananas mixed with cacao in 1982). All three provided potential arboreal habitat for *Corallus grenadensis*, although it rarely forages in bananas (RWH, pers. obs.).

In the Westerhall Estate and Mt. Hartman Bay transects on Grenada, *Corallus grenadensis* used a high percentage of tree species not native to Grenada, the West Indies, or even the Neotropics (Table 10.2). Mango (*Mangifera indica*) was introduced into the West Indies (Barbados) in 1742 (Little and Wadsworth 1964), and it was by far the most frequently used tree species by large *C. grenadensis* in the Westerhall transect. Similarly, *Acacia nilotica*, native to Africa and imported to the West Indies for the gum it produces (Barlow 1993), was widely exploited by small to medium size treeboas at both sites, and it was especially prevalent at Mt. Hartman Bay. Although largely circumstantial, and based only on contemporary evidence, the agricultural practices on Grenada may have increased the amount of exploitable edge habitat. This may have facilitated range expansion by *C. grenadensis* which is now ubiquitous from sea level to about 300 m asl on Grenada. Because it requires only a narrow corridor of trees for movements and foraging, expanses of open habitat do not preclude *C. grenadensis* as long as there is at least a single row of trees connecting larger stands of trees.

Table 10.2. Some non-native tree species commonly used by *Corallus grenadensis*. *Acacia nilotica* was introduced for the gum it produces, and *Bambusa vulgaris* was introduced to control erosion on streambanks and road cuts.

Species	Place and Year of Introduction into Caribbean Region	Source
Mango (*Mangifera indica*)	Barbados, 1742	Little and Wadsworth 1964
Breadfruit (*Artocarpus altilis*)	St. Vincent, 1793	Little and Wadsworth 1964
Nutmeg (*Myristica fragrans*)	Grenada, 1843	Groome 1970
Cacao (*Theobroma cacao*)	Trinidad, 1525	Wood 1991
Banana (*Musa* sp.)	"Caribbean," 1516	Barlow 1993
Coconut Palm (*Cocos nucifera*)	Puerto Rico, ca. 1525	Barrett 1928
Citrus (*Citrus* spp.)	Caribbean, late 1490s– early 1500s	Barlow 1993
Acacia (*Acacia nilotica*)	Uncertain	Barlow 1993
Bamboo (*Bambusa vulgaris*)	latter half of 1800s	Barlow 1993
Tamarind (*Tamarindus indica*)	Uncertain	Barlow 1993
Flamboyant (*Delonix regia*)	Uncertain	Barlow 1993

Prior to the arrival of Europeans and the introduction of *Mus* and *Rattus*, it is likely that West Indian populations of *Corallus* fed on murid rodents (Oryzomyini, probably *Oryzomys*; based on remains from cultural [archaeological] sites: Lippold 1991; Pregill et al. 1994), now extinct within the present West Indian range of *Corallus*. Thus, the primary endothermic prey of contemporary West Indian *Corallus* populations is rodents introduced to the islands with the arrival of Europeans. It is possible that the alien rodents out-competed the native species, and there may have been a transitional period of time when *Corallus* was preying on *Oryzomys*, *Rattus*, and *Mus* (but see MacPhee et al. 1999).

Similarly, the only documented predator of *Corallus grenadensis* is the introduced (Allen 1911; Morgan and Woods 1986) marsupial *Didelphis marsu-*

Table 10.3. Factors that may now impact, and impact greater in the future, the ecology of *Corallus hortulanus* complex treeboas. Populations refer to human populations.

Country	1990 Population (in 1000s)[1]	Population Density (km²) (2000)[1]	Population Growth Rate (2000–2010)[1]	Extent of Forest and Woodland (1990) (in 1000s of ha)[2]	% Annual Deforestation (1981–90) (in 1000s of ha)[2]
St. Vincent	116	336[3]	0.9	11	2.1
Grenada	85	275[3]	0	6	+5.0
Trinidad and Tobago	1281	289	1.3	155	1.9
Costa Rica	3015	58	1.6	1428	2.6
Panama	2418	38	1.4	3117	1.7
Colombia	32,978	35	1.5	54,064	0.6
Venezuela	19,735	27	2.0	45,690	1.2
Guyana	796	4	1.2	18,416	0.1
Suriname	422	3	1.3	14,768	0.1
French Guiana	?	?	?	7997	0
Ecuador	10,587	47	1.9	11,962	1.7
Peru	21,550	20	1.8	67,906	0.4
Brazil	150,368	3	1.5	561,107	0.6
Bolivia	7314	9	2.8	49,317	1.1

[1]Data from MacDonald 1992.
[2]Data from The World Resources Institute 1994.
[3]For the year 1990.

pialis. The African primate *Cercopithecus mona* (Cercopithecidae) was probably introduced to Grenada during slave trade (Groome 1970) and has been
observed molesting *C. grenadensis* at Grand Etang National Park. It is likely, of
course, that treeboas fall prey to a variety of other vertebrates (e.g., raptors),
including the mongoose (*Herpestes javanicus*) which was introduced to Grenada in 1876–1879 and to St. Vincent by 1900 (Hoagland et al., 1989), and is
known to occasionally ascend into trees (RWH, pers. obs.).

In addition to an already dramatically modified environment in the West
Indies, human population densities on Grenada and St. Vincent are among the
highest in the American tropics (although projected population growth rates are
among the lowest), and whereas percent annual deforestation is relatively high
on St. Vincent, forests are being replenished on Grenada (Table 10.3). Thus,
despite potentially catastrophic alterations in its ecology, *Corallus grenadensis*
has adjusted to an environment that includes new habitat, new prey species, and
new predators. It is possible that *C. grenadensis* and *C. cookii* are now more
abundant and occur over greater areas on Grenada and St. Vincent than they did
in the pre-Columbian and precultivation West Indies, due in large part to the
increase in the amount of edge habitat available to them.

In light of the impact of humans on treeboa ecology in Grenada, and despite the creation of more edge habitat, it is remarkable that *Corallus grenadensis*
is as widespread and locally abundant as it is. I believe that this can be attributed
to a number of factors: 1) arboreal, cryptically colored, compactly coiled on a
branch, and sheltered by leafy vegetation, it is inconspicuous to humans during
daylight hours. Being arboreal, it is able to avoid some nonhuman predators
(e.g., dogs, largely ground-dwelling mongooses), as well; 2) although it may
actively forage at night, without the aid of a light to detect the eyeshine, it
remains inconspicuous in its leafy arboreal surroundings; and 3) it preys on
common vertebrates (some commensal) that occur in high densities and wide-
ranging foraging is not mandatory for locating prey. In human-altered habitats
in coastal eastern Australia, the python *Morelia spilota* exhibits an existence
(Shine and Fitzgerald 1996) that parallels that of *Corallus* on Grenada.

Nevertheless, if areas become devoid of trees, or as patches of trees
become smaller and smaller, portions of the islands will no longer be able to
sustain *Corallus* populations. As a result of continued development, treeboas in
the West Indies will face at least local extirpations.

HUMAN HISTORY AND *CORALLUS* OUTSIDE THE WEST INDIES

Elsewhere in the range of the *Corallus hortulanus* complex, the history of
humans and treeboas is much longer than that which I have described for the

West Indies. The South American mainland was the staging ground for the dispersal of both humans and treeboas to the Lesser Antilles. Although the time of arrival of humans to the New World is a debated subject, it is probably safe to say that humans and treeboas on the neotropical mainland have shared a common history for at least 10,000–13,000 years (Moseley 1992; Richardson 1994); and although this shared history is two to three times longer than that in the West Indies, the effects are less profound because of the very wide areas occupied by *C. hortulanus* and *C. ruschenbergerii*. That is, species occupying small areas on islands are, in general, more sensitive to ecological perturbation than those with wide mainland ranges (Table 10.4). Similarly, the arrival of Europeans in Central and South America in the 1500s had a less devastating effect on the ecology of an area on the mainland than on a small island.

Among the earliest (13,000 yBP) indications of human habitation near the South American range of *Corallus ruschenbergerii* is at Taima Taima in

Table 10.4. Countries in which each species of the *Corallus hortulanus* complex occurs, and the approximate area of the total range of each species.

Species	Countries in Which it Occurs	Approximate Area (km²)
C. hortulanus	Bolivia Brazil Colombia Ecuador French Guiana Guyana Peru Suriname Venezuela	3,325,000
C. cookii	St. Vincent	311
C. grenadensis	Grenada and Grenada Grenadines St. Vincent Grenadines	357
C. ruschenbergerii	Colombia Costa Rica Panama Trinidad and Tobago Venezuela	475,000

Venezuela (just south of the Península de Paraguaná). The earliest evidence of human activity from the Amazon Basin (at Santarém) is 7000–8000 yBP, although humans had reached southeastern Brazil by 12,000 yBP (Bray 1992). Although it has been suggested that the cultivation of root crops began in the Amazon Basin about 7000 yBP, the first definite evidence comes from northern Venezuela at about 4700 yBP (Newson 1992). Evidence of small-scale forest clearance and shifting cultivation at about 4800 yBP has been found at Gatún Lake in Panama, and evidence of maize cultivation from about 7000 yBP has also been found in Panama (Bray 1992). By the time of the Spanish conquests (1492–1580), there were substantial settlements of indigenous peoples in the ranges of *C. hortulanus* and *C. ruschenbergerii*.

Using Trinidad as a focal area, I attempted to get some perspective on the ecological history of *Corallus ruschenbergerii*. The earliest radiocarbon evidence suggests that Meso-indians inhabited Trinidad about 1000 yBP, and agricultural techniques were introduced to the island by the Neo-indians (Arawak-speaking Saladoid peoples) about 2300 yBP (Newson 1976). When Columbus claimed Trinidad for Spain in 1498, it is estimated that at least 30,000–40,000 indians (probably predominantly Arawaks, but likely some Caribs also) inhabited the island, and according to Newson (1976), "There is no doubt that, relative to other West Indian islands, Trinidad was densely populated at the time of discovery ..." She estimates a population density of about 500 per 100 km². By the time of the first Spanish settlement on the island in 1592, that number had been reduced by 50% (Newson 1976; Brereton 1981).

In pre-Columbian Trinidad crops were apparently grown under a system of shifting cultivation, and the selection of plots of land for cultivation was dependent on physical and cultural factors. Except for the upper slopes of the Northern Range and lowland swamps, most of the island would probably have been considered cultivable. Primary and secondary forests were probably cleared before grasslands, as the sod-forming nature of the roots made the latter the most difficult to clear. Land was cleared by cutting, ring-barking, and burning. The foothills of the Northern Range, perhaps the best *Corallus ruschenbergerii* habitat on the island, have been described as "densely populated with cultivators," and it has been suggested that pre-Columbian burning "must have altered the structure and composition of many Trinidad forests" (Newson 1976). Root crops (e.g., manioc, sweet potato, arrowroot, yam) would probably have been grown with maize, beans, and squash, and possibly with annual pepper, pineapple, peanut, and cotton. Other crops which may have been present, and which might have provided habitat for *C. ruschenbergerii*, include plantain (*Musa paradisiaca*), coconut, and cacao (Newson 1976).

Postdiscovery, the first settlement on Trinidad was not established until 1592. By the early 1600s tobacco was the primary crop for export, but by the late 1600s and up until 1725 cocoa production was the primary industry (Newson

1976; Brereton 1981). The establishment of cacao estates required that the land be completely cleared, after which the trees would have been cultivated for at least 12 years on poor soils. Sugar was growing in Trinidad by 1570, and in 1593 Trinidad was described as being very rich in sulphur, maize, and sugarcane (Newson 1976). The sixteenth century also saw the introduction of citrus trees and the banana proper (as opposed to plantains). Again, these introductions provided potential habitat for *Corallus ruschenbergerii*. By 1777 there were 230 small plots of land in the vicinity of St. Joseph and another 59 near Port of Spain which were cultivated for long periods. This area (St. Joseph-Port of Spain) of high population density and agricultural activity was in the foothills of the Northern Range and just north of the Caroni Plain and the Caroni Swamp; certainly treeboa populations were impacted by human activity, as low elevations in the Northern Range and the Caroni Swamp still harbor *C. ruschenbergerii*. By the end of the eighteenth century (1797), the population of Trinidad was 17,718, or 3.7 persons per km².

A land-use map published in 1802 indicates that about 10% of the total land area of Trinidad was settled, primarily in the mountain valleys from Arima to Diego Martin and in the Naparimas, and in coastal areas (Beard 1946). By 1838 17,700 ha were under some form of cultivation. Sugar prices began to fall in the mid-1800s, and by 1884–1885 the sugar industry was in a depression. It hit a second depression in 1895–1897, and between 1870 and 1900 cacao overtook sugar as the leading export of Trinidad (Brereton 1981).

After the turn of the century cacao cultivation continued to accelerate, but between 1920 and 1934 cocoa prices were depressed and some estates were abandoned. According to Beard (1946), in 1938 31.8% of the area of Trinidad was permanently cultivated, representing areas of fertile soils. Beginning in the early 1900s, large areas of previously unsettled Crown Lands were sold and cleared for agriculture, thereby providing a considerable volume of timber and charcoal. As the cacao industry went into a depression, those persons who previously worked cacao started working timber for a living. When Beard (1946) did the field work for his treatise on the vegetation of Trinidad in 1941, he felt that "a reasonably large proportion of the vegetation of the Crown Lands ... has been disturbed to some extent." In his opinion the Northern Range still sustained areas that showed no signs of human interference and were "... more or less in a virgin state."

According to Beard (1946), most of Trinidad was covered with savanna in the late Pleistocene. The only extensive tract of forest was the Northern Range, with smaller tracts in the Central Range, and, on the south coast, the Trinity Hills. However, at the time of Columbus' voyages, the savannas had shrunk to their present sizes, and the island was covered largely with forests. Based on this scenario, the distribution of *Corallus ruschenbergerii* on Trinidad has probably waxed and waned for thousands of years. The late Pleistocene saw localized distributions, coincident with tracts of forest, but the species may have had a nearly islandwide distribution at the time of discovery. Postdiscovery, the range of *C. ruschenbergerii* on Trinidad has continued to shrink and to be fragmented as deforestation continued and agricultural practices changed. Today, Trinidad is still remarkably well forested (Harcourt 1996). *Corallus ruschenbergerii* has a wide, though splintered, distribution on the island, and the Northern and Central ranges and large tracts of coastal mangroves are its primary strongholds (Henderson and Boos 1993; RWH, pers. obs.).

Currently, human population densities within the ranges of *Corallus hortulanus* and *C. ruschenbergerii* range from 3 to 58 per km^2, and percent annual deforestation (in 1981–1990) ranged from 0 to 2.6%. Lowest annual rates of deforestation occurred in Guyana, Suriname, and French Guiana, as did the lowest human population densities (see Table 10.3). Projected human population growth rates within the ranges of the two species were 1.0–2.0% annually. In contrast, estimates of the human population on the eve of the Spanish conquest in lowland Costa Rica, Panama, and South America range from one to three million (Newson 1992). Armed with the knowledge that members of the *Corallus hortulanus* complex are able to adapt to radically modified environments, it seems unlikely that *C. hortulanus* or *C. ruschenbergerii* are in any danger of extinction in the foreseeable future. However, the threat of local extirpation is high in areas of clear-cutting.

CULTURAL EXPLOITATION

Today, throughout their respective ranges, species of *Corallus* are encountered by humans hundreds, perhaps thousands, of times every day. I am sure that many times these encounters result in the death of the snake from the blow of a machete, a handy stick, or even a gunshot. Why? Many people living within the range of species of *Corallus* mistakenly assume that they are venomous, confusing them with sympatric/syntopic viperid species. They do, after all, have a fairly menacing demeanor. Beebe (1946), at Kartabo, Guyana, noted that "The Indians are deadly afraid of this boa.... The number and length of the fang-like teeth, the swollen posterior portion of the head, the vertical pupils, and the unusually loud hiss of the ... tree boa, all have sinister appearances." In French Guiana, *C. hortulanus* is considered venomous, but it is also believed that killing one will bring bad luck (Starace 1998). According to W.W. Lamar (in litt., 7 May 1998), in Peru, "Locals kill them because ... they think they are *Bothrops*. However, the distinction is slender because they kill all snakes anyway. Nonetheless it is true that they specifically believe *Corallus hortulanus* to be venomous." Similarly, on Ilha de Marajó, at the mouth of the Amazon, *C. hortulanus* is considered venomous. Locals there use the same name for treeboas that they do for the bushmaster (*Lachesis muta*) (W.F. Holmstrom, in litt., 9 Nov 1997).

On Trinidad, *C. ruschenbergerii* is known as "Cascabel Dormillon," *patois* for "sleeping rattlesnake." Cascabel is the common name for *Crotalus durissus* in Venezuela (Mole and Urich 1894). Mole (1924) notes that in central Trinidad (particularly at Arima), *C. ruschenbergerii* is known as the "Mapanare," a name used to designate *Bothrops atrox* (and, presumably, *B. asper*) in Venezuela. Boos and Quesnel (1969) note that its long teeth "sometimes cause them to be mistaken for Mapepires" (= *B. asper* and *L. muta* on Trinidad). Niceforo María (1942) writes that, in Colombia, "Los llaneros suelen confundirla con serpientes muy peligrosas." On the coast of Colombia, *C. ruschenbergerii* is referred to as "Mapaná Tigre" and is considered very dangerous (Dunn 1944; Dugand 1975). It is not surprising, then, that in Venezuela, both *C. ruschenbergerii* and *C. hortulanus* are mistaken for species of *Bothrops* (Roze 1970), and in Colombia it is considerd "muy venenosa" (Medem 1968). This confusion is not limited to *Corallus hortulanus* complex treeboas, however; Schulte (1988) has suggested that one of the primary threats to *C. caninus* in Peru is the confusion with the arboreal green pit viper. *Bothriopsis bilineata.*

As pointed out by W.W. Lamar, many treeboas are killed merely because they are snakes, and for many people that is the only criterion that must be met. On the Grenada Bank, where no venomous snakes occur, *Corallus grenadensis* may still be considered dangerous. According to Dr. S.T. Danforth, based on experience in The Grenadines (in Cochran, 1938), " 'this … snake is greatly feared by the natives, who all insist it is poisonous.' " My experience on Grenada indicates that they are more often ignored as attacked. Although some Grenadians believe that they are venomous, others will kill them only because they are snakes, and still others will see them and go on about their business, letting the "serpent" do the same. I have heard from a number of Grenadians (e.g., Alan Joseph) that treeboas are not as common as they once were. Possible causes for the decline in numbers of *Corallus grenadiensis* on Grenada (in no particular order), as solicited from Grenadians, are as follows: 1) predation by mongoose (*Herpestes javanicus*); 2) predation by the common opossum (*Didelphis marsupialis*); 3) clearing of land/development (for hotels, golf courses); 4) spraying of pesticides on crops (primarily bananas) from airplanes (crop dusting); 5) chemicals in the soil as a result of bombs dropped during the 1983 "invasion."

As early as 1871, Kingsley considered *Corallus ruschenbergerii* to be a useful snake species on Trinidad and it should not be killed. Based on the Trinidad fauna, Mole (1910) divided that island's snakes into four categories from an agricultural perspective: 1) those "which are altogether useful in that

they devour rodents and insects which feed on cocoa and cane and fruit";
2) those "which destroy rats and squirrels but which vary their diet with other creatures useful to agriculturists, such as frogs, toads, and lizards"; 3) those "which are rat eaters, but which are dangerous because of their venomous powers ..."; and 4) those "which feed entirely on birds, frogs, toads and lizards, animals that are in the main all useful to the agriculturist as the destroyers of injurious insects, and which are therefore serpents which can be in no sense regarded as friends of the cultivator." Mole lamented that, although all four categories were well represented in Trinidad, every snake was killed on sight, but acknowledged "Of late years, however, a notion has been gaining ground that some snakes should be preserved as being useful inhabitants of the estates." He hoped that increased knowledge of the Trinidad snake fauna would "be of benefit to the agriculturist in that it will lead to an increase in the number of the useful snakes and to a diminution in the hordes of rats and squirrels which at present levy such heavy toll on our cocoa, cane and fruit crops." That was incredibly enlightened thinking for 1910, and likewise for 2002. *Corallus ruschenbergerii* was one of the snake species he regarded as beneficial to estate owners in Trinidad (Mole 1924).

In Grenada, where it has been honored on a postage stamp (Fig. 10.1), *Corallus grenadensis* is often carried during carnival. Benjamin (1994) de-

Figure 10.1. Postage stamp issued by Grenada depicting *Corallus grenadensis* (as *Boa enadris* [sic]).

scribed the use of serpents (the common name for *C. grenadensis* in Grenada) in the "Devil Mas" or "Jab-Jab." "Blackened to the hilt with stale molasses, tar, grease, creosote or mud and scandalously attired, they were as grotesque in appearance as they were repulsive in their dance. They paraded serpents and frogs in order to terrify onlookers and so obtain payment for their quick departure. It was not uncommon to see living serpents serving as their belts or necklaces." According to Dunn (1993), "About a week before carnival, the snakes are taken from their natural habitat. Their teeth and tongue are pulled out, so they can't bite or sense any object." Apparently the Grenada Society for the Prevention of Cruelty to Animals is trying to put a stop to the use of *C. grenadensis* during carnival. Similarly, Mole (1924), notes that *C. ruschenbergerii* "... is the snake which in Trinidad is usually exhibited at carnival time."

COMMERCIAL EXPLOITATION

In addition to the human-generated impact on the natural history of free-living treeboas, the past 25 years have put the added burden of commercial exploitation on *Corallus* populations. Although treeboas are not exploited for their hides the way larger boids are (e.g., Dodd 1986; Groombridge and Luxmoore 1991; Murphy and Henderson 1997), they are captured and exported for the pet trade. According to Dodd (1986), between 1977 and 1983, at least 4259 *Corallus "enydris"* were legally imported into the United States. I suspect that most of these came from within the range of *C. hortulanus*. In comparison, 550 *C. caninus*, and only three *C. annulatus* were imported during the same time period. More recent figures provided by the IUCN (Alison Rosser, in litt., 6 August 1998) indicate a similar trend: between 1990 and 1996, 13,416 *C. hortulanus* were exported worldwide from Guyana and Suriname, 125 *C. grenadensis* were exported from Grenada (all in 1991), and 207 *C. ruschenbergerii* were exported from Costa Rica (1) and Trinidad and Tobago (206). Again for comparison, during 1990–1996, 6830 *C. caninus* (from Guyana and Suriname) and only nine *C. annulatus* were imported (Fig. 10.2).

In 10 years I borrowed just over 600 preserved specimens of *C. hortulanus* complex treeboas from collections in the United States, Brazil, Europe, and the United Kingdom. I know there were significant collections in South America from which I saw only a small percentage of their specimens or none at all, so let us say that I borrowed only 50% of the perhaps 1200 preserved specimens available worldwide. Now comes the critical fact: Those 1200 specimens, each documented with collecting data in scientific institutions and available to many researchers worldwide, were collected over a period in excess of 100 years. They can be used over and over, and each scientist who examines them has the

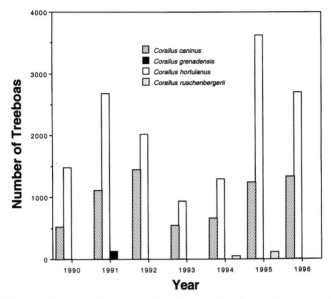

Figure 10.2. Number of snakes representing four species of *Corallus* exported between 1990 and 1996. The *C. caninus* and *C. hortulanus* were exported from Guyana and Suriname; the *C. grenadensis* were exported from Grenada, and the *C. ruschenbergerii* were exported from Trinidad and Tobago (data courtesy of IUCN).

potential of gaining new information about treeboa biology. By comparison, in a 13-year period (1978–1983, 1990–1996), more than 18,000 live *C. hortulanus* complex treeboas were taken from the wild and exported from their countries of origin. In other words, more than 15 times as many snakes were collected for commercial exploitation than for scientific collections, and in about one-tenth as much time. One wonders what became of those 18,000 treeboas, and what we learned from them.

Literature Cited

Ab'Saber, A.N. 1977. Os Dominios morfoclimáticos na América do Sul: Primeira aproximação. Geomorfologia 52:1–23.

Abuys, A. 1990. De tuinboa (*Corallus enydris enydris*) in literatuur, natuur en terrarium (2). Lacerta 48(2):38–47.

Allen, G.M. 1911. Mammals of the West Indies. Bull. Mus. Comp. Zool., Harvard University 54:173–263.

Amaral, A. 1976. Serpentes do Brasil: iconografia colorado. Universidade de São Paulo, São Paulo.

Andersson, L.G. 1899. Catalogue of Linnean type-specimens of snakes in the Royal Museum in Stockholm. Handl. Svenska Vet. Akad. Bd. 24, Afd. 4(6):1–35.

Anonymous. 1982. Land Use Map, Ministry of Agriculture, Office of Land Use, St. George's, Grenada.

Arendt, W.J. and D. Anthony. 1986. Bat predation by the St. Lucia boa (*Boa constrictor orophias*). Carib. J. Sci. 22(3–4):219–220.

Arnold, S.J. 1993. Foraging theory and prey-size - predator size relations in snakes. In: R.A. Seigel and J.T. Collins (eds.), Snakes: Ecology and Behavior, pp. 87–115. McGraw-Hill, Inc., New York.

Astor, I.N.C., J.M.S. Correia, and M.A.S. Alves. 1998. *Corallus hortulanus* (Deer Snake). Predation. Herp. Rev. 29(1):44.

Autumn, K. and D.F. De Nardo. 1995. Behavioral thermoregulation increases growth rate in a nocturnal lizard. J. Herpetol. 29(2):157–162.

Autumn, K., C.T. Farley, M. Emshwiller, and R.J. Full. 1997. Low cost of locomotion in the banded gecko: a test of the nocturnality hypothesis. Physiol. Zool. 70(6):660–669.

Barbour, K. and J.H. McAndrews. 1995. Grenada: the spice of tropical life. Rotunda, Fall 1995:25–33.

Barbour, T. 1937. Third list of Antillean reptiles and amphibians. Bull. Mus. Comp. Zool. 82(2):77–166.

Barlow, V. 1993. The Nature of the Islands. Plants and Animals of the Eastern Caribbean. Chris Doyle Publ., Dunedin, FL.

Barrett, O.W. 1928. The Tropical Crops. Macmillan Co., New York.

Barrett, R. (with appendices by P.F.A. Maderson and R.M. Meszler). 1970. The pit organs of snakes, pp. 277–300. *In* C. Gans and T.S. Parsons (eds.), Biology of the Reptilia. Vol.2, Morphology B. Academic Press, New York.

Bartecki, U. and E.W. Heymann. 1987. Field observation of snake-mobbing in a group of Saddle-back Tamarins, *Saguinus fuscicollis nigrifrons*. Folia Primatol. 48:199–202.

Beard, J.S. 1946. The natural vegetation of Trinidad. Oxford Forestry Mem. 20.

Beard, J.S. 1949. Natural vegetation of the Windward and Leeward islands. Oxford Forestry Mem. 21.

Beebe, W. 1946. Field notes on the snakes of Kartabo, British Guiana, and Caripito, Venezuela. Zoologica 31(1):11–52.

Benjamin, J. 1994. The 'olde' carnival: Jab-Jab, History Mas, wild indians, Shortknee and Pierrot, pp. 146–151. *In* Grenada, Spice Island of the Caribbean. Hansib Publ., Ltd., London.

Bierregaard, R.O., Jr. 1984. Observations of the nesting biology of the Guiana Crested Eagle (*Morphnus guianensis*). Wilson Bull. 96(1):1–5.

Boback, S.M., E. Burroughs, C. Ugarte, and J. Watling. 2000. *Boa constrictor* (Boa constrictor). Diet. Herpetol. Rev. 31:244–245.

Boos, H.E.A. 2001. The Snakes of Trinidad and Tobago. Texas A&M Univ. Press, College Station, TX.

Boos, H. and V. Quesnel. 1969. Reptiles of Trinidad and Tobago. Syncolour, Port of Spain, Trinidad.

Bray, W. 1992. The first human cultures, pp. 168–171. *In* S. Collier, T.E. Skidmore, and H. Blakemore (eds.), The Cambridge Encyclopedia of Latin America and the Caribbean, 2nd Ed. Cambridge University Press, New York.

Brennan, J.M. and E.K. Jones. 1960. Chiggers of Trinidad B.W.I. (Acarina: Trombiculidae). Acarologia 2(4):535.

Brereton, B. 1981. A History of Modern Trinidad 1783–1962. Heineman, London.

Brizan, G. 1984. Grenada: Island of Conflict. Zed Books Ltd., London.

Bullen, R.P. 1964. The archaeology of Grenada, West Indies. Contrib. Florida State Mus., Soc. Sci. 11:1–67.

Bullen, R.P. 1965. Archaeological chronology of Grenada. American Antiquity 31(2): 237–241.

Bullen, R.P. and A.K. Bullen. 1972. Archeological investigations on St. Vincent and the Grenadines, West Indies. William L. Bryant Found., American Studies 8: vi, 1–170.

Bullock, D.J. and P.G.H. Evans. 1990. The distribution, density, and biomass of terrestrial reptiles in Dominica, West Indies. J. Zool., London 222:421–443.

Bullock, T.H. and R. Barrett. 1968. Radiant heat reception in snakes. Commun. Behav. Biol., Pt. A 1:19–29.

Bustard, H.R. 1968. Temperature dependent activity in the Australian gecko *Diplodactylus vittatus*. Copeia 1968:606–612.

Bustard, H.R. 1970. Activity cycle of the tropical house gecko, *Hemidactylus frenatus*. Copeia 1970:173–176.

Campbell, J.A. and W.W. Lamar. 1989. The venomous reptiles of Latin America. Cornell University Press, Ithaca, NY.

Case, T.J. 1978. A general explanation for insular body size trends in terrestrial vertebrates. Ecology 59:1–18.

Case, T.J. and D.T. Bolger. 1991. The role of introduced species in shaping the distribution and abundance of island reptiles. Evol. Ecol. 5:272–290.

Case, T.J., D.T. Bolger, and A.D. Richman. 1992. Reptilian extinctions: the last ten thousand years, pp. 91–125. *In* P.L. Fiedler and S.K. Jain (eds.), Conservation

Biology: The Theory and Practice of Nature Preservation and Management. Chapman and Hall, New York.

Chippaux, J-P. 1986. Les Serpents de la Guyane française. Fauna Tropicale XXVII. Éditions de l'Orstom, Institut Français de Recherche Scientifique pour le Development en Coopération.

Chiras, S. 1998. Identification and husbandry of Amazon Basin emerald tree boas (*Corallus caninus*). Reptiles 69(3):48–67 + 70–75.

Chiszar, D., K. Kandler, R. Lee, and H.M. Smith. 1988. Stimulus control of predatory attack in the brown tree snake (*Boiga irregularis*). 2. Use of chemical cues during foraging. Amphibia-Reptilia 9:77–88.

Clarke, J.A., J.T. Chopko, and S.P. Mackessy. 1996. The effect of moonlight on activity patterns of adult and juvenile prairie rattlesnakes (*Crotalus viridis viridis*). J. Herpetol. 30(2):192–197.

Cochran, D.M. 1934. Herpetological collections from the West Indies made by Dr. Paul Bartsch under the Walter Rathbone Bacon Scholarship, 1928–1930. Smithsonian Misc. Coll. 92(7):1–48.

Cochran, D.M. 1938. Reptiles and amphibians from the Lesser Antilles collected by Dr. S.T. Danforth. Proc. Biol. Soc. Washington 51:147–156.

Cock Buning, T. de. 1983. Thermal sensitivity as a specialization for prey capture and feeding in snakes. Amer. Zool. 23:363–375.

Conway, J. 1998. Island gems: The Pacific boas (*Candoia*). Reptiles 6(10):48–59.

Cooper, W.E., Jr. and N. Greenberg. 1992. Reptilian coloration and behavior, pp. 298–422. *In* C. Gans and D. Crews (eds.), Biology of the Reptilia, Vol. 18 (Physiology E). University of Chicago Press, Chicago.

Coupe, B. 1997. Effects of radio-telemetric techniques on snake movement: Observations from timber rattlesnakes (*Crotalus horridus*). Abstracts, p. 104, American Soc. Ichthy. and Herpetol., 77th Ann. Mtg., University of Washington, Seattle.

Cunha, O.R. da and F.P. do Nascimento. 1978. Ofidios da Amazonia. X. As cobras da regiao leste do Para. Mus. Paraense E. Goeldi, Publ. Avul. 31:1-196.

Daltry, J.C., T. Ross, R.S. Thorpe, and W. Wüster. 1998. Evidence that humidity influences snake activity patterns: a field study of the Malayan pit viper *Calloselasma rhodostoma*. Ecography 21:25–34.

Deufel, A. and D. Cundall. 1999. Do booids stab prey? Copeia 1999(4):1102–1107.

Dirksen, L., E. Buongermini, C. Strüssmann, and T. Waller. 1998. Protective balling-posture in the genus *Eunectes* Wagler, 1830 (Serpentes: Boidae). Herpetol. Nat. Hist. 6(2):151–155.

Ditmars, R.L. 1941. Reptiles of the World. Macmillan Co., New York.

Ditmars, R.L. 1942. Snakes of the World. Macmillan Co., New York.

Dixon, J.R. 1979. Origin and distribution of reptiles in lowland tropical rainforests of South America, pp. 217–240. *In* W.E. Duellman (ed.), The South American Herpetofauna: Its Origin, Evolution, and Dispersal. Monogr. Mus. Nat. Hist. University of Kansas 7:485 pp.

Dixon, J.R. and P. Soini. 1977. The reptiles of the upper Amazon basin, Iquitos region, Peru. Part 2. crocodilians, turtles and snakes. Contribs. Biol. Geol. Milwaukee Public Mus. 12:1–91.

Dixon, J.R. and P. Soini. 1986. The reptiles of the upper Amazon Basin, Iquitos Region, Peru. Milwaukee Public Mus. viii + 154 pp.

Doan, T.M. and W.A. Arriaga. 1999. *Imantodes cenchoa* (Chunk-headed Toad Snake). Aggregation. Herp. Rev. 30(2):102.

Dodd, C.K. Jr. 1986. Importation of live snakes and snake products into the United States, 1977–1983. Herp. Rev. 17:76–79.

Duellman, W.E. 1978. The biology of an equatorial herpetofauna in Amazonian Equador. Misc. Publs. Mus. Nat. Hist. University of Kansas, 65:1–352.

Duellman, W.E. 1987. Lizards in an Amazonian rain forest community: resource utilization and abundance. Nat. Geog. Res. 3:489–500.

Duellman, W.E. 1989. Tropical herpetofaunal communities: patterns of community structure in neotropical rainforests, pp. 61–68. *In* M.L. Harmelin-Vivien and F. Bourliere (eds.), Vertebrates in complex tropical systems. Ecol. Stud., 69. Springer-Verlag, New York.

Duellman, W.E. 1990. Herpetofaunas in neotropical rainforests: comparative composition, history, and resource use, pp. 455–505. *In* A.H. Gentry (ed.), Four Neotropical Rainforests. Yale University Press, New Haven.

Duellman, W.E. and J.R. Mendelson, III. 1995. Amphibians and reptiles from northern Departamento Loreto, Peru: taxonomy and biogeography. University of Kansas Sci. Bull. 55(10):329–376.

Dugand, A. 1975. Serpentifauna de la llanura costera del Caribe. Caldasia 11(53):61–82.

Dunn, E.R. 1944. Los generos de anfibios y reptiles de Colombia, III. Tercera parte: Reptiles; Orden de las serpientes. Caldasia 3(12):155–224.

Dunn, E.R. 1949. Relative abundance of some Panamanian snakes. Ecology, 30:39–57.

Dunn, J. 1993. Grenada's serene serpents: the real story behind the tree boa. Save the Earth J. 2:8.

Emsley, M.G. 1977. Snakes, Trinidad and Tobago. Bull. Maryland Herpetol. Soc. 13: 210–304.

Eshelman, R.E. and G.S. Morgan. 1985. Tobagan recent mammals, fossil vertebrates, and their zoogeographical implications. Nat. Geog. Res. Rep. 21:137–143.

Everard, C.O.R. 1975. Endoparasites of some amphibia, reptiles and small mammals from Trinidad. J. Trinidad & Tobago Field Natur. Club 1975:72–79.

Ewel, J.J., A. Madriz, and J.A. Tosi, Jr. 1976. Zonas de Vida de Venezuela. 2nd ed. Rep. Venezuela Min. Agricult. y Cría, Caracas.

ffrench, R. 1973. A guide to the Birds of Trinidad and Tobago. Publ. No.1, Asa Wright Nature Center. Livingston Publ. Co., Wynnewood, PA.

Forsman, A. 1993. Growth rate in different colour morphs of the adder, Vipera berus, in relation to yearly weather variation. Oikos 66:279–285.

Fosberg, F.R. 1983. The human factor in the biogeography of oceanic islands. C.R. Soc. Biogéogr. 59(2):147–190.

Fritts, T.H., N.J. Scott, Jr., and J.A. Savidge. 1987. Activity of the arboreal brown tree snake (*Boiga irregularis*) on Guam as determined by electrical outages. Snake 19:51–58.

Fugler, C.M. 1986. La estructura de una comunidad herpetologica en las selvas Benianas en la Estacion de Sequia. Ecol. Bolivia 8:1–20.

Garman, S. 1887. On West Indian reptiles in the Museum of Comparative Zoology at Cambridge, Mass. Proc. American Phil. Soc. 24:278–286.

Gerhardt, R.P., P.M. Harris, and M.A.V. Marroquín. 1993. Food habits of nesting Great Black Hawks in Tikal National Park, Guatemala. Biotropica 25(3):349–352.

Gibbons, J.W. and R.D. Semlitsch. 1987. Activity patterns, pp. 396–421. *In* R.A. Seigel, J.T. Collins, and S.S. Novak (eds.), Snakes: Ecology and Evolutionary Biology. Macmillan Co., New York.

Gray, J.E. 1849. Catalogue of the Specimens of Snakes in the collection of the British Museum. British Mus., London.

Greene, H.W. 1977. Phylogeny, convergence, and snake behavior. Unpubl. Ph.D. Diss. Univ. Microfilms Int., Ann Arbor, MI, xii + 112 pp.

Greene, H.W. 1983a. Dietary correlates of the origin and radiation of snakes. Amer. Zool. 23:431–441.

Greene, H.W. 1983b. *Boa constrictor* (Boa, Béquer, Boa Constrictor), pp. 380–382. *In* D.H. Janzen (ed.), Costa Rican Natural History. University of Chicago Press, Chicago.

Greene, H.W. 1997. Snakes: The Evolution of Mystery in Nature. University of California Press, Berkeley.

Greene, H.W. and G.M. Burghardt. 1978. Behavior and phylogeny: constriction in ancient and modern snakes. Science 200:74–77.

Groombridge, B. and R. Luxmoore. 1991. Pythons in South-east Asia: A review of distribution, status, and trade in three selected species. CITES, Lausanne, Switzerland.

Groome, J.R. 1970. A Natural History of the Island of Grenada. Caribbean Printers Ltd., Arima, Trinidad.

Guppy, H.B. 1917. Plants, Seeds, and Currents in the West Indies and Azores. Williams and Norgate, London. 531 pp.

Hall, D. 1982. The Caribbean Experience: An Historical Survey 1450–1960. Heinemann Educational Books, London.

Harcourt, C. 1996. Trinidad and Tobago, pp. 144-150 *In* C.S. Harcourt and J.A. Sayer (eds.), The Conservation Atlas of Tropical Forests, the Americas. Simon and Schuster, London.

Hardy, J.D. 1957. Bat predation by the Cuban boa, *Epicrates angulifer* Bibron. Copeia 1957:151–152.

Hedges, S.B. 1996. The origin of West Indian amphibians and reptiles, pp. 95–128. *In* R. Powell and R.W. Henderson (eds.), Contributions to West Indian Herpetology: a Tribute to Albert Schwartz. Soc. Study Amphib. Rept., Ithaca, NY. Contrib. Herpetol., Vol. 12.

Henderson, R.W. 1990a. Tree boas on Grenada: the colorful puzzle. Bull. Chicago Herpet. Soc. 25(2):21–24.

Henderson, R.W. 1990b. Correlation of environmental variables and dorsal color in *Corallus enydris* (Serpentes: Boidae) on Grenada: some preliminary results. Carib. J. Sci. 26(3–4):166–170.

Henderson, R.W. 1992. Consequences of predator introductions and habitat destruction on amphibians and reptiles in the post-Columbus West Indies. Carib. J. Sci. 28(1–2):1–10.

Henderson, R.W. 1993a. *Corallus enydris*. Catalogue of American Amphibians and Reptiles 576:1–6.

Henderson, R.W. 1993b. Foraging and diet in West Indian *Corallus enydris* (Serpentes: Boidae). J. Herpetol. 27(1):24–28.

Henderson, R.W. 1993c. On the diets of some arboreal boids. Herpetol. Nat. Hist. 1(1):91–96.

Henderson, R.W. 1994. A splendid quintet: the widespread boas of South America. Lore 44(4):2–9.

Henderson, R.W. 1996. Searching for tree boas high, low, and in-between. Lore 46(1): 18–23.

Henderson, R.W. 1997a. A taxonomic review of the *Corallus hortulanus* complex of neotropical tree boas. Carib. J. Sci. 33:198–221.

Henderson, R.W. 1997b. An irascible aerialist: the common tree boa of the American tropics. Fauna 1(1):16–25.

Henderson, R.W. 1998. Back to the future: tree boas, collections, and history. Lore 48(1):4–11.

Henderson, R.W. and H.E.A. Boos. 1993. The tree boa (*Corallus enydris*) on Trinidad and Tobago. Living World, J. Trinidad & Tobago Field Natur. Club 1994–1994:3–5.

Henderson, R.W. and B.I. Crother. 1989. Biogeographic patterns of predation in West Indian colubrid snakes, pp. 479–517. *In* C.A. Woods (ed.), Biogeography of the West Indies: Past, Present, and Future. Sandhill Crane Press, Gainesville, FL.

Henderson, R.W. and S.B. Hedges. 1995. Origin of West Indian populations of the geographically widespread boa *Corallus enydris* inferred from mitochondrial DNA sequences. Molec. Phylogen. Evol. 4:88–92.

Henderson, R.W. and K.F. Henderson. 1995. Altitudinal variation in body temperature in foraging tree boas (*Corallus enydris*) on Grenada. Carib. J. Sci. 31:73–76.

Henderson, R.W. and M.A. Nickerson. 1976. Observations on the behavioral ecology of three species of *Imantodes* (Reptilia, Serpentes, Colubridae). J. Herpetol. 10:205–210.

Henderson, R.W., and R. Powell. 1999. West Indian herpetoecology, pp. 223–268. *In* B.I. Crother (ed.), Caribbean Amphibians and Reptiles. Academic Press, San Diego, CA.

Henderson, R.W. and R.A. Winstel. 1992. Activity patterns, temperature relationships, and habitat utilization in *Corallus enydris* (Serpentes: Boidae) on Grenada. Carib. J. Sci. 28(3–4):229–232.

Henderson, R.W. and R.A. Winstel. 1995. Aspects of habitat selection by an arboreal boa (*Corallus enydris*) in an area of mixed agriculture on Grenada. J. Herpetol. 29: 272–275.

Henderson, R.W. and R.A. Winstel. 1997 [1998]. Daily activity in tree boas (*Corallus grenadensis*) on Grenada. Herpetol. Nat. Hist. 5(2):175–180

Henderson, R.W., J.R. Dixon, and P. Soini. 1978. On the seasonal incidence of tropical snakes. Milwaukee Public Mus. Contrib. Biol. Geol. (17):1–15.

Henderson, R.W., J.R. Dixon, and P. Soini. 1979. Resource partitioning in Amazonian snake communities. Milwaukee Public Mus. Contrib. Biol. Geol. 22:1–11.

Henderson, R.W., R.A. Sajdak, and R.A. Winstel. 1998. Habitat utilization by the arboreal boa *Corallus grenadensis* in two ecologically disparate habitats on Grenada. Amphibia-Reptilia 19:203–214.

Henderson, R.W., R.A. Winstel, and J. Friesch. 1996. *Corallus enydris* (Serpentes: Boidae) in the post-Columbian West Indies: new habitats, new prey species, and new predators, pp. 417–423. *In* R. Powell and R.W. Henderson (eds.), Contributions to West Indian Herpetology: A Tribute to Albert Schwartz. Soc. Study Amphib. Rept., Ithaca, NY. Contrib. Herpetol. Vol. 12.

Henderson, R.W., M. Höggren, W.W. Lamar, and L.W. Porras. 2001. Distribution and variation in the neotropical treeboa *Corallus annulatus* (Serpentes: Boidae). Stud. Neotrop. Fauna Environ. 36(1):39–47.

Henderson, R.W., T.A. Noeske-Hallin, J.A. Ottenwalder, and A. Schwartz. 1987. On the diet of the boa *Epicrates striatus* on Hispaniola, with notes on *E. fordi* and *E. gracilis*. Amphibia-Reptilia 8:251–258.

Henderson, R.W., T.A. Noeske-Hallin, B.I. Crother, and A. Schwartz. 1988. The diets of Hispaniolan colubrid snakes II: prey species, prey size, and phylogeny. Herpetologica 44:55–70.

Henderson, R.W., T. Waller, P. Miccuci, G. Puorto, and R.W. Bourgeois. 1995. Ecological correlates and patterns in the distribution of neotropical boines (Serpentes: Boidae): a preliminary assessment. Herpetol. Nat. Hist. 3(1):15–27.

Hertz, P.E. 1981. Adaptations to altitude in two West Indian anoles (Reptilia: Iguanidae): field thermal biology and physiological ecology. J. Zool. Soc. London 195: 25–37.

Hoagland. D.B., G.R. Horst, and C.W. Kilpatrick. 1989. Biogeography and population biology of the mongoose in the West Indies, pp. 611–633. *In* C.A. Woods (ed.), Biogeography of the West Indies: Past, Present, and Future. Sandhill Crane Press, Gainesville, FL.

Hoge, A.R. and P. Souza Santos. 1953. Submicroscopic structure of "stratum corneum" of snakes. Science 118:410–411.

Hoge, A.R., S.A.R.W.D.L. Romano, and C.L. Cordeiro. 1976/77 [1978]. Contribuiçao ao conhecimento das serpentes do Maranhão, Brasil [Serpentes: *Boidae, Colubridae e Viperidae*]. Mem. Inst. Butantan 40/41:37–52.

Hoogmoed, M.S. 1979. The herpetofauna of the Guianan region, pp. 241–279. *In* W.E. Duellman (ed.), The South American Herpetofauna: Its origin, Evolution, and Dispersal. Monogr. Mus. Nat. Hist. University of Kansas 7:485 pp.

Hoogmoed, M.S. 1983 [1982]. Snakes of the Guianan region. Mem. Inst. Butantan 46: 219–254.

Hopkins, H.C. and M.J.G. Hopkins. 1982. Predation by a snake of a flower-visiting bat at *Parkia nitida* (Leguminosae; Mimosoideae). Brittonia 34(2):225–227.

How, R.A. and D.J. Kitchener. 1997. Biogeography of Indonesian snakes. J. Biogeog. 24:725–735.

How, R.A., L.H. Schmitt, and A. Suyanto. 1996. Geographical variation in the morphology of four snake species from the Lesser Sunda Islands. eastern Indonesia. Biol. J. Linn. Soc. 59:439–456.

Howard, R.A. 1952. The vegetation of the Grenadines, Windward Islands, British West Indies. Contrib. Gray Herb., Harvard University 174:1–129.

Hueck, K. and P. Seibert. 1972. Vegetationskarte von Südamerika. Gustav Fischer Verlag, Stuttgart.

Huey, R.B., P.H. Niewiarowski, J. Kaufmann, and J.C. Herron. 1989. Thermal biology of nocturnal ectotherms: is sprint performance of geckos maximal at low body temperatures? Physiol. Zool. 62(2):488–504.

Iturralde-Vinent, M.A. and R.D.E. MacPhee. 1999. Paleogeography of the Caribbean region: implications for Cenozoic biogeography. Bull. Amer. Mus. Nat. Hist. 238.

Jes, H. 1984. Beobachtungen an einigen ovovipar gebärenden Riesenschlangen (Boidae). Salamandra 20(4):268–269.

Kingsbury, R.C. 1960. Commercial geography of the Grenadines. Dept. Geog., Tech. Report. 1:iv + 1–39. Indiana University, Bloomington.

Kingsley, C. 1871. At Last: A Christmas in the West Indies. Macmillan & Co., New York.

Kirschner, A. and H. Seufer. 1995. Der Königspython. Pflege und Zucht. Kirschner and Seufer Verlag, Keltern-Weiler, Germany.

Klauber, L.M. 1939. Studies of reptile life in the arid Southwest. I. Night collecting on the desert with ecological statistics. Bull. Zool. Soc. San Diego 14:1–100.

Kluge, A.G. 1991. Boine snake phylogeny and research cycles. Misc. Publs. Mus. Zool. University of Michigan, No. 178.

Kornacker, P.M. 1999. Checklist and Key to the Snakes of Venezuela. PaKo Verlag, Rheinbach, Germany.

Kreutz, R. 1989. Ballstellung bei der Gartenboa *Corallus enydris* (Linnaeus, 1758). Salamandra 25:115–116.

Lancini V., A.R. 1979. Serpientes de Venezuela. Graficas Armitano, Caracas.

Lancini, A.R., and P.M. Kornacker. 1989. Die Schlangen von Venezuela. Verlag Armitano Edit., Caracas.

Lehr, E. 2001. New records for amphibians and reptiles from departamentos Pasco and Ucayali. Herpetol. Rev. 32:130–132.

Lemke, T.O. 1978. Predation upon bats by *Epicrates cenchris cenchris* in Colombia. Herp. Rev. 9(2):47.

Lescure, J. 1987. Le peuplement en reptiles et amphibiens des Petites Antilles. Bull. Soc. Zool. France 112(3–4):327–342.

Lillywhite, H.B. 1987. Temperature, energetics, and physiological ecology, pp. 422–477. *In* R.A. Seigel, J.T. Collins, and S.S. Novak (eds.), Snakes: Ecology and Evolutionary Biology. Macmillan Co., New York.

Lillywhite, H.B. and R.W. Henderson. 1993. Behavioral and functional ecology of arboreal snakes, pp. 1–48. *In* R.A. Seigel and J.T. Collins. (eds.), Snakes: Ecology and Behavior. McGraw-Hill, Inc., New York.

Linnaeus, C. 1758. Systema naturae per regna tria naturae, secundum classes, ordines, genera, species, cum characteribus, differentiis, synonymis, locis. Tomus I. Editio duodecima, Reformata. Laurentii Salvii, Holmiae.

Lippold, L.K. 1991. Animal resource utilization by saladoid peoples at Pearls, Grenada, West Indies, pp. 264–268. *In* E.N. Ayubi and J.B. Haviser (eds.), Proceedings of the 13th International Congress for Caribbean Archeology. Rept. Archeol.-Anthropol. Inst. Netherlands Antilles, No. 9.

Little, E.L. and F.H. Wadsworth. 1964. Common Trees of Puerto Rico and the Virgin Islands. Vol. 1. U.S. Dept. of Agricult., Agricult. Hdbk. 249, Washington, DC.

Longland, W.S. and M.V. Price. 1991. Direct observations of owls and heteromyid rodents: can predation risk explain microhabitat use? Ecology 72:2261–2273.

MacDonald, J.S. 1992. Contemporary size and distribution of population, pp. 151–157. *In* S. Collier, T.E. Skidmore, and H. Blakemore (eds.), The Cambridge Encyclopedia of Latin America and the Caribbean, 2nd ed. Cambridge University Press, New York.

Machado, O. 1945. Observaçoes sôbre ofídios do Brasil. Bol. Inst. Vital Brazil 27:61–64.

MacPhee, R.D.E., C. Fleming, and D.P. Lunde. 1999. "Last occurrence" of the Antillean insectivore *Nesophontes*: new radiometric dates and their interpretation. Amer. Mus. Novitates 3261.

Madsen, T. and M. Osterkamp. 1982. Notes on the biology of the fish-eating snake (*Lycodonomorphus bicolor*) in Lake Tanganyika. J. Herpetol. 16:185–188.

Malhotra, A. and R.S. Thorpe. 1991. Microgeographic variation in *Anolis oculatus*, on the island of Dominica, West Indies. J. Evol. Biol. 4:321–335.

Marques, O.A.V. and J. Cavalheiro. 1998. *Corallus cropanii* (NCN). Habitat and diet. Herp. Rev. 29(3):170.

Martins, M. 1996. Defensive tactics in lizards and snakes: the potential contribution of the neotropical fauna, pp. 185–199. *In* Del Claro, K. (ed.), Anais do XIV Encontro Anual de Etologia. Soc. Brasileira de Etologia, Univ. Fed. Uberlandia, Brasil.

Martins, M. and M.E. Oliveira. 1998 [1999]. Natural history of snakes in forests of the Manaus Region, Central Amazonia, Brazil. Herpetol. Nat. Hist. 6(2):78–150.

Mason, R.T. 1992. Reptilian pheromones, pp. 114–228. *In* C. Gans and D. Crews (eds.), Biology of the Reptilia, Vol. 18 (Physiology E). University of Chicago Press, Chicago.

Maury, R.C., G.K. Westbrook, P.E. Baker, Ph. Bouysse, and D. Westercamp. 1990. Geology of the Lesser Antilles, pp. 141–166. *In* G. Dengo and J.E. Case (eds.), The Caribbean region. Geol. Soc. North America, Boulder, CO.

McCoy, C.J. and E.J. Censky. 1992. Biology of the Yucatan hognosed viper, *Porthidium yucatanicum*, pp. 217–222. *In* J.A. Campbell and E.D. Brodie, Jr. (eds.), Biology of the Pitvipers. Selva, Tyler, TX.

McDiarmid, R.W., J.A. Campbell, and T'S. Touré. 1999. Snake Species of the World. Vol. 1. Herpetol. League, Washington, DC.

McDiarmid, R.W., T'S. Touré, and J.M. Savage. 1996. The proper name of the tropical American tree boa often referred to as *Corallus enydris* (Serpentes: Boidae). J. Herpetol. 30(3):320–326.

Medem, F. 1968 [1969]. El desarrollo de la herpetologia en Colombia. Rev. Acad. Colombiana Cienc. Exact., Fis. y Nat. 13(50):149–199.

Miller, G.S., Jr. 1904. Notes on bats collected by William Palmer in Cuba. Proc. U.S. Nat'l. Mus. 27:337–348.

Miller, T.J. 1983. *Corallus enydris enydris* (Garden Tree Boa). Food. Herp. Rev. 14(2):46–47.

Mole, R.R. 1910. Economic zoology in relation to agriculture. Pt. 1. Snakes. Dept. Agricult. Trinidad Bull. 9(65):140–141.

Mole, R.R. 1924. The Trinidad snakes. Proc. Zool. Soc. London 1924: 235–278.

Mole, R.R. 1926. The snakes of Trinidad. Port of Spain Gazette, serial: January 10–July 25.

Mole, R.R. and F.W. Urich. 1891. Notes on some reptiles from Trinidad. Proc. Zool. Soc. London 1891:447–449.

Mole, R.R., and F.W. Urich. 1894. Biological notes upon the Ophidia of Trinidad, B.W.I., with a preliminary list of the species recorded from the island. Proc. Zool. Soc. London 1894:499–518.

Montgomery, G.G. and A.S. Rand. 1978. Movements, body temperature and hunting strategy of a *Boa constrictor*. Copeia 1978:532–533.

Moonen, J., W. Eriks, and K. van Deursen. 1979. Surinaamse slangen in kleur. C. Kersten & Co., Paramaribo.

Morgan, G.S. and C.A. Woods. 1986. Extinction and zoogeography of West Indian land mammals. Biol. J. Linnean Soc. 28:167–203.

Moseley, M.E. 1992. The Incas and Their Ancestors. Thames and Hudson, New York.

Murphy, J.C. 1997. Amphibians and Reptiles of Trinidad and Tobago. Krieger Publ. Co., Malabar, FL.

Murphy, J.C. and R.W. Henderson. 1997. Tales of Giant Snakes: A Historical Natural History of Anacondas and Pythons. Krieger Publ. Co., Malabar, FL

Newson, L. 1992. Pre-Columbian settlement and population, pp. 128–132. *In* S. Collier, T.E. Skidmore, and H. Blakemore (eds.), The Cambridge Encyclopedia of Latin America and the Caribbean, 2nd ed. Cambridge University Press, New York.

Newson, L.A. 1976. Aboriginal and Spanish Colonial Trinidad. Academic Press, London.

Niceforo Maria, H. 1942. Los ofidios de Colombia. Rev. Acad. Colombiana Cienc. Exact., Fis. y Nat. 5:84–101.

Nichols, H.A. 1891. A trip through the Grenadines. Unpublished diary. Gray Herb. Library, Harvard University, Cambridge, MA.

Noble, G.K. and A. Schmidt. 1937. The structure and function of the facial and labial pits of snakes. Proc. American Philosoph. Soc. 77:263–288.

Owen, D.F. 1963. Polymorphism and population density in the African land snail, Limicolaria martensiana. Science 140:666–667.

Oxtoby, G.P. 1989. Zwangerschap van een uitzonderlijk jonge Cooks tuinboa (*Corallus enydris cookii*). Lacerta 47:112–116.

Parker, H.W. 1963. *Snakes.* Norton, New York.

Parker, M. 1990. Study of Laughing Falcons (*Herpetotheres cachinnans*) in Tikal National Park, Guatemala. Raptor Res. Found., Allentown, PA.

Parker, W.S. and M.V. Plummer. 1987. Population ecology, pp. 253–301. *In* R.A. Seigel, J.T. Collins, and S.S. Novak (eds.), Snakes: Ecology and Evolutionary Biology. Macmillan Co., New York.

Pendelbury, G.B. 1974. Stomach and intestine contents of *Corallus enydris*: a comparison of island and mainland forms. J. Herpetol. 8:241–244.

Pendleton, R.C. 1947. A snake "den" tree on Guadalcanal Island. Herpetologica 3:189–190.

Pérez-Santos, C. and A.G. Moreno. 1988. Ofidios de Colombia. Monografia VI, Museo Regionale di Scienze Naturali, Torino.

Peterson, C.R., A.R. Gibson, and M.E. Dorcas. 1993. Snake thermal ecology: the causes and consequences of body-temperature variation, pp. 241–314. *In* R.A. Seigel and J.T. Collins (eds.), Snakes: Ecology and Behavior. McGraw-Hill, Inc., New York.

Plummer, M.V. 1981. Habitat utilization, diet and movements of a temperate arboreal snake (*Opheodrys aestivus*). J. Herpetol. 15:425–432.

Plummer, M.V. 1997. Population ecology of green snakes (*Opheodrys aestivus*) revisited. Herpetol. Monogr. 11:102–123.

Porras, L.W. 1997. Photo of *Atheris s. squamiger*. Fauna 1(2):33.

Porras, L.W. 1999. Island boa constrictors (*Boa constrictor*). Reptiles 7(12):48–61.

Portig, W.H. 1976. The climate of Central America, pp. 405–478. *In* W. Schwerdtfeger (ed.), Climates of Central and South America. Elsevier Scientific Publishing Co., Amsterdam.

Pough, F.H., R.M. Andrews, J.E. Cadle, M.L. Crump, A.H. Savitzky, and K.D. Wells. 1998. Herpetology. Prentice Hall, Upper Saddle River, NJ.

Pregill, G.K., D.W. Steadman, and D.R. Watters. 1994. Late Quaternary vertebrate faunas of the Lesser Antilles: historical components of Caribbean biogeography. Bull. Carnegie Mus. Nat. Hist. 30:iii, 1–51.

Price, R.M. 1982. Dorsal snake scale microdermatoglyphics: ecological indicator or taxonomic tool? J. Herpetol. 16(3):294–306.

Prior, K.A. and R.C. Gibson. 1997. Observations on the foraging behavior of the Jamaican Boa, *Epicrates subflavus*. Herp. Rev. 28:72–73.

Puorto, G. and R.W. Henderson. 1994. Ecologically significant distribution records for the common tree boa (*Corallus enydris*) in Brazil. Herpetol. Nat. Hist. 2(2):89–91.

Quelch, J.J. 1897. The boa-constrictors. Timehri 2(11):294–313.

Ratisbona, L.R. 1976. The climate of Brazil, pp. 219–293. *In* W. Schwerdtfeger (ed.), Climates of Central and South America. Elsevier Scientific Publishing Co., New York.

Richardson, J.B., III. 1994. People of the Andes. St. Remy Press, Montreal.

Rivas, J. 1999. Tracking the anaconda. National Geogr. 195(1):62–69.

Rivas, J.A., M.D.C. Muñoz, J. Thorbjarnarson, W. Holmstrom, and P. Calle. 1995. A safe method for handling large snakes in the field. Herp. Rev. 26(3):138–139.

Rivero-Blanco, C. and J.R. Dixon. 1979. Origin and distribution of the herpetofauna of the dry lowland region of northern South America, pp. 281–298. *In* W.E. Duellman (ed.), The South American Herpetofauna: Its Origin, Evolution, and Dispersal. Monogr. Mus. Nat. Hist. University of Kansas 7:485 pp.

Rodda, G.H. 1992. Foraging behaviour of the brown tree snake, *Boiga irregularis*. Herpetol. J. 2:110–114.

Rodda, G.H., T.H. Fritts, and D. Chiszar. 1997. The disappearance of Guam's wildlife. BioScience 47(9):565–574.

Rodda, G.H., T.H. Fritts, M.J. McCoid, and E.W. Campbell III. 1999. An overview of the biology of the Brown Treesnake (*Boiga irregularis*), a costly introduced pest on Pacific islands, pp. 44–80. *In* G.H. Rodda, Y. Sawai, D. Chiszar, and H. Tanaka (eds.), Problem Snake Management: the Habu and the Brown Treesnake. Comstock Publ. Assoc., Ithaca, NY.

Rodrigues, M.T. 1996. Lizards, snakes, and amphisbaenians from the Quaternary sand dunes of the Middle Rio São Francisco, Bahia, Brazil. J. Herpetol. 30(4):513–523.

Rodríguez, G. and D.P. Reagan. 1984. Bat predation by the Puerto Rican boa (*Epicrates inornatus*). Copeia 1984:219–220.

Rodríguez, L.B. and J.E. Cadle. 1990. A preliminary overview of the herpetofauna of Cocha Cashu, Manu National Park, Peru, pp. 410–425. *In* A.H. Gentry (ed.), Four Neotropical Rainforests. Yale University Press, New Haven.

Rodríguez-Duran, A. 1996. Foraging ecology of the Puerto Rican Boa (*Epicrates inornatus*): predation, carrion feeding, and piracy. J. Herpetol. 30:533–536.

Rodríguez-Robles, J.A. and H.W. Greene. 1996. Ecological patterns in Greater Antillean macrostomatan snake assemblages, with comments on body-size evolution in *Epicrates* (Boidae), pp. 339–357. *In* R. Powell and R.W. Henderson (eds.), Contributions to West Indian Herpetology: A Tribute to Albert Schwartz. Soc. Study Amphib. Rept., Ithaca, NY. Contrib. Herpetol. vol. 12.

Ross, R.A. and G. Marzec. 1990. The Reproductive Husbandry of Pythons and Boas. Instit. Herpetol. Res., Stanford, CA.

Roth, V. 1960. Anaconda produces 16 babies. J. British Guiana Museum and Zoo 26:54.

Roughgarden, J. 1995. Anolis Lizards of the Caribbean: Ecology, Evolution, and Plate Tectonics. Oxford University Press. New York.

Roughgarden, J., D. Heckel, and E.R. Fuentes. 1983. Coevolutionary theory and the biogeography and community structure of *Anolis*, pp. 371–410. *In* R.B. Huey, E.R. Pianka, and T.W. Schoener (eds.), Lizard Ecology: Studies of a Model Organism. Harvard University Press, Cambridge, MA.

Rouse, I. 1989. Peopling and repeopling of the West Indies, pp. 119–136. *In* C.A. Woods (ed.), Biogeography of the West Indies: Past, Present, and Future. Sandhill Crane Press, Gainesville, FL.

Roze, J.A. 1964. La herpetologia de la Isla Margarita, Venezuela. Mem. Soc. Cienc. Nat. La Salle 24:209–241.

Roze, J.A. 1966. La taxonomía y zoogeografía de los ofidios en Venezuela. Univ. Cent. de Venezuela, Edic. Biblio., Caracas.

Roze, J.A. 1970. Ciencia y fantasía sobre las serpientes de Venezuela. Edit. Fondo Cult. Cientifica, Caracas.

SAS Institute Inc. 1990. SAS/STAT User's Guide, Version 6, 4th ed. SAS Institute, Inc., Cary, NC.

Sazima, I. 1988. Um estudo de biologia comportamental de jararaca, *Bothrops jararaca*, com uso de marcas naturais. Mem. Inst. Butantan 50(3):83–99.

Sazima, I. 1992. Natural history of the jararaca pitviper, *Bothrops jararaca*, in southeastern Brazil, pp. 199–216. *In* J.A. Campbell and E.D. Brodie, Jr. (eds.), Biology of the Pitvipers. Selva, Tyler, TX.

Schmidt, K.P. and R.F. Inger. 1957. Living Reptiles of the World. Doubleday & Co., Inc., Garden City, NY.

Schoener, T.W. and G.C. Gorman. 1968. Some niche differences in three Lesser Antillean lizards of the genus *Anolis*. Ecology 49:819–830.

Schulte, R. 1988. Observaciones sobre la boa verde, *Corallus caninus*, en el Departamento San Martín-Perú. Bol. Lima 55:21–26.

Schwaner, T.D. 1985. Population structure of black tiger snakes, *Notechis ater niger*, on offshore islands of South Australia, pp. 35–46. *In* G. Grigg, R. Shine, and H. Ehmann (eds.), Biology of Australian Frogs and Reptiles. Royal Zool. Soc. New South Wales, Australia.

Schwaner, T.D. and S.D. Sarre. 1988. Body size of tiger snakes in southern Australia, with particular reference to *Notechis ater serventyi* (Elapidae) on Chappell Island. J. Herpetol. 22:24–33.

Schwartz, A. and R.W. Henderson. 1991. Amphibians and Reptiles of the West Indies: Descriptions, Distributions, and Natural History. University of Florida Press, Gainesville.

Scott, N.J. 1976. The abundance and diversity of the herpetofauna of tropical forest litter. Biotropica 8:41–58.

Secor, S.M. 1995. Ecological aspects of foraging mode for the snakes *Crotalus cerastes* and *Masticophis flagellum*. Herpetol. Monogr. 9:169-186.

Seutin, G., N.K. Klein, R.E. Ricklefs, and E. Bermingham. 1994. Historical biogeography of the Bananaquit (*Coereba flaveola*) in the Caribbean region: a mitochondrial DNA assessment. Evolution 48:1041–1061.

Sexton, O.J. 1958 [1956/57]. The distribution of Bothrops atrox in relation to food supply. Bol. Mus. Ciencias Nat. (Caracas) 2/3:47–54.

Sexton, O.J., and H.F. Heatwole. 1965. Life-history notes on some Panamanian snakes. Carib. J. Sci. 5:39–43.

Shephard, C. 1831 [1971 reprint]. An historical account of the island of Saint Vincent. Frank Cass and Co., Ltd., London.

Shine, R., Ambariyanto, P.S. Harlow, and Mumpuni. 1998. Ecological divergence among sympatric colour morphs in blood pythons, *Python brongersmai*. Oecologia 116: 113–119.

Shine, R. and M. Fitzgerald. 1996. Large snakes in a mosaic rural landscape: the ecology of carpet pythons *Morelia spilota* (Serpentes: Pythonidae) in coastal eastern Australia. Biol. Conserv. 76:113–122.

Shine, R. and T. Madsen. 1996. Is thermoregulation unimportant for most reptiles? An example using water pythons (*Liasis fuscus*) in tropical Australia. Physiol. Zool. 69:252–269.

Shine, R. and T. Madsen. 1997. Prey abundance and predator reproduction: rats and pythons on a tropical Australian floodplain. Ecology 78(4):1078–1086.

Shine, R. and D.J. Slip. 1990. Biological aspects of the adaptive radiation of Australasian pythons (Serpentes: Boidae). Herpetologica 46:283–290.

Silva, N.J., da. 1993. The snakes from Samuel Hydroelectric Power Plant and vicinity, Rondônia, Brazil. Herpetol. Nat. Hist. 1(1):37–86.

Silva-Taboada, G. 1979. Los murciélagos de Cuba. Editorial Academia, La Habana, Cuba. 423 pp.

Sironi, M., M. Chiaraviglio, R. Cervantes, M. Bertona, and M. Río. 2000. Dietary habits of *Boa constrictor occidentalis* in the Córdoba Province, Argentina. Amphibia-Reptilia 21:226–232.

Smith, H.M. and C. Grant. 1958. New and noteworthy snakes from Panama. Herpetologica 14:207–215.

Snow, J.W. 1976. The climate of northern South America, pp. 295–478. *In* W. Schwerdtfeger (ed.), Climates of Central and South America. Elsevier Scientific Publishing Co., Amsterdam.

Stafford, P.J. and R.W. Henderson. 1996. Kaleidoscopic Tree Boas: the Genus *Corallus* of Tropical America. Krieger Publ. Co., Malabar, FL. x + 86 pp.

Starace, F. 1998. Guide des Serpents et Amphisbènes de Guyane française. Ibis Rouge Ed., Guyane.

Strimple, P.D. 1993. Overview of the natural history of the green anaconda (*Eunectes murinus*). Herpetol. Nat. Hist. 1(1):25–35.

Strussmann, C. 1997. Hábitos alimentares da sucuri-amarela, *Eunectes notaeus* Cope, 1862, no pantanal matogrossense. Biociências 5(1):35–52.

Strüssmann, C. and I. Sazima. 1991. Predation on avian eggs by the boid snake, *Eunectes notaeus*. Herp. Rev. 22(4):118–120.

Thomas, M.E. 1974. Bats as a food source for *Boa constrictor*. J. Herpetol. 8:188.

Tolson, P.J. 1988. Critical habitat, predator pressures, and the management of *Epicrates monensis* (Serpentes: Boidae) on the Puerto Rico Bank: a multivariate analysis, pp. 228–238. *In* R.C. Szaro, K.E. Severson, and D.R. Patton (eds.), Management of Amphibians, Reptiles, and Small Mammals in North America. USDA Forest Serv., Gen. Tech. Rep. RM-166. Ft. Collins, CO.

Tolson, P.J. and R.W. Henderson. 1993. The Natural History of West Indian Boas. R & A Publ., Somerset, UK.

Underwood, G. 1962. Reptiles of the Eastern Caribbean. Carib. Affairs (n.s.), 1. Dept. Extramur. Affairs, University of the West Indies, Port-of-Spain.

Underwood, G. 1964. Reptiles of the Eastern Caribbean. 1st Supplement. Carib. Affairs. Dept. Extramur. Affairs, University of the West Indies, Port-of-Spain.

Underwood, G. 1993. A new snake from St. Lucia, West Indies. Bull. Nat. Hist. Mus. (Zool.) 59(1):1–9.

Underwood, H. 1992. Endogenous rhythms, pp. 229–297. *In* C. Gans and D. Crews (eds.), Biology of the Reptilia. Vol. 18 (Physiology E). University of Chicago Press, Chicago, IL.

Urich, F.W. 1933. Snake v. mongoose. Trop. Agric. 10:5.

Valderrama, X. and J.B. Thorbjarnarson. 2001. *Eunectes murinus* (Green Anaconda). Diet. Herpetol. Rev. 32:46–47.

Vanzolini, P.E. 1988. Distributional patterns of South American lizards, pp. 317–342. *In* P.E. Vanzolini and W.R. Heyer (eds.), Proceedings of a Workshop on Neotropical Distribution Patterns. Acad. Brasileira Ciências, Rio de Janiero.

Vergner, I. 1993. Pozor na hadi boje v terariu ["Beware of duels between snake males in vivarium"]. Ziva 41(4):176–177.

Villa, B. and W.F. Lopez. 1966. Cinco casos de predación de pequeños vertebrados en murciélagos de México. An. Instit. Biol. Univ. Natl. Mexico 37:187–193.

Villa, J.D. and J.R. McCranie. 1995. *Oxybelis wilsoni*, a new species of vine snake from Isla de Roatán, Honduras (Serpentes: Colubridae). Rev. Biol. Trop. 43(1–3):297–305.

Vitt, L.J. 1996. Ecological observations on the tropical colubrid snake *Leptodeira annulata*. Herpetol. Nat. Hist. 4:69–76.

Vitt, L.J. and L.D. Vangilder. 1983. Ecology of a snake community in northeastern Brazil. Amphibia-Reptilia 4:273–296.

Vitt, L.J. and P.A. Zani. 1997. Ecology of the nocturnal lizard *Thecadactylus rapicauda* (Sauria: Gekkonidae) in the Amazon region. Herpetologica 53(2):165–179.

Waller, T., E. Buongermini P., and P.A. Micucci. 2001. *Eunectes notaeus* (Yellow Anaconda). Diet. Herpetol. Rev. 32:47.

Walls, G.L. 1942. The vertebrate eye and its adaptive radiation. Cranbrook Inst. Sci., Bull. 19.

Wehekind, L. 1974. Notes on the foods of the Trinidad Snakes. Br. J. Herpetol. 2:9–13.

Westermann, J.H. 1953. Nature preservation in the Caribbean. Publ. Found. Sci. Res. Surinam and Neth. Antilles 9:1–106.

Willard, D.E. 1977. Constricting methods of snakes. Copeia, 1977: 379–382.

Williams, K.L. 1988. Systematics and Natural History of the American Milk Snake, *Lampropeltis triangulum*. Milwaukee Public Mus. x + 176 pp.

Wood, G.A.R. 1991. A history of early cocoa introductions. Cocoa Growers Bull. 44:7–12.

World Resources Institute. 1994. World Resources 1994–95. Oxford University Press, New York.

Wunderle, J.M., Jr. 1981a. An analysis of morph ratio cline in the Bananaquit (*Coereba flaveola*) on Grenada, West Indies. Evolution 35:333–344.

Wunderle, J.M., Jr. 1981b. A shift in the morph ratio cline in the Bananaquit on Grenada, West Indies. Condor. 85:365–367.

Yamagishi, H. 1974. Observations on the nocturnal activity of the Habu with special reference to the intensity of illumination. Snake 6:37–43.

Zimmerman, B.L. and Rodrigues, M.T. 1990. Frogs, snakes, and lizards of the INPA-WWF preserves near Manaus, Brazil, pp. 426–454. *In* A.H. Gentry (ed.), Four Neotropical Rainforests. Yale University Press, New Haven.

Additional *Corallus hortulanus* Complex Literature

Abuys, A. 1981. De systematiek en kenmerken van de slangen van het genus *Corallus*. Litt. Serp., 1(6):222–237.

Abuys, A. 1988. De tuinboa (*Corallus enydris*) in literatuur, natuur, en terrarium (1). Lacerta, 46:194–198.

Amaral, A. do. 1948. Ofidios do Pará. Bol. Mus. Paraense E. Goeldi 10:149–159.

Austin, C.C. 2000. Molecular phylogeny and historical biogeography of Pacific island boas (*Candoia*). Copeia 2000(2):341–352.

Barbour, T. 1914. A contribution to the zoogeography of the West Indies, with especial reference to amphibians and reptiles. Bull. Mus. Comp. Zool. 44:209–359.

Barker, D. and T. Barker. 1998. A report of a tree boa hybrid. Reptiles 6(3):14–17.

Bartlett, R.D. 1986. Comments on the Amazonian tree boa (*Corallus enydris ssp.*). Notes from NOAH, 14(2):3–6.

Bartlett, R.D. 1988. The Amazonian tree boa: a study in color diversity, pp. 232–234. *In* R.D. Bartlett, In search of reptiles and amphibians. E.J. Brill, New York.

Becak, W. 1965. Constitucao cromossomica e mecanismo de determinacao do sexo em ofidios sul-Americanos. I. Aspectos cariotipicos. Mem. Inst. Butantan 32:37–78.

Beddard, F.E. 1908. A comparison of the neotropical species of Corallus, C. cookii, with C. madagascariensis; and on some points in the anatomy of Corallus caninus. Proc. Zool. Soc. London 1908:135–158.

Boettger, O. 1898. Katalog der Reptilien-Sammlung im Museum der senckenbergischen naturforschenden Gesellschaft in Frankfurt am Main. II. Theil (Schlangen). Frankfurt a. M. ix + 160 pp.

Boulenger, G.A. 1893. Catalogue of Snakes in the British Museum (Natural History). Vol. 1., containing the familes Typhlopidae, Glauconiidae, Boidae, Ilysiidae, Uropeltidae, Xenopeltidae, and Colubridae aglyphae, part. British Mus. (Nat. Hist.), London.

Branch, W.R. 1981. Hemipenes of the Madagascan boas *Acrantophis* and *Sanzinia*, with a review of hemipeneal morphology in the Boinae. J. Herpetol. 15:91–99.

Briceño Rossi, A.L. 1934. El problema del ofidismo en Venezuela. Bol. Minist. Salubr. Agric. Cria, Venezuela Año II [Vol. 1] (14):1079–1177.

Carpenter, C.C. and G.W. Ferguson. 1977. Variation and evolution of stereotyped behavior in reptiles, pp. 335–554. *In* C. Gans and D.W. Tinkle (eds.), Biology of the Reptilia, Vol. 7, Ecology and behaviour A. Academic Press, New York.

Carrillo de Espinoza, N. 1966. Contribucion al conocimiento de los boideos Peruanas (Boidae, Ophidia, Reptilia). Publ. Mus. Hist. Nat. "Javier Prado," Ser. A., Zool. 21: 86–136.

Carillo de Espinoza, N. 1970. Contribucion al conocimiento de los reptiles del Peru. Publ. Mus. Hist. Nat. "Javier Prado," Ser. A., Zool. 22:1–64.

Chiras, S. 1998. Hybrid tree boa. Reptiles 6(3):68.

Cope, E.D. 1876. Batrachia and Reptilia of Costa Rica. J. Acad. Nat. Sci. Philadelphia 2:93–157.

Cundall, D. and A. Deufel. 1999. Striking patterns in booid snakes. Copeia 1999(4): 868–883.

Daudin, F.M. 1803. Histoire Naturelle des Reptiles, Vol. 5. Paris.

Donndorff, J.A. 1798. Zoologische Beytrage zur XIII. Ausgabe des Linneischen Natur-systems. Vol. 3. Wiedmannsche Buchandlung, Leipzig.

Duméril, A.M.C. and G. Bibron. 1844. Erpétologie Générale ou Histoire Naturelle Complète des Reptiles. Vol. 6. Librairie Encyclopédique de Roret, Paris.

Dunn, E.R. and J.R. Bailey. 1939. Snakes from the uplands of the Canal Zone and of Darien. Bull. Mus. Comp. Zool. (Harvard) 86(1):1–22.

Eerden, H. van der. 1986. Striking behaviour of *Corallus enydris enydris* in the terrarium. Litt. Serp. 6(4):126.

Eerden, H. van der. 1987. The breeding of *Corallus enydris enydris* in a terrarium. Litt. Serp. 7(5):243–246.

Foekema, G.M.M. 1974. Enkele notities over *Corallus enydris* (slanke boomboa), met een verslag over verzorging en gedrag van drie *Corallus enydris cookii* in een huiskamerterrarium. Lacerta 32(9–10):151–164.

Forcart, L. 1951. Nomenclature remarks on some generic names of the snake family Boidae. Herpetologica 7:197–199.

Frazzetta, T.H. 1959. Studies on the morphology and function of the skull in the Boidae (Serpentes). Pt. 1. Cranial differences between Python sebae and Epicrates cenchris. Bull. Mus. Comp. Zool. 119(8):453–472.

Frazzetta, T.H. 1975. Pattern and instability in the evolving premaxilla of boine snakes. Amer. Zool. 15:469–481.

Gasc, J-P. and M.T. Rodrigues. 1980. Liste préliminaire des serpents de la Guyane française, Bull. Mus. Natn. Hist. Nat., Paris 4th ser. 2, sec. A, no. 2:559–598.

Gorman, G.C. and F. Gress. 1970. Chromosome cytology of four boid snakes and a varanid lizard, with comments on the cytosystematics of primitive snakes. Herpetologica 26:308–317.

Gray, J.E. 1842. Synopsis of prehensile-tailed snakes, or family Boidae. Zool. Misc. 41–46

Greene, H.W. 1988. Antipredator mechanisms in reptiles, pp. 1–152. *In* C. Gans and R.B. Huey (eds.), Biology of the Reptilia, Vol. 16, Ecology, Defense and Life History. Alan R. Liss, Inc., New York.

Gunther, A.C.L.G. 1895. Biologia Centrali-Americana. Reptilia and Batrachia. Porter, London.

Hardy, J.D., Jr. 1982. Biogeography of Tobago, West Indies, with special reference to amphibians and reptiles. Bull. Maryland Herpetol. Soc. 18:37–142.

Haslewood, G.A.D. 1967. Bile Salts. Methuen, London.

Haslewood, G.A.D. and V.M. Wootton. 1951. Comparative studies of bile salts. 2. Pythocholic acid. Biochem. J. 49:67–71.

Henderson, K. 2001. The snake hunters. Milwaukee Mag. 26(7):48–55.

Henderson, R.W. 1988. The kaleidoscopic tree boa: *Corallus enydris* in the West Indies. Lore 38(4):25–30.

Henderson, R.W. 1991. Distribution and preliminary interpretation of geographic variation in the neotropical tree boa *Corallus enydris*: a progress report. Bull. Chicago Herpet. Soc. 26(5):105–110.

Henderson, R.W. 1993. *Corallus*. Catalogue of American Amphibians and Reptiles 572:1–2.

Henderson, R.W. and G. Puorto. 1993. *Corallus cropanii*. Catalogue of American Amphibians and Reptiles 575:1–2.

Henderson, R.W., J. Daudin, G.T. Haas, and T.J. McCarthy. 1992. Significant distribution records for some amphibians and reptiles in the Lesser Antilles. Carib. J. Sci. 28(1–2):101–103.

Hudson, R. 1983. The reptile reproduction program at the Fort Worth Zoo, pp. 328–349. *In* D.L. Marcellini, (ed.), Proceedings of 6th Annual Reptile Symposium on Captive Propogation and Husbandry. Thurmont, MD.

Huff, T.A. 1980. Captive propogation of the subfamily Boinae with emphasis on the genus *Epicrates*, pp. 125–134. *In* Reproductive Biology and Diseases of Captive Reptiles. SSAR Contrib. Herpet. 1.

Jan, G. and F. Sordelli. 1864. Iconographie generale des ophidiens. Vol. 1, livr. 7. Milan.

Lacepede, B.G.E. 1802. Naturgeschichte der Amphibien, oder der eyerlegenden vier-fussigen Thiere und der Schlangen. Aus dem Franzosischen ubersetzt und mit Anmerkungen und Zusatzen versehen von Johan Matthaus Bechstein. Vol. 4. Industrie-Comptoirs, Weimar.

Laszlo, J. 1983. Further notes on reproduction patterns of amphibians and reptiles in relation to captive breeding. Int. Zoo Yb. 23:166–174. Zoological Society of London, London.

Laurenti, J.N. 1768. Austriaci viennensis Specimen medicum, exhibens synopsin reptilium mendatum cum experimentis circa venena et antidota reptilium austriacorum. Joan. Thom. Nob de Trattnern, Viennae.

Lescure, J. 1978. Singularité et fragilité de la faune en vertébrés des Petites Antilles. C.R. Soc. Biogeogr. 482:93–109.

Maderson, P.F.A. 1970. The distribution of specialized labial scales in the Boidae, pp. 301–304. *In* C. Gans and T.S. Parsons (eds.), Biology of the Reptilia, Vol. 2, Morphology B. Academic Press, New York.

Mendez, D. 2000. Neotropical tree boas. Vivarium11(2):18, 20.

Mertens, R. 1973. Eine für Tobago neue Riesenschlang. Salamandra 9(3–4): 163.

Meszler, R.M. 1970. Correlation of ultrastructure and function, pp. 305–314. *In* C. Gans and T.S. Parsons (eds.), Biology of the Reptilia, Vol. 2, Morphology B. Academic Press, New York.

Mijares-Urrutia, A. and A. Arends R. 2000. Herpetofauna of Estado Falcón, northwestern Venezuela: a checklist with geographical and ecological data. Smithsonian Herpetol. Infor. Serv. 123.

Mole, R.R. and F.W. Urich. 1894. A preliminary list of the reptiles and batrachians of the island of Trinidad. J. Field Nat. Club 2(4):77–90.

Molenaar, G.J. 1992. Anatomy and physiology of infrared sensitivity of snakes, pp. 367–453. *In* C. Gans and P.S. Ulinski (eds.), Biology of the Reptilia, Vol. 17 (Neurology C). University of Chicago Press, Chicago.

Moonen, J. 1977. Enkele veldwaarnemingen op Trinidad en Tobago. Lacerta 35: 187–196.

Monteiro, L.R. 1996. Osteologia craniana de *Corallus caninus* (L., 1758) e *Corallus enydris* (L., 1758) (Serpentes-Boidae). Naturalia, São Paulo 21:187–200.

Monteiro, L.R. 1998. Ontogenetic changes in the skull of *Corallus caninus* (L., 1758) and *Corallus enydris* (L., 1758) (Serpentes-Boidae), an allometric study. Snake 28: 51–58.

Morales, V.R. and R.W. McDiarmid. 1996. Annotated checklist of the amphibians and reptiles of Pakitza, Manu National Park Reserve Zone, with comments on the herpetofauna of Madre de Dios, Peru, pp. 503–522. *In* D.E. Wilson and A. Sandoval (eds.), Manu: The Biodiversity of Southeastern Peru. Smithsonian Institution, Washington, DC.

Murphy, J.C. 1996. Crossing Bond's Line: the herpetological exchange between the eastern Caribbean and mainland South America, pp. 207–216. *In* R. Powell and R.W. Henderson (eds.), Contributions to West Indian Herpetology: A Tribute to Albert Schwartz. Soc. Study Amphib. Rept., Ithaca, NY.

Nascimento, F.P. do, T.C.S. de Avila Pires, and O.R. da Cunha. 1988. Répteis Squamata de Rondônia e Mato Grosso coletados através do Programa Polonoroeste. Bol. Mus. Paraense E. Goeldi Ser. Zool. 4(1):21–66.

Nobuo Yuki, N. and R.M. dos Santos. 1996 [1998]. Snakes from Marajó and Mexiana islands, Para State, Brazil. Bol. Mus. Paraense E. Goeldi Ser. Zool. 12(1):41–53.

O'Shea, M.T. 1990. The herpetofauna of Ilha de Maracá, state of Roraima, northern Brazil. Reptiles: Proc. 1988 U.K. Herpetol. Soc. Symp. Captive Breed. pp. 51–72.

Parker, H.W. 1935. The frogs, lizards, and snakes of British Guiana. Proc. Zool. Soc. London 1935:505–530.

Pérez-Santos, C. and A.G. Moreno 1991. Serpientes de Ecuador. Monografia XI, Museo Regionale di Scienze Naturali, Torino.

Pols, J.J. van der. 1981. Care and breeding of *Corallus enydris enydris*. Litt. Serp. 1(6):238–245.

Prado, A. and A.R. Hoge. 1947. Notas ofiológicas. 21. Observaçoes sobre serpentes do Perú. Mem. Inst. Butantan 20:283–295.

Rentfro, A. 1997. Comments on the incidence of interspecies hybridization in wild populations of boas of the genus *Corallus*. Notes from Noah 24(11):5–7.

Reuss, A. 1834. Zoologische Miscellen, Reptilien Ophidier. Mus. Senck. 1:129–162.

Rivas F., G.A. and O. Oliveros G. 1997. Herpetofauna del Estado Sucre, Venezuela: Lista preliminar de reptiles. Mem. Soc. Cienc. Nat. La Salle 57(147):67–80.

Rocha, C.F.D., H.G. Bergallo, and C. Strussmann. 1991. *Corallus enydris* (Deer Snake). Herp. Rev. 22(1):26.

Sajdak, R. 2001. The cascabels of Caroni Swamp. Reptiles 9(2):10–12, 14, 16, 18, 20–21.

Schmidt, K.P. 1933. Amphibians and reptiles collected by the Smithsonian Biological Survey of the Panama Canal Zone. Smithson. Misc. Coll. 89(1):1–20.

Schmidt, K.P. 1943. Peruvian snakes from the University of Arequipa. Field Mus. Nat. Hist., Zool. Ser. 24(26):279–296.

Schwaner, T.D. and H.C. Dessauer. 1981. Immunodiffusion evidence for the relationships of Papuan boids. J. Herpetol. 15(2):250–253.

Seba, A. 1734. Locupletissimi rerum naturalium thesauri accurata descriptio, et iconibus artificiosissimis expressio, per universam physices historiam...., Vol. 1. Janssonio-Waesbergios & J. Wetstenium & J. Smith, Amsterdam.

Seba, A. 1735. Locupletissimi rerum naturalium thesauri accurata descriptio, et iconibus artificiosissimis expressio, per universam physices historiam...., Vol. 2. Janssonio-Waesbergios & J. Wetstenium & J. Smith, Amsterdam.

Sentzen, U.I. 1796. Ophiologische Fragmente. Meyer's Zool. Arch. pp. 49–74.

Spix, J.B. von. 1824. Serpentum brasiliensium species novae ou histoire naturelle des especes nouvelles de serpens, recueillies et observees pendant le voyage dans l'interieur du Bresil dans les annees 1817, 1818, 1819, 1820, execute par ordre de sa majeste le Roi de Baviere. Typis Franc. Seraph. Hubschmanni, Monachii.

Stafford, P.J. 1981. Observations on the captive breeding of Cook's tree boa (*Corallus enydris cookii*). The Herptile, 6(4):15–17.

Stafford, P.J. 1986. Notes on the distribution, habits and various colour morphs of Cook's tree boa (*Corallus enydris cookii* Gray). Litt. Serp. 6(4):147–154.

Staton, M.A. and J.R. Dixon. 1977. The herpetofauna of the central llanos of Venezuela: noteworthy records, a tentative checklist and ecological notes. J. Herpetol. 11(1): 17–24.

Stejneger, L. 1901. An annotated list of batrachians and reptiles collected in the vicinity of La Guaira, Venezuela, with descriptions of two new species of snakes. Proc. U.S. Nat'l. Mus. 24:179–192.

Stemmler, O. and Z. Vesely. 1968. Eine interesante Form der Gartenboa (*Corallus enydris* ssp. non det) von Venezuela. Aqua. Terra. 5:38–39.

Stimson, A.F. 1969. Liste der rezenten Amphibien und Reptilien. Boidae (Boinae + Bolyerinae + Loxoceminae + Pythoninae). Das Tierreich, Berlin 89: xi + 49 pp.

Stull, O.G. 1935. A check list of the family Boidae. Proc. Boston Soc. Nat. Hist. 40(8): 387–408.

Tolson, P.J. 1987. Phylogenetics of the boid snake genus *Epicrates* and Caribbean vicariance theory. Occ. Pap. Mus. Zool. University of Michigan (715)1–68.

Underwood, G.L. 1967. A contribution to the classification of snakes. British Mus. Nat. Hist.

Underwood, G.L. 1976. A systematic analysis of boid snakes, pp. 151–175. *In* A.d'A. Bellairs and C.B. Cox (eds.), Morphology and Biology of Reptiles. Academic Press, New York.

Wallach, V. 1998. The lungs of snakes, pp. 93–295. *In* C. Gans and A.S. Gaunt (eds.), Biology of the Reptilia, Vol. 19 (Morphology G). Soc. Study Amphib. Rept., Ithaca, NY.

Winstel, A. 1987. Breeding the Amazon tree boa *(Corallus enydris enydris)*. Litt. Serp. 7(6):267–271.

Winstel, A. 1988. The Amazon tree boa's amazing colors. Vivarium, 1(3):5–7.

Winstel, A. 1989. Herpetoculture of the Amazon tree boa. Vivarium, 1(4):12–14.

Winstel, A. 1990. Husbandry and display potential of the Amazon tree boa (*Corallus enydris enydris*). Anim. Keepers Forum 17:386–387.

Winstel, A. 1992. Observations on the care and management of Amazon and Cook's tree boas (*Corallus enydris*). Rept. Amphib. Mag., Sept.–Oct. 1992:2–13.

Winstel, A. 1995. Tree boas on a tropical isle. Reptiles 2(5):16–22.

Winstel, A. 1998. Cultivating the garden tree boa. Reptile Hobbyist 4(1):10–18.

Zenneck, J. 1898. Die Zeichnung der Boiden. Tübinger Zool. Arb. 3(4):1–384 + 8 pl.

Index

References to the four species in the *Corallus hortulanus* complex (*C. cookii*, *C. grenadensis*, *C. hortulanus*, and *C. ruschenbergerii*) are not indexed.

193

Notes

Notes

Notes

Notes